Managing Information Technology

Francisco Castillo

Managing Information Technology

 Springer

Francisco Castillo
Paranaque
Philippines

ISBN 978-3-319-81769-9   ISBN 978-3-319-38891-5   (eBook)
DOI 10.1007/978-3-319-38891-5

Printed on acid-free paper

This Springer imprint is published by Springer Nature
The registered company is Springer International Publishing AG Switzerland

Preface

In 2011, I started my career as CIO of a large Philippine company; during that time, the first thing I wanted to do was to set the organization right, in terms of its structure, as well as processes, as this would set the pace for the many years to follow. Got it wrong, and I would have had to live with that mistake for many years. What was clear to me at that time is that there were two very different components in IT: Strategy, which is long term; and tactical and operational concerns, which is short term. One cannot do without the other, and I was expected to address both, knowing the fact that I only had a very limited honeymoon period in my hands. I could not address long term without fixing the operational issues first, and yet, strategy would always be in the back of my mind.

The other very apparent difference for me was that of managing operations versus projects, and I wondered if what many companies were doing at that time was right: Mixing resources to do both. So I did what I always do when unsure, which is to research to support some of my suspicions, and I came out relatively empty handed. Yes, I was already aware at that time of some of the industry standards, but these were high level and difficult to interpret on how to actually execute them, worst of all, I did not have any time to do that. And so, I did the next thing I would usually do, which was to roll-up my sleeves, put on my thinking cap, and try to dissect and understand what really would make sense. This was the start of my practical experience that is reflected in this book.

The book starts with just that: Discussing the ideal/suggested table of organization in an IT department, and the rationale of why I have reached such a conclusion. It separates distinctly strategy from day-to-day operations, as well as projects from operations, the two most important functions of a CIO. It goes on, discussing the most pressing need: Managing operations in Chap. 4. This chapter is based on some of the best industry standards and their nomenclature in the field, with a difference: I try to explain exactly what each party is to do, and how it should be done at a very practical level. The theory exists out there, but how to make it practical is a different matter. For in operations, once the structure is correct, the next challenge is how to handle tickets (e.g., requests and incidences), which are the basic day-to-day of the operations team. This means how to record changes, escalate them, address them, test them, release them, and possibly roll them back if necessary. This brings us to the typical lifecycle for operations' services: Planning

& Design—Release—Maintain—Retire. Each of these phases has its own distinct aspects which should be monitored and managed, including availability and capacity management. Operations are also linked to IT strategy, and we discuss when this strategy translates to a project, or to operational changes, and if the former, how these project(s) link to operations.

Chapter 5 discusses projects, the other lifeline of IT, and in this chapter we make a marked distinction between the methodologies to be used in projects with that to be used in operations. It is not recommended to mix these, and as such discuss IT project management in detail. We first start with the basic project management principles, but zero in on the way these general principles are to be used in IT projects. IT projects are perhaps one of the most difficult projects to manage because they deal only with intangibles. Furthermore, the people that usually define the success of a project are the end users which the CIO has no control of, but who must influence using some special people skills (so-called change management). We spend time discussing some of the most critical parts of IT projects: Analysis, design, cut-over period, and go-live and support phases. Each of these requires its own particular documentation and techniques. Included in this chapter is a discussion on some of the most failure-prone components of a project: Customizations, testing, and people change management.

Documentation is discussed at length for both operations and projects, because adapting to the waterfall standard of project methodology, it is really the lifeline for IT to be sustainable, as well as projects transferable to operations.

What I also learned during my stint as CIO was that the cut-over from projects to operations was many times the most critical. People from these two distinct teams did not like to talk to one another, but is necessary for the sustainability of the service that has just been designed. Likewise I searched for material and found very little on this subject, so I decided to develop our own guidelines and procedures, these are shared in Chap. 6. Starting with a discussion on the typical different environments (development, testing, training, production), and then aspects which seem like common sense and are usually taken for granted, but are actually very much project-specific: Backup and restore procedures, release management procedures, data migration, data quality, interfaces, and most importantly, roles and responsibilities of operations, project personnel, and third parties during the go-live and support phase. We have come up with a checklist of tasks to be undertaken before the go-live to increase its probability of success, which have been refined throughout the years, the basis for this chapter.

Once operations and projects are in place and the fire-fighting is finished, the next thought that should be in a CIO's mind is how to sustain this, as well as how to minimize issues. Fire-fighting and addressing issues should consist of less than 20 % of one's time, but in order for that to happen, the proper governance should be put in place, which is discussed in Chap. 7. We first start on how company governance is related to IT governance, and how these in turn are related to policy, and international standards such as ISO20000, ISO9001. Operations governance is actually embedded as part of the processes by which operations works with, but project governance is somewhat more "loose", so that the chapter delves mainly on project governance. Governance in projects refers to what must be ensured by the Project Manager, and once more, is based on the minimum required documentation that must be produced at different phases of a project. Documentation standardization is in fact the key in making projects successful, as this is the tool necessary to monitor status, and manage accordingly. We discuss the proposed four basic documents for any project: Project plan, issue registry, request registry, and project deliverables checklist. We also discuss the roles and responsibilities of different personnel in an IT project, because oftentimes, projects also fail because of unrealistic expectations in the project team, or mismatch between expected and actual skills and roles.

Chapter 8 is an overview on one of the hottest topics in IT project management methodologies today: Agile-Scrum. The surprising thing for me is that although many of the topics laid out above do not have much reference material, a lesser (at least from my point of view) subject like Agile-Scrum has tons of material written on it. As such, I do not attempt to write about Agile-Scrum in detail, but merely to contrast it with the waterfall approach (which is the basic precept for much of my material), and identify when it would be useful to use.

Operations, projects, and governance, how does all this glue together? If the number of projects and the breadth of operations are huge, it is suggested to have ad hoc portfolio managers that will oversee these according to specialty. If not, the ultimate portfolio manager is the CIO herself. From the point of view of the portfolio manager, he is interested in knowing how his operations and projects are performing, but would not be interested in the details unless he needs to dive into them (e.g., there are issues to be resolved). As such, he defines the governance for his set of operations and projects so that he can get accurate and timely information from which to act. One of his main tasks as well is to think beyond the projects and see if the projects are still meaningful or not to the company, and if new projects or operational initiatives need to be defined in order to align IT to company strategy. The portfolio management as discussed in the Chap. 9, can be defined as a cycle once more: Planning and design, assessment and communicating, and portfolio rebalancing. On top of this cycle is portfolio governance by which the different portfolio components are to comply with, as well as his monitoring and control tools.

Well, this is all for now. I have written this book to hopefully bridge the gap which I think still exists today, so that anyone who is in the same situation I was 5 years ago would have a much easier time.

Lastly, anyone interested in receiving a copy of my templates in MS office format, please contact me at my email below and I will gladly reply.

Many thanks and good luck with all your IT operations!

Francisco Castillo
kikocas88@yahoo.com

Acknowledgments

I would like to acknowledge the many people that supported me while preparing this book.

First, I would like to thank my very supportive bosses, Ricky Vargas and Herbert Consunji, who gave me the opportunity to apply all these learnings in the corporate world. Mon Fernandez, who also encouraged me when he took over as President of the company, and Manny Pangilinan, for giving his employees the leeway and opportunity to think beyond just the short term.

To my parents, who made all this possible.

To my IT staff Jenny, Noel, Ces, Konch, Jamie, Elaine, Gera, Mac, Jelle, and Sheena, whom I taught and learned from at the same time.

To my wife Rina and daughter Linda, my main inspiration, and who heartened me and had all the patience in seeing me toil on this book during many weekends and holidays.

I also want to dedicate this book to the Filipino engineers and IT professionals, who bring innovation, order, and process in a country not particularly famous for it.

Francisco Castillo

Contents

Introduction

When speaking of IT functions, two distinct ones come to mind: the day-to-day Operations and Maintenance (what I will refer to as O&M), and Projects. O&M, as the name implies, deals with maintaining all of the IT services available, keeping things running, and dealing with the request for changes that are raised by the different users of the IT systems, whether these are purely internal and within the company organization, or external customers. Projects, as implied by the name, refer to new deployments of IT services in the form of systems, applications and infrastructure. A CIO is expected to handle both, and to know a bit of everything: software, processes, user change management, servers, networking, programming, etc., and he is also expected to know how to handle operations, and handle projects.

In truth, handling operations is very different from handling projects, and the methodologies used and best practices for each differ considerably. Both IT and Project Management standards exist out there, but as standards, are high level and fail to tell really how you can practically apply these. Concretely, if one is to setup an IT organization, immediate concerns would come to mind: how to structure the organization, what are their roles and responsibilities, how to divide and distribute work, how and when to specialize, and what are the management tools that need to be set-up for these.

In this book I have attempted to do just that, take the fundamental principles of IT Service Management (ITSM) and best practices in project management, and come up with a single, seamless reference for IT Managers and Professionals. I have tried to make it as practical as possible, talking about how to actually apply these principles based on my experience in the industry. Making these practical is the first and most import step, but is not enough. Long-term sustainability requires that these principles also be framed in governance policies and procedures, and so I also discuss what aspects should necessarily be captured in these policies and procedures.

© Springer International Publishing Switzerland 2016
F. Castillo, *Managing Information Technology*,
DOI 10.1007/978-3-319-38891-5_1

IT Areas and Functions

2

2.1 Projects Versus Operations, Strategy Versus Operations

Projects and Operations & Maintenance (O&M) are the two distinct, yet necessary functions in any IT Organization. Projects have distinct properties as compared to operations. First and foremost, projects have a very distinct start and finish, while operations are continuous in nature, and this is true no matter what industry it is being applied on. Because of this, the ways projects are managed are quite distinct from operations, and yet, that interface between projects and operations is a crucial link for projects to be ultimately successful, and an area which commonly fails.

Projects also have very distinct phases, in which they initiate-plan-execute and close, while operations are continuous, and have no distinct phases within them. IT Project outputs may lead to additional services, which will then need to be supported by O&M thereafter, and will form part of operations' service catalog. O&M can also request and initiate a project as part of its effort to continuously improve (PDCA), yet the treatment of this project will follow that of standard projects.

Some more differences between the two are shown in Table 2.1.

Though as will be discussed, project governance has its own particular policies and guidelines, every project is different, so that each project has its own charter, organization, and goals, its main purpose is in fact to CHANGE something, while that of operations is more of status quo, with its semi-permanent (though improvements do exist) charter, organization and overall goals. Projects are put up to produce a very concrete IT service, while operations are mainly to support and operate an existing, predefined service that is part of its service catalog. Projects have a definite timeline, after which they cease to exist, while operations never end.

A very important characteristic is that deliverables or outputs of a project are progressively elaborated, something which is very important and will be discussed in detail under scope management, and which means, that unlike operations, the final detailed outputs are not clear from the very beginning, but are progressively defined and refined in terms of detail as the project progresses.

© Springer International Publishing Switzerland 2016
F. Castillo, *Managing Information Technology*,
DOI 10.1007/978-3-319-38891-5_2

Table 2.1 Projects versus operations comparison

Projects	Operations
Creates its own charter, organization, and goals	Semi-permanent charter, organization, and goals
Purpose of change	Purpose of status quo
Unique product or service	Predefined and approved product or service
Heterogeneous team	Heterogeneous teams
Definite start-definite end	Ongoing (continuous)
Progressively elaborated process deliverables	Fully known process deliverables

Table 2.2 Roles and responsibilities for Operations and Projects

CIO (overall)	Operations	Projects
Strategy	Head for operations	Portfolio managers (information systems head, IT infrastructure head)
Delivery functions	O&M team	Project manager

Just from some of these differences, it becomes apparent that the way projects are to be handled differs considerably from that of operations.

On the other hand, strategic decisions need to be made for both projects and operations, many times, these cannot be made separately (especially so for infrastructure). Table 2.2 shows a typical matrix of roles in the organization and their corresponding responsibilities.

Strategy consists of planning and initiating projects or other initiatives that either improves the service to the end users or provide additional services to them. It must be aligned with the overall company focus and direction, and must provide some concrete benefit or address concrete requirements needed by the company. Generally speaking, a new initiative should

- Increase revenue
- Decrease operational cost
- Improve customer service
- Address legal and regulatory requirements or
- Minimize risk.

These are of course very broad, and it is up to the CIO, Head for Operations, as well as the Heads for the Portfolios to align and translate business requirements from the organization to concrete initiatives that need to be started in IT. The portfolio managers depicted above may be several, depending on the size and structure of the organization. At the very least, it requires one to handle new applications (Head for

Table 2.3 Roles in projects and O&M

Responsible area/function	O&M	Projects
Overall management	Operations head, CIO	PM, portfolio Mgr., CIO
Applications	Application management (AM)	Business analysts
Programming	Developers (under AM)	Developers
Operations	IT operations management (ITOM)	n/a
User support, service desk	User support (US), Service Desk (SD)	n/a
Technical infrastructure	Technical management (TM)	Technical support

Information Systems - IS), and another to handle hardware and infrastructure (Head for IT infrastructure - II). For larger organizations, IS and II roles may be further broken down into separate portfolios. These personnel are the key in conceptualizing, proposing, and designing new projects. They also are responsible for all the different projects that fall within their portfolio, as well as applying governance over the different projects and overseeing Project Managers (PMs) under them.

The operations Head's strategic initiatives mainly focus on how to improve operations by reducing costs, making it more efficient, resilient, and minimizing risk, and in some case how to cater to the different regulatory and legal requirements. These improvements may be small in scope and breadth, so that they can be handled directly by the O&M team, or may be treated as a separate project altogether. In case of the latter, it then falls under one of the portfolio manager's responsibility and is treated much like any other project.

Table 2.3 details further the roles for O&M and projects.

As one may appreciate, there are counterparts in projects for the roles in O&M, except for those roles that really only appear once the system is in operations: IT Operations Management (ITOM), and User Support (US). The first does not exist because they are in charge of regularly executing programs that produce outputs for the end users. As a project is by nature not yet operating, there are no end users yet to speak of, thus there is no role equivalent for ITOM. The same holds true for User Support.

A portfolio manager may have O&M as part of his portfolio, and this is true as well for the CIO. Not only is he overall head for the IT Department and drives strategy, he is also the overall portfolio manager which also contains O&M as part of his portfolio. Some other organizations do not differentiate their IT structure between projects and operations, but rather, mix these according to functional area. This has its own advantages and disadvantages, some of which are discussed in Chap. 3; however in general, this is not a best practice. Main advantage of a functional organization is that if the portfolio manager has been long with the organization, he may have a deep functional knowledge of the portfolio he is handling, disadvantage is that he will have to learn how to apply two distinct methodologies, and learn how and when to switch from one to the other. This setup may be appropriate for very large organizations which require very specialized functional expertise, and regularly have update projects in that functional area, but other than that, it is better off to separate projects from operational responsibility.

The problem in having both an Operations and a Project hat at the practical level is that since both methodologies are distinct, the person does not easily "switch" mentality. Take for example a role in which the team lead for the sales system is getting a large number of tickets due to incidences in the sales process which has been now declared obsolete due to circumstances, while at the same time, management is pushing some new sales modules which need to be developed and implemented in the next month. Although the team lead has all the necessary resources: business analysts familiar with the application, developers, technical architect, he has a problem in allocating resources for each, and making sure that the project is monitored in accordance with Project Management best practices, while tickets are replied on time and with full details and documentation as also required by operations best practices.

On the other hand, having separate teams has one major challenge that of transferring projects into O&M, what I refer to as cut-over (also referred to as hand-over, transitioning, etc.), and requires special procedures so as to guarantee its success.

It is important to remember that success or failure of projects and initiatives is to be seen from the business point of view, meaning, whether the project has delivered the intended benefit to the business. Oftentimes, IT Departments have a narrow vision of success: project completed on time, project completed within budget, and yet, due to other factors, the delivered service is not actively used by the users. Common issues include

- People change management issues
- Project does not really reflect the needs of the users
- Project does not reflect the need of the business
- The project is already obsolete due to the new direction taken by the business.

The first point is taken further in its respective section; the second refers to scope management, while the last two are the main jobs of the portfolio manager, and is explained in its respective section.

Take for example this typical, real-life situation. A big corporation is given a huge budget to modernize its IT systems, starting with its reporting system. Having seen several vendor presentations, they settle for one of the fastest, most sophisticated data storage, reporting system, and corresponding hardware. The project is awarded and started, making sure all the software components are correctly installed and the architecture at par with the best performing data storage systems in the world, however, the consultants and IT manage the whole process from a technology point of view, having in-depth user requirements defined as an afterthought. In fact, they apply "Agile" techniques in which the users are presented with reports and dashboards and asked for their concurrence, to which they do, however, they fail to go into the details of the different indicators being presented and how they are calculated. The project hits a major snag when the first set of deliverables is presented to the users, which they reject because they do not concur in the way several KPIs are being measured. The project team is at a loss and after tweaking and re-tweaking the reports, gives up after 1 year, when the IT Manager is fired and the whole project shelved.

2.2   Systems, Processes, and People

It is commonly said that IT is made up of three main components: systems, processes, and people. Unfortunately, all three are intangibles, so they are very hard to define and manage.

- **Systems**: refers to the applications, infrastructure, and other assets which execute and automate particular business functions.
- **Processes**: refers to the way in which the systems are setup to conduct a particular business function.
- **People**: refers to the IT Department's staff, as well as, all end users making use of the systems in conducting their normal business operations.

Each of these three needs to be managed by IT, and in degree of increasing complexity (normally) are systems, processes, and people. To explain each by means of an example, let us take a common application, say a financial application that handles General Ledger (GL), Accounts Payable (AP), and Accounts Receivables (AR)

- System—in this case would refer to the specific brand and version of the financial package bought.
- Process—would refer to the configuration and setup of the different modules in the system. For example, for Accounts Payables (AP), it would refer as to how the Accounts Payable processes these accounts and payments, in step by step fashion and in accordance with how business is conducted using the system.
- People—refers to IT and the finance department using the application.

For any application to succeed, all three need to be addressed, for example by:

- **System**: purchasing a brand and version that meets the end user requirements in finance (this means, that the system is CAPABLE of delivering the desired functionality).
- **Process**: the specific configurations on the system so that it meets the end user requirements. These requirements need to be defined in detail so that the configurations match these requirements. If the system chosen must have the capability to deliver the functionalities, the actual process design and configuration of the system are what *enable* and *deliver* the desired functionality. A system delivered with a certain process in place is referred to as an application.

- **People**: even though the right system was chosen and the right process mapped unto it, it is still useless if the people do not understand it and do not use the application correctly, unless otherwise, the success of the application is doomed.

Systems are bought from a vendor, processes are configured into the system by the consulting and System Integration companies contracted, and people are trained both by the System Integrator and by IT in the use of the application. The reason why people are usually the most difficult component is that first, it is the users that need to define the process they need. This poses several problems, for one, the users may not really know or cannot really express what they need. Second, assuming that the consulting company is very experienced in eliciting their requirements, the users may not be able/may not want to dedicate sufficient time to this endeavor. This may be especially true during the testing phase, as it must be the end users to test and verify whether the system adheres to the specifications that they require. Finally, there is the people change management aspect. People change management refers to the process of managing change in an organization, in our case, brought about by a new application or new process to be released. People are inherently resistant to change, it causes insecurity and fear in them, and the natural reaction is pushback. Pushback manifests itself in making it difficult for the change to succeed, delaying approvals, continuously raising issues, ignoring meetings, and may manifest in many more ways. It may also be unintentional and the fault of the IT Department, in not explaining enough (not just about the application, but what It means for the business), not enough training, or focusing too much in transactional training rather than disseminating to the users the rationale and know-how on how the processes are designed to work.

In summary, the IT Department needs a strange combination of many skills: technical, operations, project management, processes, technical management, and people skills. It is for this reason that many IT initiatives fail; putting all these skills together in a concerted fashion is a very difficult task indeed. Furthermore, structure and procedures make a lot of difference in ensuring success, the other being experience, something which is not taught nor written in any book (but hopefully addressed, even if partially by this book).

Take the following problematic examples:

Example 1: A new sales system is bought by IT as requested by the Sales Department. The system is selected based on demos and features shown by the vendor which were appreciated by the end users, however, when the project starts, the Sales Department is too busy to dedicate time in sitting it out with IT and the System Integrator (SI) in defining the correct sales processes, sending instead some very junior staff which together with IT, define the blueprint. Upon going live, the system does not work in accordance with what sales wants and the whole application is junked.

Example 2: A new enterprise resource planning (ERP) system is bought as higher management has decided to "modernize" without clearly understanding what this means or implies. The services for implementing the system are bid out as a turn-key contract and awarded to an experienced SI. IT, however, is inexperienced with this type of system, and most especially the industry best practices in terms of the processes covered. In the course of the project, some hard decisions are to be made, including streamlining the invoice payment process from a purely manual process, in which currently payments are approved by means of an approval form physically signed by different authorized signatories, to 3-way matching in which everything is paperless. 3-way matching means matching an invoice received from the vendor with the actual purchase order released to him, and the acceptance of the goods upon delivery (Goods Receipt-GR), which guarantees that payment takes effect only if the 3 "match". The SI presents this process, however, the users are very resistant to the change, and IT being unknowledgeable, is unable to defend the proposed process change. As the SI has a project to finish, and sensing the mounting resistance, conveniently accedes to the request of not implementing 3-way matching to avoid lengthy discussion and conflict, proposing instead a change request for customizing the payment process based on the users' liking. This situation is a losing proposition for the customer in not utilizing the power of an industry best practice, and for IT, in customizing a very standard process in the ERP, which will get back to them eventually.

Organization and Human Resources

3

From the point of view of operations versus projects, there are several variations on the type of organizations employed. Typical operations-focused organizations have a very rigid hierarchy, based mainly on the functional roles for each position under IT as shown in Fig. 3.1.

Functional managers would be concerned with their particular area of responsibility, whether this would be a series of applications, or organized based on the type a skills they handle. A typical IT operations-focused organization would look like that shown in Fig. 3.2.

The role and function of each of these teams are explained further in the sections under O&M, however, to briefly describe:

- **Technical Management (TM)**—is in charge of the general upkeep of all infrastructure components. This includes network, storage, servers' resources, as well as, technical components of the different software, typically the technical implementation of the applications, databases, and operating systems.
- **Application Management (AM)**—is in charge of updating and maintaining all application configurations. They typically modify these based on incidences and request requirements. The difference with the involvement of TM in the applications is that AM handles everything that affects processes and their behavior, while TM handles all technical aspects.
- **IT Operations Management (ITOM)**—responsible for the day to day management and maintenance of the IT Infrastructure, batch processes and other repetitive functions needed to deliver the necessary IT services to the end users
- **User Support (US)**—is the interface between IT and the users, so that users need not know anybody else but the US personnel interfacing with them. It is in charge of first level support to the users and attempts at their resolution. It handles all requests and incidences reported by end users.

© Springer International Publishing Switzerland 2016
F. Castillo, *Managing Information Technology*,
DOI 10.1007/978-3-319-38891-5_3

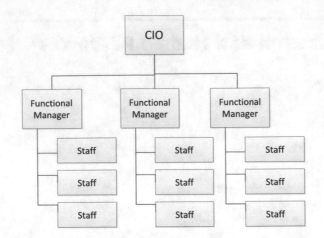

Fig. 3.1 Functional organizational structure

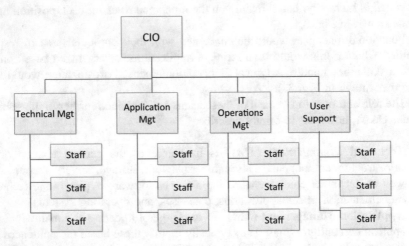

Fig. 3.2 Typical IT functional structure

If we now further define the table of organization one level down, we then have the TO shown in Fig. 3.3.

Technical Management has its different distinct teams in charge of networks, system administration, and Database Administration. The Application Management team will have business analysts specialized in the different applications, and typically a pool of developers (programmers) in charge of customizations. The Business Analysts may not be broken down into specialized groups but may also be a pool, which can service different applications, depending on their skill sets. IT Operations Management will have different batch operator teams that run and monitor the different batch processes, and the facilities management team in charge of the regular upkeep of IT facilities such as data center, common facilities, and the

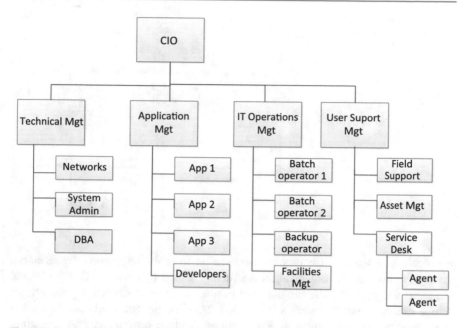

Fig. 3.3 Typical IT functional structure with details for each team

like. User Support is further broken down to Field Support (FS) Asset Management, and Service Desk (SD). Service Desk is manned by agents who receive and process the requests and incidences from the users, and are the users' single point of contact. They man the Service Desk system and attempt to address the request or resolve the customer's issue immediately, but if unable will then escalate this to the proper team. Field support refers to personnel that distinct from the rest of the teams, may actually travel to where the user is in attempting to service a request or incident. They commonly address requests and issues related to the endpoint devices, including repairs. The reason for placing field support under user support is that although it may seem that it is more technical and would belong to technical management, most requests and incidences are generated directly from the service desk by end users and need close coordination with the service desk personnel. Asset Management here refers to the reception, storage, and disposal of IT assets, which is under User Support as the bulk of these items correspond to end user requested or assigned devices.

On the other end of the spectrum is the project-oriented organization as shown in Fig. 3.4.

Wherein each manager is focused toward his particular project(s), and there is no operational focus whatsoever. This is typically found in consulting companies, system integrators, and engineering companies which have a very lean internal operational function (sales, administration, and marketing...). As most IT organizations need a mix of both, the question is what would be the proper Table of Organization (TO) for an all-encompassing IT organization? My recommended

Fig. 3.4 Typical
project-oriented structure

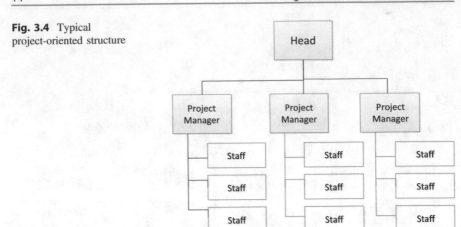

approach is to separate the project organization from the operations organization, giving the operational organization a structure which follows the IT Operational structure above, while the project organization is focused toward a pure project setup, similar to what is shown in this last TO. The project heads would have a more strategic role, in coming up with medium and long-term plans, and translating these into actual projects that are aligned with the company's overall (changing) strategy. These project heads would be managing the portfolio of projects and continuously aligning them to the company strategy. An example of this organization is shown in Fig. 3.5.

In this organization, the head for IS is in charge of strategy and new projects related to software applications, while the Head for IT infrastructure is his

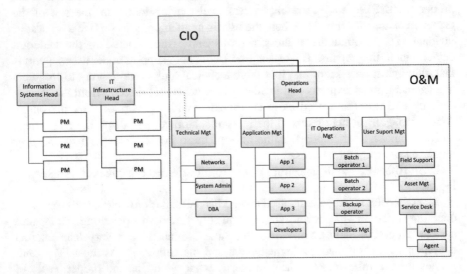

Fig. 3.5 Project and operations combined IT structure

counterpart for infrastructure, which includes all hardware and technology components. The IT infrastructure Head must coordinate very closely with the technical management team under O&M due to their interrelationship, and definitely all projects must be closely coordinated between Projects and O&M for turn-over.

The philosophy of the company in undertaking projects should also be considered. If projects are fully contracted out, then each of the PMs will interface with each vendor PM and have no personnel under it. If projects are done in-house, then the PM will have to "borrow" resources from the line organization either full-time or part-time. This is only possible if the company's IT headcount is considerable, so that the O&M team can afford to lend to the project teams, but is rarely the case. Part-time borrowing has the problem mentioned during the book's introduction, in which the personnel will lack focus and would be confused as to the methodology to use. In this case, he shall also be reporting to at least two bosses, and may not actually be evaluated by both, nor the boss from O&M appreciative of his work in the project. Due to these reasons, and unless the company is developing its own software platforms for outside sale, it is recommended to fully contract projects. This also has the advantage that the project can be contracted to a specialist in the project products without having to hire them full-time (as the project has a definite duration anyhow).

Managing Operations

4

4.1 Information Technology Service Management

IT service management (ITSM) is the process of aligning enterprise IT services with the business needs with the intention of delivering to the end-user a service at its desired performance level. ITSM ensures that the right processes, people, and technology are in place so that the organization can meet its business goals through the service provided by IT. One standard that has become a sort-of de facto in the IT industry is ITIL (Axelos 2011) which defines many of the nomenclature used in the IT industry today for managing IT operations including much of the nomenclature used here, as well as the philosophy of how to handle operations. In this chapter, we adapt many of these principles but recommend concrete and practical ways of setting-up and managing your operations which most of the current standards do not define [some other relevant standards includes Microsoft Operating Framework, ISO 20,000 (ISO 2011), and COBIT (ISACA 2015)].

We shall limit the use and definition of ITSM to cover that of operations only, and exclude projects as these have their own distinct methodology. We shall also be using the Table of Organization shown in Fig. 3.5 from here onwards as our reference, and refer to operations as O&M to contrast it from ITOM (IT Operations Management).

It may seem obvious, that O&M should have precedence over all decisions made, especially with respect to managing releases (changes) into production, yet sometimes this is not practiced to the letter. Since O&M has a commitment in delivering a certain Service Level Agreement (SLA) to its end-customers, it has to ensure that no disruption to operations occurs. Projects, once cut-over into production almost always have some risk and disruption, so the timing, manner and preparation for the cut-over needs to be carefully worked on, and coordinated with O&M. Any release by any project will always need to be cleared with O&M before proceeding. For now, it suffices to say that under all circumstances, the Head of Operations needs to be consulted and should be in agreement with the cut-over of the project into production, more of this is discussed in detail in Chap. 6 under cut-over strategy.

© Springer International Publishing Switzerland 2016
F. Castillo, *Managing Information Technology*,
DOI 10.1007/978-3-319-38891-5_4

Below, we discuss the specific and detailed roles and responsibilities of each team shown in the Table of Organization.

4.1.1   Service Desk (SD)

Service Desk is the single point of contact for all users within an organization with IT for any request or incidence. This means that from their point of view, they need not understand the underlying Table of Organization, roles and responsibilities of each individual within the IT organization, but merely be aware of service desk, due to its customer-facing roles and responsibilities. When a user has an inquiry, request or incidence, he only needs refer to the service desk to obtain the necessary explanation, service, or resolution. A user would also expect that this is done within a reasonable amount of time. A service desk is handled by agents which would open tickets in accordance with what is being reported.

Different channels may be used for contacting the Service Desk

- Phone
- Email
- Web (self-service)
- App (self-service)

The service desk is also responsible for attempting First Call Resolution; this means its ability to resolve the inquiry or incident right on the instant when reported by the user. This means that the ticket can be closed much faster than if it is escalated, and also uses less technical and expensive resources (Service Desk agents) handle the resolution versus more expensive and specialized ones if escalated (AM, TM personnel).

Tickets opened by the Service Desk should follow the following classification:

- **Incidence**—any event which impairs the use of a service. It may also be an event that has not yet impaired service, but will do so if left unattended.
- **Request**—User's request for information, advice, for change, or for access to an IT Service.

Tickets may be generated by both end-users, or internally by the IT staff. Best practice is that once the ticket is resolved, it goes back to Service Desk for confirmation of closure from the user thus closing the loop in making the Service Desk the single point of contact.

The Service Desk is responsible for ensuring that tickets are opened with all the necessary information before escalation

- **Complete description of the incidence or request**. This may include screenshots and detailed description of the issue, or a complete description of the request. It is the Service Desk's responsibility to understand what information is needed before escalation, so as to avoid the ticket from delaying

- **Understanding who is requesting for the ticket**. This may be automatic (if through Web or email), but will not be if by phone, for example.
- **Classifying the ticket correctly**. Service Desk determines (either automatically by the Service Desk (SD) system, or manually by the agent) the team to which the ticket should be escalated, the approver, the information details required for the ticket, and this also sets in motion the count which will be used in calculating the SLA.

In order to maximize the amount of tickets resolved via First Call Resolution, an FAQ is usually facilitated to the Service Desk along with training and regular updates. Incidences are highest whenever a new project is released into production, so that Service desk agents must be trained thoroughly before the go-live of a project.

Once the ticket is escalated, it will follow its normal pre-determined flow until the ticket is resolved or canceled. Incidences should be resolved within the allowable time, however, it may be that the incidence's root cause cannot be easily identified either because it is totally new, is of a complex nature, or may be due to many possible factors. In such a case, a problem ticket is created by the assigned team (AM, TM, ITOM, US) and will remain open until the final root cause is identified. A problem ticket may also be referenced by several incidences, wherein all these incidences are related to a common problem (More of this is explained under Sect. 4.5.3).

Even if the problem ticket remains open, it is important to resolve the incident as soon as possible, and that means that work-arounds may need to be applied, so that at least the service can still be delivered. Thus, once the work-around is effectuated, the incidence ticket is closed, but the problem ticket shall remain open. If, upon further investigation, the root cause of the problem ticket can still not be identified, several options exist (which may also be undertaken simultaneously)

- Consultation between different teams. As the root cause may reside in a gray area between the different responsibilities.
- Escalation to next level support. This may be to the software or hardware vendor's technical support team.
- Recreation of the scenario in a sandbox environment for simulation and testing.

It is important to fill-out details of resolution of incidences and problems in the company's Knowledge Base (KB). These resolved problems and incidences with work-arounds are called Known Errors, and help in applying the resolution identified whenever the same incidence is encountered again. A properly designed Knowledge Base allows the different IT teams to search through it by content, ticket type, date, user, etc., quickly identifying past issues which are similar to the current, accessing the work-arounds and root cause and applying these to the current issue for final resolution. On the other hand, the process for the handling of problems is called Problem Management.

Not all requests and incidences are treated equally nor should they be given the same criticality, due to

- **Impact on services (severity)**. Incidences which have a higher impact are more severe. As an example, a network incidence may affect only one user, a whole department, or the whole company, and therefore the priority given based on these should correspondingly increase.
- **User**. Not all users are created equal, and thus, requests and incidences reported by top management have a higher priority overall (VIPs), followed by managers, and rank and file, for example.
- **Type of incident or request**. The type of ticket being requested may also have an influence on the priority, this may be due to the known impact such a type of ticket may have over the business (affects customer service, for example), the expected response time for such type of tickets (request for password email reset for example should not take very long). It may also be related to the complexity of what is being asked, for example, a modification on the functionality of a program (which goes to AM), typically requires several man-hours analysis and therefore is not immediate, so it is of little avail to assign it a high priority.

The usual way for calculating the overall severity of the ticket (High–Normal–Low, or whatever other classification has been designed) is to come up with a matrix that calculates the overall criticality based on the priority assigned (from the above) as well as severity. See the example shown in Fig. 4.1.

The severity would be dependent on another similar table classification as shown in Fig. 4.2.

Thus, the overall severity will be based on a formula or table which defines the overall classification based on the above. For example, the formula may say that severity will be urgent for as long as the impact level is high or priority is high, minor severity incidences may be those with low priority, and so forth. It is important that once the ticket is routed, all users accessing the ticket have visibility over its classification, so that they can give due priority. Even better if the service desk system automatically calculates the due date and displays this information as well.

Proper training of service desk personnel is crucial for the process flow to execute correctly. It is the service desk that will identify the impact the ticket has by means of their understanding of the issue, through interactive dialog, as well as whether the requestor is a VIP or not. Though the VIP tag may be automatically calculated depending on the ID of the user, take note that VIPs may not be the ones personally reporting to the Service Desk (i.e., their secretary or staff), so that needs to be captured correctly. It is also the Service Desk that will classify the ticket correctly so that the overall severity calculation takes place and proper routing is done by the system.

Consider the situation in which a new proxy server was deployed by TM's networks group and propagated the change to the end-users' web browser, but failed to properly inform Service Desk. Upon going live, some users have issues with the change and are unable to connect to internet, so they report this to SD, however, because SD was not properly briefed, it merely escalates the issues to TM, which is now swamped with tickets. This could have been

Catego ry	Sub Category 1	Sub Category 2 (Incident)	Incident /Request	Priority	Assignment
H/W	Printer	Can't print	Incident	Low	Service Desk
		Can't detect printer/printer not connected to network	Incident	Low	Service Desk
		Dirty Print Out	Incident	Low	Field Support
		Paper Jam	Incident	Low	Field Support
		Continiously printing	Incident	Low	Service Desk
		Printing inconsistent colors	Incident	Low	Field Support
		Printer not working/malfunctioning	Incident	Low	Service Desk
		Beeping sound	Incident	Low	Service Desk
	Servers	Blue screen	Incident	High	Technical Mgt1
		Infected with virus	Incident	High	Technical Mgt1
		Windows License Not Activated	Incident	Medium	Technical Mgt1
		Can't Boot/Corrupted OS	Incident	High	Technical Mgt1
		Beeping sound	Incident	High	Technical Mgt1
		Can't power on/ no power	Incident	High	Technical Mgt1
		Always restarts	Incident	High	Technical Mgt1
	UPS	Not working/malfunctioning	Incident	Medium	Field Support
				Low	Field Support
				High	Technical Mgt1
	Biometrics	Can't detect / not connected to network	Incident	Medium	Service Desk
	Switches	No power	Incident	Medium	Network Mgt
		Ports not working	Incident	Medium	Network Mgt
		No connection	Incident	Medium	Network Mgt

Fig. 4.1 Sample category matrix for a service desk

avoided by simply devoting sufficient time in briefing SD, which would then be able to resolve this under first call resolution.

4.1.2   Technical Management (TM)

The technical management team, as it's name implies, is in charge of the IT infrastructure. Normally this includes

- System Administration. In charge of Operating systems and applications.
- Database Administration

Fig. 4.2 Sample severity
level calculation based on
impact, priority, and type of
user

Priority:	VIP:	Impact:	Severity:
High	Yes	Enterprise	Critical
High	Yes	Whole zone	Critical
High	Yes	Whole office	Critical
High	Yes	Single user	Critical
High	No	Enterprise	Critical
High	No	Whole zone	Urgent
High	No	Whole office	Important
High	No	Single user	Important
Medium	Yes	Enterprise	Urgent
Medium	Yes	Whole zone	Urgent
Medium	Yes	Whole office	Urgent
Medium	Yes	Single user	Urgent
Medium	No	Enterprise	Urgent
Medium	No	Whole zone	Important
Medium	No	Whole office	Minor
Medium	No	Single user	Minor
Low	Yes	Enterprise	Important
Low	Yes	Whole zone	Important
Low	Yes	Whole office	Important
Low	Yes	Single user	Important
Low	No	Enterprise	Important
Low	No	Whole zone	Minor
Low	No	Whole office	Minor
Low	No	Single user	Minor

- Network Management
- Management of Servers and Storage

Some of the functions above, depending on the size and complexity of the organization, may be shared by different team members, such as the system administrator also performing functions related to the management of servers and storage, but take note that the skills required for each is quite distinct.

Two of the main preoccupations of TM are

- Availability Management
- Capacity Management

Which are explained in more detail in Sects. 4.5.6 and 4.5.7, however, to describe them simply, TM's first and foremost role is to keep things running, with minimal disruption to the service (availability management). On the other hand, capacity management refers to the allocation of resources to the different applications so as to ensure that there is no performance degradation to the service. Capacity management is especially relevant during the go-live phase of a project as it is the moment of truth in terms of how much resources are actually needed by the new system. During the lifecycle of a service, capacity requirements will also change due to the changing environment in which the service is used. Some of these aspects will be explained briefly in the next few sections.

4.1.2.1   System Administration

Main functions of the System Administrator (SysAd) are related to availability management and security. As new patches and versions are released for many of the different Configuration Items (CIs) periodically, the System Administrator needs to determine whether these need to be installed or not and when. Priority are security patches, installation of modules or versions which are to become outdated or support is to be ceased, as well as patches to address known issues. Next in the priority list are new versions which have functionalities required by AM due to a request or a planned change. Other patches and upgrades may be set aside until a more relevant event triggers their required deployment.

These activities are related to Availability management as failure to install and deploy these changes may result to incidences, or security breaches, as the case may be. It must be kept in mind that all new releases, and to a lesser extent patches, must be properly tested before release to production, and such testing, depending on the application, may be quite complex. If testing is complex, a comprehensive upgrade and test plan may be required.

In complex systems such as ERPs or core banking, modules within these applications are interdependent, so that a change in one module affects the other. It is for this reason that failures will most likely be in the FRICEW (see Sect. 5.3) when upgrading, as these customizations divert from the standard modules (and therefore interfaces between modules) released by the vendor (which of course, we hope were properly and exhaustively tested by the vendor before release, but actually may not be so). The proper planning for release management and upgrades is beyond the scope of this book, and is in fact quite dependent on the application, but take note that all customizations have a higher risk of failure when being upgraded as compared to standard functions.

One other very important function of the System Administrator (SysAd) is releasing changes into the different environments (QA, PROD), keeping track of these, and having readily-available roll-back procedures. One particular special release is user roles and authorizations. These are not normally authorized, nor determined by the SysAd, but are necessarily executed by him.

As an example of an incident related to improper testing, take the case of a patch being released by the ERP vendor to address known issues in its Java components. The patch update is then deployed by the SysAd immediately in the DEV, QA, and

PROD servers, only to find out that some customized Java displays in the portal that interfaces to the ERP are now not functioning.

Ideally, the O&M team needs to assess beforehand what is easier to undertake, either a straight deployment without thorough testing (maybe some very basic testing only of commonly used affected transactions), or a staged DEV + checking, QA + thorough testing, and then deployment to PROD once all the testing has passed. If the former is selected, a simple roll-back procedure should be identified prior to the deployment of the patch. If the latter, then a complete test plan and test scripts should be developed as well. The final selection of release strategy will depend on the risks, impact, and overall effort. Obviously if the risk and impact of a nonworking deployment is small but the testing effort is big, then a straight-through deployment makes sense, while if either the roll-back procedure is complicated or the impact of wrong transactions is high, then thorough testing should be done before deployment to PROD.

4.1.2.2 Database Administration

Database performance, after proper allocation of server resources, is perhaps the second most common reason why a system performs poorly. Unlike most of the other resources which may need to be revisited as part of the capacity management process, DB administration is not as much related to capacity management as it is to regular tuning and maintenance activities. Database tuning and indexing are functions that should regularly be performed by the Database Administrator (DBA). Indexing also has to be taken into account by the programmers in the form of best practices for coding, otherwise no matter how much tuning and indexing is done by the DBA, performance will still be bad (again, a topic beyond the scope of this book). Wherever possible, the DBA may also flag to the developer (through AM) issues and improvements he/she sees that can be made on the code. A variety of tools exist for determining when and how DB tuning and re-indexing is to be performed, and are generally application and DB brand-dependent. In general, the way these tools work is that they generate statistics as to the usage of different DB tables in terms of frequency, and their corresponding response time. Tables that are commonly accessed but are slow are prime candidates for indexing. Again, the DBA can only do so much as the manner of coding is equally important. Expensive statements which have many conditions on table entries while searching through many entries are very expensive, and may have to be written in a more efficient manner.

It is important to note that it is of tremendous help if the DBA understands the nature and behavior of the application that is accessing the DB. Different applications behave in different ways, and this helps in understanding the patterns of reads and writes that go into the DB, tables being accessed. For example, take a datawarehouse setup which extracts data from a transactional system as shown in Fig. 4.3.

In which the Extraction Transformation Loading (ETL) program extracts raw data from the ERP system and loads it into the Datawarehouse. Afterwards, the report generation kicks-in, transforming the data into a format the different

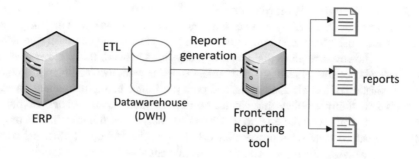

Fig. 4.3 Sample datawarehouse architecture

reporting tools need, and stores these report formats into the DWH database. If, for example, the following schedules are observed:

- ETL: 1:00–6:00 am, weekly
- Report generation: 6:00–8:00 am
- Access to the reports by users: 8:00 am

Then, this will help the DBA understand that massive writes into the datawarehouse will occur during 1–6 am period that is run weekly, report generation which is a combination of read (mainly) and writes at 6–8 am, and massive read transactions at 8 am. He/She can also drill down to understand what tables are accessed by each process, and relate this to when slow performance occurs and in which part of the process.

The system administrator, now understanding the patterns may make suggestions on how to improve performance

- Tune commonly accessed tables by each process
- Suggest on how to segregate different ETL batch processes. For example, if two batch processes are reading from the same set of tables, it would be faster to run them separately rather than concurrently so as to speed them up, as accessing the same tables simultaneously usually results in performance degradation. He/She may also opt to run some of the ETLs which have no interdependence in separate application servers while running them in parallel, in this way taking advantage of parallelism capabilities of your hardware infrastructure.
- Can suggest that certain reports be generated immediately after their ETL batch processes have finished, even while other ETL processes are still running but for which the reports' data are not dependent on, reducing the overall execution time for the whole process.

These are just examples, the specific architecture, ETL jobs, reports, and the manner the tools work will determine the approach to take.

4.1.2.3   Network Management

This involves both availability and capacity management. Nowadays with the advent of many tools used for monitoring network traffic, actual usage can easily be determined, this, however, requires quite a bit of analysis, as network traffic may not be all legitimate and not always readily identifiable. Proper network availability management is a combination of technical, analysis, and policy, all three being intertwined, there is no point in defining a policy that cannot be implemented because either the proper tools are not in place or there is no capability to analyze the traffic. Without proper policy and enforcement (also proper network design), the traffic will always grow to saturate the network, every upgrade being insufficient shortly after deploying.

For availability management, tools exist now which send SMS and emails to personnel whenever a link or switch goes down, facilitating response time. Most important in network management is the proper configuration of the switches, as well as the network topology and configuration. Nowadays with Network Management Tools, the job of identifying the CI details for each switch and router is made much easier, as well as the deployment of changes remotely. New patches and firmware versions are deployed according to priority (similar to what was discussed for the SysAd). One of the difficulties in network management is that the dependencies are network-wide, such that a change in one switch can actually affect the whole network. Another difficulty is that although lab deployment and testing is recommended for major changes, lab environments cannot capture the full condition of the actual environment once deployed, so that testing is limited at best.

An actual experience we had with a firewall was that although it worked perfectly well in a contained environment, once deployed it started degrading over time due to ever increasing memory utilization in the firewall appliance. This was in fact due to a memory leak (memory which would not release after it ceased to be utilized by a process), and after much investigation, was found to be due to blocked web pages' memory not being released properly. This was not detected in the contained environment as the number of such transactions was relatively small, but in the real-world example, was huge enough to make the problem apparent after a few days of having a lot of pages blocked. The bug fix was then released by the vendor's support and applied.

Sufficient capacity, on the other hand, should always be cross-checked to determine if the traffic is

- Legitimate
- Due to a security breach/oversight
- Due to improper network configuration, especially loops or traffic taking very long routes
- Defined Quality of Service is proper (or necessary)

These should be addressed first before allocating additional bandwidth. Aside from capacity in terms of MBps, another important parameter that needs to be inspected is latency, which may also be due to

- Improper configuration: switches, routers, and appliance involved in the path need to have their configuration properly set, any one of them along the path causing the delay, delays the whole path.
- Non-optimal network design: wherein for example the paths traveled through the network are very long, having to go through many switches before reaching the final destination.
- Overcapacity: switches may have been undersized (e.g., an edge switch used in distribution switch configuration), or appliances in the path having reached their limit.

Sometimes, the latency may be thought to be purely network-related, but may reside in a gray area and not be so apparent. This may be especially true for intermittent slowdowns experienced by users. A good example of this is a problematic DNS server which takes very long to respond, affecting users intermittently. This issue normally cannot be seen by simply monitoring network traffic, and if no proper tools are available, will require lengthy analysis, also with the SysAd team until finally identified.

Also, illegitimate traffic may not be so easy to detect. Take for example a network in which policy allows the downloading and sharing of videos due to the nature of the business. Though firewall policy may be in place, this is still no guarantee that the videos being shared (which eat a lot of bandwidth) are in fact work-related, unless one physically inspects the videos themselves. This is where policy is important, as it is impossible to police all traffic 100 %, but policy should state that any infraction to which a user is caught shall carry severe penalties.

4.1.2.4   Management of Servers and Storage

These are most important during the go-live of a new service, since as indicated before is the moment of truth, in which the hardware requirements defined during the design phase are confirmed to be those actually needed. After going live, server and storage resources need to be monitored and tweaked, until the desired performance is attained. It is very important, however, that proper design be conducted from the very start before deployment, as is for example the proper design of the storage LUNs, or a very common mistake: assigning the wrong drives for the data and logs (C: is commonly used as the default, which is where the OS resides, and therefore not appropriate).

Unless environmental conditions change dramatically (e.g., number of users, patterns of usage) then availability should not degrade over time. Capacity management is, however, very important and though it also does not commonly change very fast, it is susceptible to a number of factors

- Change in the number of end-users
- Growth of data over time (disk storage)

- Additional application modules being deployed
- Change in the schedule of batch processes. New schedule may coincide with some other operations that consume a lot of CPU and memory.

Part of IT Service Continuity management as well roll-back procedures is regular backup. The definition of the backup procedures will still reside with TM, including restoration procedures.

4.1.2.5   Technical Management

The head of the technical management team has a very important role which includes

- Making sure skills are up-to-date and relevant. If necessary, conducting hand-holding, internal and external sessions and ensuring these are scheduled and conducted.
- HR resource capacity management. Should be sufficient for the work on hand, and should have sufficient resiliency and redundancy in case of resignations or prolonged sickness
- Overall understanding of the technical architecture, including management of its corresponding documentation
- ITSM documentation custodian and overall Quality Assurance supervisor
- Compiling all major CIs requests that translate into additional procurement requests
- Assignment of tickets to personnel within the team, in case these have not been routed directly
- Monitoring of team's compliance to the SLAs

Aside from this, he has to interface exhaustively with the Head of IT infrastructure, in assisting projects that will be phased into production. Unlike software projects, infrastructure projects cannot usually be separated from existing operations as they need to take into account the overall existing architecture and design. Testing for infrastructure projects before deployment will also be a major time-consuming role for TM.

As an example, imagine a project which needs 10 new servers to be provisioned. Though the existing capacity may be able to meet this new requirement, TM needs time to understand the requested architecture and scrutinize the requirements before proceeding to provision these. The project may also be competing with other projects for the infrastructure or even the time devoted by the TM team.

4.1.3   Application Management (AM)

The Application Management (AM) team is in charge of all CIs related to software. They also have a very important role, which is to act as the bridge translating business requirements into technical specifications. They must be knowledgeable of the functional aspects of the different applications, including possibilities and limitations, so that when translating these functional specifications, they are aware on what can be done, and how it can be done, with minimal customizations if possible.

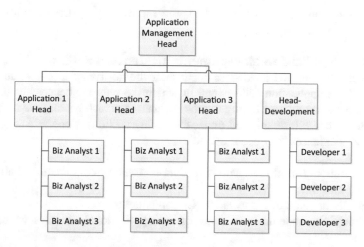

Fig. 4.4 Structure for application management team

An AM team can be structured according to application type as shown in Fig. 4.4.

So that specialists occur for each particular application 1, 2, 3, and also a general pool of programmers exists that can work on specific tickets (versus applications), depending on the programming technology required. If the changes for the different applications are few, then a full-time head per application may not be required, and resources may be shared, thanks to cross-skilling, so that Business Analyst 1, for example, may be the same person for both Application 2 and 3, as the number of tickets for these two applications is low, and he/she has the skills to maintain both, resulting in the structure shown in Fig. 4.5.

Availability management is not very relevant to the AM team, and capacity management only in terms of resources. On the other hand, ticket handling by the AM team is of crucial importance as incidences and requests sent to this team are

Fig. 4.5 Alternate structure for application management team

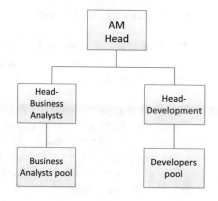

usually more complex in nature and require more analysis. Let us analyze incidences and requests separately.

4.1.3.1 Application Management: Incidence Handling

Most application-related incidences occur after the go-live of a project due to the
novelty of the application and system, in which the only incidences already identified are those discovered during the testing phases, which seldom are really very
complete in nature (as explained under the testing section). Long after going live,
additional incidences may occur due to

- Not commonly used transactions or data-transaction combinations being used
  for the first time
- Upgrades in some of the technical CI components
- Modifications undertaken in some of the applications' modules which affect
  others

As an example of a modification which affects other modules, take a utility
billing system where new potential customers are created upon their application for a service. Provisioning of the utility service, however, requires an
initial payment from the customer AFTER it is ensured that the customer's
location can be provisioned with the service. Inadvertently, if this initial
payment is created as a receivable in the finance module and it takes a
considerable time to validate the application and receive the payment, this
may cause a bloating of receivables which may not necessarily reflect the true
state of the business. Eventually either this is paid after a considerable amount
of time, or may need to be reversed due to nonavailability of the utility
service or failure for the potential customer to pay. This means that they were
not actual receivables in the true sense of the word, but actually more of an
anticipation of payment from the potential customer.

Incidences may be of differing nature

- Program gives an error and cannot proceed
- Program does not perform intended functionality, giving a different output from
  what is expected

The second type of incidence is usually harder to analyze and resolve.

Take a timekeeping system which feeds into payroll. Imagine that its configuration is such that employees working overtime are to be paid a special rate, and
that the timekeeping system is built such that all extension beyond 8 am–5 pm
period is calculated as overtime pay. It is, however, overlooked that there is a night
shift which actually starts work at 5 pm, which is not entitled to this overtime pay,

but an altogether different pay scale. This is an example of a program failing to give the desired functionality, but not a hard error.

AM-related incidences are usually harder to resolve as they may occur only based on certain conditions (data), and this data may not be always used by the transaction that is failing. It may be necessary to reproduce (simulate) the error for the purpose of testing and analysis, and sometimes this may not be so easy. In case the incidence cannot be resolved immediately, workarounds must be given until the final resolution is determined. A problem ticket may also need to be raised if the root cause is not determined within a reasonable amount of time, and assistance may be sought from second level support.

As for requests, these also require sufficient effort to analyze, oftentimes because the request is incomplete in terms of specifications, and then requires an interaction between the business analyst and the end-user to determine exact requirements. For this purpose, documentation on the request is to be filled-out, together with details filled-up by the analyst in terms of implication, whether this is a configuration, and what needs to be done in order to address this request, and if it requires some customization, at what level: code, fields, tables, objects, and the corresponding man-day effort. Oftentimes, the code may be a modification over an existing standard code, so that the standard code is referenced. More information on the suggested documentation is specified in Sect. 4.4.1.2.

Any modifications related to the application will raise a change request (CR) and trigger the change management process, which normally should also be handled by the service desk system. Change management triggers an approval process which is dependent on the company's IT policy. This is discussed in detail in its corresponding section.

4.1.3.2 Application Management: Development

It is best practice that developers be shielded from the end-users and should only receive instructions on what is to be coded from the corresponding Business Analysts. As the developers are usually a pool (unless many of the applications are custom-coded and require an almost full-time dedication), their assignment to different applications will be on a case to case basis based on the tickets generated, programming skills required, and the load of each developer. Best practices in terms of coding standards and security should be imparted by the developers' head and disseminated and improved by the team.

4.1.3.3 Application Management: Overall

Among the roles of the AM Head are:

- Making sure skills are up-to-date and relevant. If necessary, hand-holding, internal and external sessions are to be scheduled and conducted
- Personnel capacity management. Should be sufficient for the work on hand, and should have sufficient resiliency and redundancy in case of resignations or prolonged sickness
- ITSM documentation custodian and overall Quality Assurance supervisor

- Assignment of tickets to personnel within the team, in case these have not been routed directly
- Monitoring of team's compliance to the SLAs
- Maintaining coding standards
- Maintaining configuration standards and guidelines
- Improving on the documentation needed in determining scope
- Assignment of tasks to developers (if there is no development head)

4.1.4   IT Operations Management (ITOM)

IT operations management is the "heart" of IT, as it manages all aspects that directly concern the end-users: the day-to-day activities that ensure to the users the availability of the different IT services. Of all the teams, it is perhaps the least technical, and yet, is the most critical in terms of perceived impact by the users.

It has two main functions

- IT Operations Control, which can be further subdivided into

    - Console Management
    - Job scheduling
    - Backup and restore
    - Print and output
    - Report generation
    - Data investigation and resolution

- Facilities Management

    - Data centers
    - Recovery sites
    - Contracts (for the facilities)
    - Consolidation
    - Common facilities management

In other words, the first set of functions under IT Operations Control are functions related to batch processes that are scheduled and run as part of normal IT Operations. ITOM checks for the successful completion of these as part of its functions, and analyzes errors, reports them for resolution (usually to AM or TM if they cannot get to the root cause) and rerun these batch processes as required. An important function as well is to investigate issues which are data-related that impede from some ITOM job from proceeding. Incorrect data is usually attributed to causes at the source (end-user or external third party) and are typically due to

- Incorrect transactions being undertaken
- Wrong procedure by the end-user
- Incorrect data being provided by a third party (such as a bank, outsourced provider, etc.)
- Errors in some of the source files being utilized

ITOM will investigate the source of the data error and either fix it directly, or coordinate with the concerned party for them to correct.

On the other hand is the facilities management function. In many organizations, this function has not been fully turned-over to the ITOM group and may still reside with TM due to the skill set, as well as for historical reasons. End-user common facilities that should also be handled by ITOM are those common to many end-users

- Timekeeping systems
- Deployed general-use PCs (versus those assigned to specific users)
- Displays and PCs in common-use areas of the company
- Others

ITOM should ensure their availability in terms of the hardware, as well as their content.

The table of Organization for ITOM is typically that shown in Fig. 4.6.

In this diagram and depending on the number of batch processes, operators may be separated into different teams, with or without a head per team. If the number of batch processes is few, then all operators are placed in a common pool, and each operator may undertake different functions.

Fig. 4.6 Structure for IT operations management team

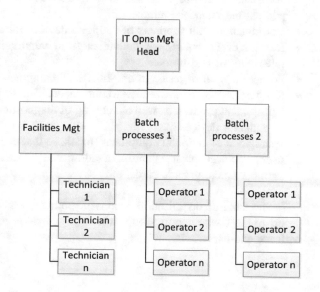

The facilities' technicians will also work according to specialization, as for example, those assigned to the data centers will monitor data center parameters like air conditioning, electricity consumption, etc.

4.1.5   Field Support (FS)

This refers to the team that conducts the troubleshooting, configuration, and repair of endpoints (user's assets such as PCs, smartphones, laptops, printers, and other peripheral devices). Common functions of the field support team are

- Configuration of endpoint devices. This may be done

    – On-site: meaning, the technician will be physically present where the user is
    – Remotely: by means of remote support tools, such as

        Remote desktop
        Remote patch deployment software
        Remote antivirus deployment engines
        Etc.

- Repair of endpoint devices. This may be first level support and repair for out-of-warranty devices, especially for small repairs like replacement of common components (capacitors, resistors), replacement of power supply, cords, etc. This may include pulling out of the units and bring to the repair shop.
- Installation of baseline configuration (the standard software and configurations) for new endpoint devices before releasing to the users
- Assistance to end-users on field if service desk is unable to service the request or address the incidence remotely
- Coordination with suppliers of endpoint devices for their repair or replacement
- Receipt of IT equipment deliveries from vendors, storage, and subsequent release to the end-users
- Proper disposal or resale of end-of-life IT equipment
- Regular Endpoints' Preventive Maintenance. This may include cleaning of PCs, laptops, and printers, as well as running of diagnostic tools and defragmentation of endpoint devices.
- Installation of endpoint equipment (for those that cannot be simply done by the users), as well as installation of additional hardware to endpoints (such as memory cards, graphic cards, etc.)

In the table of organization proposed, both the service desk and field support report to the User Support group, which in general is in charge of all interactions with the end-users.

4.1.6   Operations Head

The operations head is the person overall responsible for O&M as depicted in the Table of Organization shown in Fig. 3.5. The duties and responsibilities of the Operations Head are

- Overseeing the Service Level Agreement (SLA) that measures the effectiveness of the O&M team toward the end-users.
- Overseeing and managing the Operational Level Agreement (OLA) that measures the internal agreement between the IT Management and the O&M team. This OLA is typically more stringent than the SLA to allow for some buffers and slippage.
- Ensuring compliance to Operations' governance policies, as well as tuning and improving these policies and implementing guidelines in order to make operations more effective and responsive to end-user needs.
- Overseeing competencies and skills of the O&M team, ensuring they are attuned to the needs of operations, identifying skill gaps and conducting actions that decrease these gaps. These may include internal trainings, hand-holding, external trainings, immersion programs, etc.
- Planning for and managing trainings, in accordance with the skill gaps identified previously.
- On-boarding for new team members. Consists basically of the preparation of material for quick on-boarding, as well as a training and hand-holding plan for them to quickly ramp-up and be productive in the shortest possible time.
- Regular performance review of team members, and identifying corrective actions for those with deficiencies.
- Skilling-up, researching for new techniques to further improve operations, and implementing these.
- Driving continuous improvement to the team via PDCA (see chapter 4.8 for more details).
- Fostering an environment of learning and growth, as well as good team relationships.
- Coordinating with the IS and II Heads on projects that are being transitioned into Operations, and identifying the correct O&M resources that need to be involved in the cut-over.
- Providing the necessary resources to IS and II for support to projects which necessitate O&M involvement.
- Overall caretaker of the Business Processes that all the different applications are using. In this aspect, the Operations Head should ideally be very familiar with the existing Business Processes so that he/she can critique any new change to the existing BP and see if applicable.

Of all the three heads, Operations Head, IS Head and II Head, the Operations head has the most power as she/he has the authority to veto any project or initiative from IS and II which may go into production, or affect operations. This is because ultimately he/she is responsible for the SLA to the end-users and must ensure that these are met.

As indicated, the operations head is also in charge of governance and ensuring that O&M complies with it, this means

- Ensuring ITSM policies are strictly enforced
- Ensuring security policies are complied with both the IT team, as well as the end-users.
- Reporting and communicating any breaches to the CIO

Communication to the CIO on the above is done on an as-need basis, however, day-to-day monitoring and management of operations usually involves:

- Regular operations meetings with the O&M team and CIO (usually weekly), in which the tickets for the last time period are reviewed and analyzed. This analysis includes

  - Number of tickets created: incidences, requests, and problems
  - Number of tickets resolved. Operations needs to ensure that there is no increasing backlog of tickets, which will result in an ever increasing backlog as time goes on.
  - Analysis of tickets per team. These are monitored for unusually heavy activity and analyzed for the underlying reason.
  - Repetitive incidence tickets which usually point to an underlying problem causing multiple generation of incidences.
  - Status of incidence tickets after a major project has been implemented. Usually, incidences will spike after go-live but should continuously decrease afterwards.
  - First call resolution. FCR should be maximized so as to avoid escalation which results in delayed ticket closure.

- Team leads' Operational reports, which normally is done as part of the Operations meeting, in which each team reports activities conducted for the period, issues, and resolutions. Team may also ask for guidance on matters they are unsure on how to proceed.
- PDCA or continuous improvement.

4.1.7   Operations Management Office

This is the office wherein the head for Operations is, which oversees all operations under her. This office is composed of:

- Operations Head: in charge of the whole O&M to which the AM, TM, ITOM, US heads report to
- Support staff

The support staff functions include:

- Producing all SLA and regular operations reports
- Design, drafts and implements the different operational policies
- Internal audit (for the O&M group) to ensure compliance
- Regular review of policies
- On-boarding to new members coming into the team
- Debriefing and clearance for departing team members

On the other hand, the Operations head is the primary responsible party for managing and ensuring that the O&M team complies with the prescribed SLA. Her primary duty includes:

- Regular reporting to the portfolio manager. He/She ensures also the accuracy of the reports; this also entails discussion and finalization of the SLA KPIs attained by the team.
- Internal Billing and availability reporting
- Ensuring that the skills needed by O&M are met. This includes resource matching, sourcing and releasing of human resources.
- Updating the O&M team on policies.

4.1.8 Information Systems (IS) Head

As described in Sect. 2.1, a best practice is to separate day-to-day operations from strategy and especially, projects, reason being that the methodologies for managing IT operations and projects differ considerably. Also, software projects can in fact be totally isolated (usually) from operations, in a different environment, a different team, and even in content and scope, so it makes more sense to have a separate team in charge of these altogether.

The Information Systems Head is in charge of all software-related projects, and therefore is its portfolio manager. He is in charge of managing these from conceptualization through development and execution until these projects go-live and is transitioned to O&M during the support phase.

His main duty for all software projects includes

- **Planning and strategizing**: determine what new projects are needed in order to meet the company's plans, objectives, and strategies. This is a normal function of a portfolio manager, and is a continuous process.

- **Overseeing the portfolio of projects**. This includes all those responsibilities described under portfolio management for its whole lifecycle of the portfolio. Most importantly, the monitoring and control of the projects, regular communication with the stakeholders, as well as ensuring that portfolio governance is followed.
- **Coordination and proper turn-over to O&M**. This is done from an IT technical and functional aspect as discussed in chapter 6, but also from a business aspect, meaning, he/she has to maximize the success of the project once it goes into operations in delivering the business benefit(s) it was designed for.

With regards to human resources, the IS Head may dispose of full-time project managers under him, or just manage Project Managers (PMs) as their respective projects are assigned under his portfolio (part-time resources for the duration of the project). As for resources under their respective PMs, these may be fully contracted out as turn-key projects, may be using in-house resources which have been mobilized and assigned for the duration of the project, or a combination of in-house and outsourced. Only in the first case are resources wholly managed by the contractor's PM, for all other cases (and sometimes even for the first), the project resources will have to be fully managed by the customer PM.

Governance is an aspect of outmost important to the IS Head, as it determines all aspects in which his/her portfolio is to be managed (more in Chaps. 7 and 9)

- How projects are to be monitored? These are the tools given to each PM in monitoring and controlling the projects, which in turn are reported to the portfolio manager (IS Head).
- How results are communicated to stakeholders? In which manner, periodicity, and channels used are defined.
- Conditions and steps in starting a project. A project may be requested from an end-user organization or internally initiated, the procedure and conditions for initiating a project need to be properly defined.
- Minimum documentation and deliverable requirements. These should be in the form of templates which the PMs can easily adapt to their respective projects.
- How changes in scope (and change requests) are to be raised, analyzed, and approved.
- How to transition a project into operations
- Project closure

Software projects affect both operations and hardware projects, so that there needs to be close coordination between all three. Specifically for operations the turn-over activities specified in Chap. 6 need to be followed by all PMs. Specifically,

- During the start-up phase of the project, O&M needs to be informed of the project and given a high-level overview of the project

- All infrastructure requirements need to be discussed with TM and/or II Head for the provisioning and capacity planning during the beginning of the project. This also includes operational aspects such as backup and restoration procedures, security, among others.
- Training and hand-over right before going live (with TM, ITOM, AM)
- In-depth discussion of technical and process information also before going live with the O&M team
- Briefing to SD before going live
- Post go-live Support scheme to be used involving the project team, O&M, as well as first and second level product support from the principal.

The infrastructure requirements of the different projects under the IS Head need to be discussed even before the project has started, so that planning, provisioning, and in some cases purchasing of additional capacity or special hardware can be done in time for the project. This discussion needs to take place with the IT infrastructure Head (next section), as he/she will ensure the overall technical architecture to meet the projects' requirements, while at the same time ensuring operations, as well as TM, which will be the team to do the actual provisioning.

4.1.9   IT Infrastructure (II) Head

The IT infrastructure (II) Head is the direct counterpart of the IS Head. In the same manner that the IS Head is in charge of all software projects, the II Head is in charge of all infrastructure projects. This includes, but is not limited to

- Servers
- Storage
- Network devices
- Security appliances and software
- Databases
- Virtualization
- Cloud technology
- Operating systems
- As well as all components that may fall into the above

Besides projects, the II Head has to ensure coherence of the overall architectures for the different applications, whether these are in operations, in projects, PROD, QA, or DEV. For this reason, his responsibility spans across both operations and projects.

Among his duties are

- **Planning and strategizing**: defining what new projects are needed in order to meet the company's plans, objectives, and strategies. This is a continuous process, and he is responsible for the portfolio of all infrastructure projects

- **Overseeing the portfolio of projects**. This includes all those responsibilities described under portfolio management for its whole lifecycle. Most importantly, the monitoring and control of the projects, regular communication with the stakeholders, as well as ensuring that portfolio governance is followed.
- **Capacity planning**. Reviewing current capacity, usage projections, and triggering procurement for additional capacity as may be needed. This applies to servers, storage, network, as well as software components.
- **Availability management**. Reviewing availability of infrastructure components with TM and O&M in general, and proposing new strategies in order to meet the required availability.
- **Security**. Reviewing and proposing new security policies, guidelines, as well as appliances and software that may be needed in order to meet the security requirements of the organization.
- **Resource skills management**. Ensuring that the skills and competencies of the team (both O&M and projects team) are commensurate with requirements, will flag and plan for required trainings, additional personnel whether long-term or contractual, as well as personnel which may be taken out of the team (if outsourced).

As all IS projects require infrastructure, regular meetings should be held with the IS Head to plan for the necessary capacity

- **Annual capacity review**. This may be done more often, depending on the speed in which requirements come, and is conducted together with the IS and Operations Head, ensures that for the next time horizon, hardware capacity will be sufficient, or if otherwise, will initiate a procurement process.
- **Provisioning based on IS Project requirements**. Any new project will require additional hardware resources, and so these will be requested formally through an infrastructure request form which will trigger review and provisioning. It is recommended, however, that a meeting at the start of the project be conducted to review the proposed architecture, hardware requirements, so as to ensure that these are acceptable and a good understanding on both sides occurs. It is very common for project teams to overdesign the specifications, so this meeting is conducted in order to rationalize these.

Another important duty of the II Head is with regards to security. Security is a concern that spans the whole organization, and cannot rest only on one individual or group; however, the II Head together with the CIO must take the lead in promoting good security practices. Ensuring a secure environment is a combination of

- Overall Policy
- Governance and oversight
- Implementation of the policies
- Configuration of the different servers, applications, and appliances

- Architecture
- Use of security appliances, software

Thus, if only a few of the above is addressed, this would not be sufficient to guarantee a secure environment. In spite of security being everyone's concern, most of its implementation resides on the infrastructure side, so it is logical that the II Head be the lead in defining and implementing security, unless a full-time Chief Security Officer is deemed necessary by the organization, which would normally report to the CIO. A Chief Security Officer (CSO) is also called for in business environments where security are of primary importance, such as in banks, financial institutions and retail which regularly transact and hold confidential customer information. Whatever the case, these would have to coordinate together with the Head of Operations and IS Head, to ensure that the policies are viable, as well as to regularly review the security policies and their enforcement.

Similar to the IS Head, the II Head is in charge of all hardware-related projects, and is therefore its portfolio manager. Once more, he/she is in charge of managing these projects from conceptualization through development and execution until these projects go-live and is transitioned to operations during the support phase.

His/Her main duty for all infrastructure projects includes

- **Planning and strategizing**: defining what new projects are needed in order to meet the company's plans, objectives, and strategies. This is a normal function of a portfolio manager, and is a continuous process.
- **Overseeing the portfolio of projects**. This includes all those responsibilities described under portfolio management for its whole lifecycle of the portfolio. Most importantly, the monitoring and control of the projects, regular communication with the stakeholders, as well as ensuring that portfolio governance is followed.
- **Coordination and proper turn-over to O&M**. This is to guarantee that from the moment of go-live, the infrastructure can be taken over and maintained by TM. Proper training as well as hand-holding is necessary for this to become a reality.

Similar to the IS Head's setup, resources may be full-time or part-time depending on the philosophy and Table of organization. Another similar, important aspect is that of governance, which for infrastructure projects, again resides with the II Head. Governance rules and project templates should generally be the same as that for IS so that they are in concordance, but may have its own, small particularities. Generally, the II templates are much simpler than that of IS'. Refer to the governance roles described under the IS Head, as these are directly applicable as well for the II Head.

Important aspects on II projects (or infrastructure components in IS projects) that need to be coordinated with O&M (TM specifically) are:

- During the start-up phase of the project, O&M needs to be informed of the project and given a high-level overview of the project
- Overall architecture of the new project being initiated. This must be approved by both the II Head and TM.
- Also during project start, discuss with TM all infrastructure requirements for provisioning.
- Backup and restoration procedures for the specific application being implemented.
- Release management procedures. These are going to be executed by TM, so it is imperative that TM understand and approve these.
- Training and hand-over right before going live (TM, ITOM, AM)

4.2   IT Services Lifecycle

In general, IT services are planned, designed, created, released, maintained and operated, then retired, so these can be broken down into four distinct phases:

- Planning and Design phase
- Release phase
- Maintain phase
- Retirement phase

These can be represented conceptually by the diagram shown in Fig. 4.7

Initially, a service is planned for and designed accordingly; this may come from a user's request, may be internally escalated, or may be a transition from a project. Release phase refers to that of placing these new IT services or changes into operations as part of the roster of applications in production, which render the service to the end-users. During the course of delivering this IT service, the service needs to be supported and from time to time enhanced (maintenance phase), which may entail additional releases. Finally, if there is no need for the IT service, it is uncatalogued and decommissioned under the retirement phase.

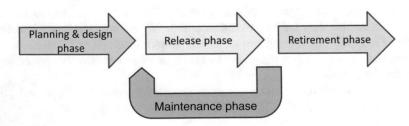

Fig. 4.7 The IT services lifecycle

Table 4.1 IT versus end-user point of view in the delivery of services

Example of technical services (IT's viewpoint)	Example of IT services (users' viewpoint)
Network availability	Email
Servers' availability	Financial Management Sys
Storage response time	Billing services
Report application's availability	Reports
Firewall availability	Internet

IT services are therefore created, deployed, maintained and improved, and eventually, retired.

What is exactly an IT service? The key to the answer is in thinking not from the point of view of IT (technical perspective), but from that of the users', which is IT's customer. The service must be something of value to the users. Thus, for example, the servers and storage being maintained by IT may be thought of as a service by IT, but indeed, it is not from a customer's perspective. This is because the customer does not care about the availability of the storage, servers and their components, her concern will be on the availability of the financial management system application (for example) which runs on servers, storage and the network, and which she needs in order to conduct her work properly. Thus, from the customer's perspective, it is the availability and adequacy of the financial management system as a whole that is a service to her. To understand this further, take a look at Table 4.1 which shows some examples (note that the left hand column does not have a one to one correspondence with the right hand column).

So, in fact, for every service indicated on the right hand side of the table, their availability and usage actually depend on many different technical services in order to be able to render the desired and expected performance. Thus, for the example earlier, the financial management system, if the concern is availability and response time of the application, it in turn depends on the availability of the network, servers, storage, application, as well as their corresponding aggregate response time.

The compendium of all services which are delivered to the end-customers is thus called the service catalog, and it is this list of services in the catalog which are maintained throughout the whole service cycle (planning/design-release-operate/maintain-retire).

4.3   Planning and Design Phase

Services are created for the purpose of servicing a demand by the users, and in this sense, must be planned and designed accordingly. A service catalog is that compilation of IT services being offered, which is added, modified and deleted accordingly. However, offering the service is not enough, the performance of the service must be guaranteed as needed by the users, and this performance agreement between the users and IT is called the Service Level Agreement (SLA) which governs the levels of performance for each service being rendered. This will be expounded more under its corresponding subsection, so we park it for now.

In planning and designing for a new service, several questions come to play

- What need will it address?
- What service level must be guaranteed?
- What is the needed infrastructure? Is it available and should just be provisioned or should it be procured? This may trigger a capacity planning review.
- What resources are needed? (High level) Are they available? By when? How many man-days effort will this be?
- What will be the approximate duration to deliver the service?
- Will this be treated as a change request for O&M to handle or a new project? This would depend on IT's policy. Generally speaking, anything beyond a certain number of man-days or anything requiring a new system or major infrastructure (not just provisioning) would be treated as a project.

Two possible outcomes when designing

- **Project**. If the number of man-days to undertake the change is significant (depending on policy), then it will be treated as a project and shall follow the normal path for a project (normally outside the scope of O&M); or
- **Change**. In such a case, it will follow the change management procedure as described in the next section.

New services may be the result of a planning exercise or may be due to a request. Take the two following examples:

Example 1: The finance department requests for the enablement of online payments. In this case, it has been an end-user department to request for the service, the enablement of this service may be treated as a project or merely as a change request to O&M, depending on the effort, complexity, as well as policy for treating requests as projects or changes handled by O&M.

Example 2: At the end-of-the year during the planning session, it was decided to offer by Q2 of the following year a new service allowing customers to view their bill online. This was subsequently treated as a change request which O&M handled.

4.3.1   Change Management

Change management (Schiesser 2001) refers to the process of changing any Configuration Items (CI) in accordance with a request that may be either initiated internally by IT, or by the user through a request ticket. It defines the process for handling the request for change, while ensuring that the change requests follow proper procedure.

All request for changes normally originate from the Service Desk System in the form of a ticket assigned to a Business Analyst under the AM team (or a TM personnel). The Business Analyst then comes up with a design document which basically records:

- **Reason for the change**. This should be explained in simple, nontechnical terms. If the user is initiating the change, then he should be interviewed to understand the reason for the request, and whether this is due to an incident, or is an enhancement.
- **Applications and infrastructure affected by the change**. In other words, this should explain the configuration items that will change. It should necessarily include a nontechnical explanation of how the CI will be affected, as well as a technical portion for subsequent reference by the technical team. If the change is at its initial analysis phase, the technical portion may not yet be complete, but will be successively refined. The technical portion should contain information such as

  - Application affected
  - Module
  - Table and field affected/created/modified
  - Code utilized (if any)

- Initial effort estimated in man-days and type of resources needed
- Information needed by the Change Advisory Board (explained later) should be clear so that approval can proceed without delays. This will include:

  - Change due to request or incident?
  - Impact: companywide/department wide/limited impact. This will include a description of the impact
  - Risk in releasing the change

A change will undergo the normal evaluation and approval process as defined by the policy. Approval may be needed from the Change Advisory Board (CAB) (Burges 1984) as explained hereafter.

The CAB is the body which approves/disapproves changes on all Configuration Items that are of primary importance. Not all CI changes need to be approved by the CAB, and would depend on the organization's policy. Changes that are routine and known to have little negative risk can be approved at the lower levels (Operations Head), but if there is an inherent risk in the change or if it has a major impact to the organization, then these shall require CAB approval. The overall approval process may be illustrated by the diagram as shown in Fig. 4.8.

The CAB will usually be composed of the Head for AM, Head for Operations, and if required, the CIO herself, other members may be called to participate as the need arises. Among the aspects evaluated will be:

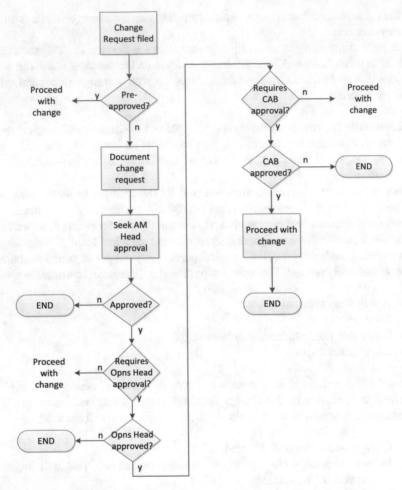

Fig. 4.8 Change request approval flow

- Risk in conducting the change.
- Cost of the change (either in $ terms or in man-hours)
- Need for the change
- Complexity of the change (which normally affect both risk and cost)

Some of the criteria determining the complexity of the change are:

- Does it affect more than one department?
- Does it divert from standard process?
- Does it necessitate customization (FRICEW)? (FRICEW is explained in Sect. 5.3 but basically refers to customizations on the application)
- Does it require policy change?

- Does it need approval from other departments (especially important would be finance, legal, HR, and procurement)?

On the other hand, factors that are taken into account in evaluating risk are:

- Inherent risk in disrupting operations
- financial impact to the organization
- legal or regulatory impact
- Changes that require customization. Because customization is an expensive and error-prone process, this is inherently riskier than a mere configuration change.
- Requires Interfaces to different systems, again due to their inherent complexity (and therefore, risk).
- Major changes in master data structure
- Requires access to confidential or restricted data

The CAB may decide to approve, reject or defer the change. Deferment may be just a delay in its deployment, an instruction to seek further clarification from the user/analyst, or a request to consult second level support. This may be due to

- Insufficient clarity on the possible impact (and risk)
- Insufficient justification on the need for the change
- Insufficient clarity on whether a customization is really needed
- Insufficient documentation

As an example of a request with insufficient detail, take a request lodged for serializing the official receipts generated by the system, wherein the number series depends on geographic location, with no clear indication on why this change is requested, other than this being a finance request. This change has a very large impact and effort, as well as a major risk (affects tax compliance). It was also flagged as a customization, and offhand would seem like a major one, especially taking into account that exhaustive testing would be needed so as to minimize possible negative impact, that has possible regulatory penalty implications. The decision to approve this was therefore deferred pending a more complete explanation on the reason for the need, analysis of its impact, as well as a need to explore alternative ways of doing this without the use of customization.

In the case changes need to be applied urgently, and Emergency Change Advisory Board (ECAB) may be called just for the purpose, and if justified, the documentation may be done after release.

As an example of how the CAB may work, take a request for change involving the modification of the address master to add a special subcategory called "Sub district" which is non-standard, and necessitates the use of a table and field in the address master. AM's Business Analyst suggests the use of a table and field designed for another purpose (Block area). The CAB convened and discussed this at length, this being a customization which involves the use of a standard field but for other purposes. Given this, the CAB decided to disapprove it, due to the possible risk that this field may be needed some time in the future, even if unused today.

4.3.1.1   Prioritization

As several request for changes will arrive simultaneously, a prioritization should be made at the very beginning when capturing the details of the change.

Prioritization of changes should take into accounts several factors:

- Is it to address an incident or a problem? Or is it an improvement or request from a user?
- Perceived urgency by the line organization
- Possible disruption to Operations in case of not proceeding

If the priority cannot be well-established by the Business Analyst, then it will be escalated for consultation to the AM Head, and if still not determined clearly, to the Operations Head.

Again, highly urgent changes can be routed directly to the Emergency Change advisory board (ECAB) for immediate action, and if very urgent, it may be decided that the corresponding documentation be deferred till after deployment. Take note, however, that these should be exceptions rather than the rule; otherwise, it defeats the purpose of having a proper Change Management process.

4.3.2   Service Level Agreement (SLA)

Again, the agreement should capture what the users require, and also what IT can provide. In other words, it is useless to target (and invest in) very high service levels, if the users do not in fact require it, while on the other hand it is futile to target very high performance if IT (people, infrastructure, etc.) has not been dimensioned accordingly (nor IT's budget). Take as an example the availability of a reporting system. If this system is not to be used over the weekends, there is no point in targeting 24×7 availability when in fact the weekends may actually be used for maintenance purposes of the application and related components.

The SLA is a covenant agreement between the two parties, and a commitment for IT to provide the necessary performance levels described in it. Common performance metrics used for service level include:

- Availability —indicates the (usually %) amount of time that the application is available for use.
- Response time—the time for the application to return the requested output.
- Correctness—of reports, data uploads (for example, from external systems)
- Resolution time—time needed to resolve an issue
- Timeliness—delay or % of time a particular output is available
- Completeness—usually of documentation that is used in supporting operations such as Knowledge Base documents, work-instructions, manuals, etc.
- Customer Satisfaction–by means of surveys

Thus, all services must be designed according to the agreed-upon SLA, which means that all the different components needed in order to deliver the necessary service level must also be designed accordingly. Thus, for response time, resolution time and other metrics which use time, the following calculation is used:

$$\text{Total time for delivery of the service} = t_1 + t_2 + t_3 + \cdots + t_n$$

This means that the total time for delivering the service is equal to the sum of each component. Similarly, the overall availability will depend on the product of each individual's availability component:

$$\text{Overall availability for the service} = A_1 * A_2 * A_3 * \ldots A_n$$

The formula above is applicable when nonredundant/non high-availability components are used. Thus, for example, the overall availability of the financial management system will be the resulting availability of the product between the availability of the network, availability of the servers, availability of the storage, and availability of the application itself. On the other hand, its response time would be the response time of each individual component: network (summation of each switch's latency involved in the routing), server response time (application server, database server), and other components utilized.

The service catalog is thus a list of services that is provided to the end-users as defined in the SLA between IT and the users. It is imperative that this SLA be presented and approved by higher management, as it comprises of IT's commitment to deliver. As services change with time, the service catalog needs to be updated by adding services, deleting them, as well as updating the SLA based on new requirements, changing strategy, or changing environment.

IT in turn may be contracting several parties to undertake the services being delivered. As such, these subcontracted services need to also commit to certain service levels that conform to the overall SLA. These underlying contracts are thus governed by a similar mechanism, but are called Operational Level Agreement (OLA) which should be more stringent than the overriding SLA so as to allow IT to meet the SLA commitments with some buffers.

Suppliers that may form part of the delivery of the agreed services includes outsourced service providers, hardware maintenance providers, network and

Fig. 4.9 SLA versus OLA

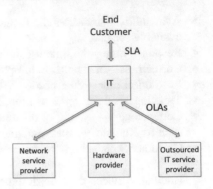

telecommunication providers, software developers, and the like, and each should have its OLA governing their services which should tie-up to the overall SLA. This is shown diagrammatically in Fig. 4.9.

4.4 Release Phase

The release phase refers to the different tasks and aspects that need to be undertaken before and during the release of the change into production. This release may be a new service or a change to an existing service.

A change must be managed properly, in that it:

- Be conducted with the right quality, time and cost
- Have minimal unpredicted impact on production
- Reduce errors and minimize risks due to transitioning to the new or changed services

Any change undertaken means that a corresponding configuration item (CI) has changed. A configuration item refers to any asset, service component or other item which needs to be controlled in order to deliver a service or services. Thus, any deviation from the baseline situation is considered a change that has to undergo proper release management.

In order to minimize the impact to production, releases must be tested thoroughly and properly before release. This means that aside from the production environment, proper development and testing (also called Quality Assurance) environments should be used, and this brings us to the topic of testing.

4.4.1   Testing

Testing is explained more exhaustively in Sect. 5.5; however, there are some basics of testing worth mentioning here. Firstly is the need to have separate environments for Development, Quality Assurance (Testing) and Production. Under absolutely no circumstances will any releases be done directly into the production environment

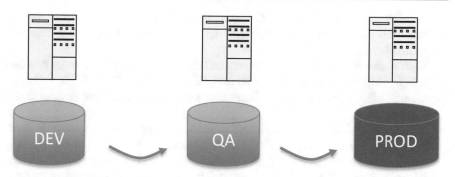

Fig. 4.10 Typical release lifecycle

without prior testing in the QA environment, while at the same time, all changes are to be initiated in the DEV environment. The diagram in Fig. 4.10 depicts a typical release's lifecycle.

A typical change is initiated in DEV by the Business Analyst and/or developer, and unit testing is undertaken here. If successful, then the release procedure is called (and executed by TM) so that the change is now released into the QA environment, where he will proceed with a more exhaustive testing (unit testing, regression testing, integration testing, and whatever else has been determined to be necessary). If and when it passes all these testing by the Business Analyst, he may then call (depending on the type of change) for the users for their round of testing. As a rule of thumb, users should generally be called for them to test when:

- They were the requestors for the change; or
- They are the ones commonly using the said transaction or function; or
- Involves transactions too complex for IT to understand or recreate due to unfamiliarity with the data, or manner in which the transactions are to be conducted.
- If unsure, the best rule is that it be the end-users to test

In other words, since the users are the experts in using these transactions and measuring their impact, they should be the ones to determine whether the change has been successful or not. Failure to involve the users during testing can result in grave consequences.

Take as an example a report produced with written-off accounts. This report was requested by finance for use by different departments including sales, however, the rules of how to write-off the accounts necessarily needs to come from finance, as they are the only ones capable of attesting to the veracity and accuracy of the reports, and also have intrinsic authority in officiating these reports.

Once all testing has passed in QA, then the final release to production may be initiated, this has to be in accordance with the plan determined, especially if there is downtime involved.

It is TM that actually undertakes (executes) the release, but it is normally AM and ITOM (or projects) that initiates the request for release into QA, PROD. From the description of how the different environments work, take note as well that normally:

- **DEV**: contains all changes that were initiated, regardless of whether these were released, were canceled or deferred. For this reason, it is important to have a backup of the configurations stored in DEV. The data, however, is relatively irrelevant, as it is usually scant, and created by the testers only for the purpose of simple unit testing.
- **QA**: should be a reflection of PROD in terms of configuration (except for those changes in QA pending release to PROD). It should normally contain data that is quite similar to PROD for testing purposes, and this is why many times, the data from PROD is copied regularly into QA, so as to maintain it current so that the testing can be more accurate.

There are several risks in having DEV and QA not properly maintained. Consider the following problematic scenarios:

- **QA does not have some of the Configuration Items that are in PROD** (aside from the CIs being tested): that means that the testing environment in QA does not reflect the same as PROD, which defeats the purpose of testing, as you wish to test in an environment as close to as possible to PROD, before you release into PROD. This has the implication that although testing may pass in QA, it may ultimately fail in PROD.
- **Data in QA is very old**: data, same as CIs, affect the behavior of the environment. Though it is impossible to have all PROD data in QA at any given time, the data in QA must be refreshed periodically so that the environment stays relevant (and similar to PROD), to make the testing effective.
- **CI in QA did not come from DEV**: In this scenario, the QA was properly configured directly without it coming from DEV. This means that the development package is not tracked (it should always originate in DEV) and may be lost in the next QA refresh. Ultimately this means that something in PROD will not be reflected in DEV and QA which may cause errors in the future. Furthermore, these CIs will be hard to trace and if and when identified, will need to be manually reproduced in DEV, and subsequently released to QA.

4.4.2   Configuration Items

As explained, changes mean modification on configuration items, where configuration items mean the details on the setup of an application, system, or asset to deliver an IT service(s). Examples of configuration items are:

- **in a server**: the operating system used, patches and versions applied, memory, number of CPUs
- **in a network switch**: operating system used, its version, firmware version, Network Access Tables, number of ports, connectivity of the ports to other devices, etc.
- **in an application**: the different modules, tables with their configuration entries, custom programs used, tables and fields in the DB, etc.

Configuration Item changes must form part of the documentation produced during the planning and design phase, and must be updated subsequently if any additional changes are made. It is also important to note that Configuration Item changes have the effect that they may in fact affect more than one asset, so that the impact of such changes need to be analyzed and tested thoroughly before actually releasing to production.

As a particular configuration item may affect many different assets or services, the relationship between configuration items is to be recorded in a so-called Configuration Management Database (CMDB) (Michael Brenner 2006; Axelos 2011). This database records the relationship between all the different configuration items.

An example of a configuration item change that affects others is shown in Fig. 4.11, which depicts a network switch attached to two servers.

Any change on Switch 1 (say the routing rules) therefore has a potential impact on server1 and server2, which in turn have a relationship to the FMS and procurement systems, and the HR system, respectively. Thus, ideally this relationship between the switch and the other assets should be captured (as part of the CMDB), along with the properties and characteristics of each component.

Fig. 4.11 Example for a switch and the effect of a CI change

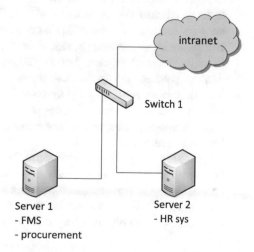

4.4.3   The Configuration Management Database (CMDB)

A Configuration Management Database (CMDB) refers to a record of all Configuration Items (CI) for the company, meaning, all assets and their respective configurations as well as their interdependency with other assets and in turn their own CIs. As an example, a software called "Easy software" version 1.2 is related to other assets, for example, the server it resides on, a Dell PowerEdge R220 Rack Server, the O/S it is running on, Windows 7, the DB which is MS-SQL 2014, and so forth. These assets by themselves will carry more details, such as the MS-SQL 2014, which would have information on its version, patches applied, etc. Relationship between assets may be quite complex, as for example in the case where we have a switch connected to several servers, the connection between these assets needs to be captured as well.

CMDB for the longest time has been a panacea and has been tracked by means of manually recording this information. However, new tools are now available in the market which allow for the "auto discovery" of these assets. CMDB software scan servers, network, as well as endpoint devices to display the interrelationship between them, and the CIs for every asset.

In its conceptual form, the CMDB is a logical representation and relationship between services, assets and the infrastructure and which records the relationship between configuration items. This is conceptually shown in Fig. 4.12.

In many cases, however, the CMDB will not be a one and unique central repository, because for all practical purposes, different tools will be more efficient in discovering different types of assets:

- **Network Management system (NMS)**: will act as the CMDB of all network-related assets such as switches, routers and the like. The NMS' CMDB is in fact just a subset of the NMS' main function, which is to manage the network seamlessly from a single console.
- **Endpoint Device Management System**: system that manages the endpoints (mainly PCs and laptops, but nowadays also tablets and smartphones), and deploys patches and upgrades to them.
- **Mobile Device management system**: This is an endpoint device management system specific to mobile devices (e.g., tablets and smartphones).
- **Asset Management system**: may encompass some of the above functionalities, but additionally also servers.
- **Excel sheets**: these may have information on the above (especially if no system is used for them), additionally, contractual and supplier information and maintenance information (such as when it will expire) will be stored here.
- **Integrated CMDB software**: in which all the above functions are encompassed by means of auto discovery agents.

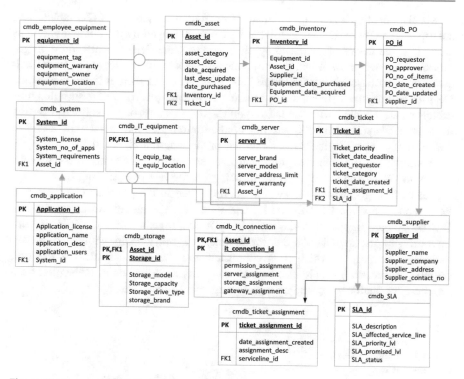

Fig. 4.12 Sample CMDB logical structure (partial structure only)

Benefits of a complete CMDB are:

- Easier troubleshooting
- Easier renewal of maintenance
- Management and control of licenses
- Easier release management and impact analysis

Again, pros and cons need to be evaluated in determining the extent and depth in which to deploy a CMDB solution.

Another important and related concept is that of the Baseline Configuration. A configuration baseline is defined as the configuration of a service, product or infrastructure that has been formally reviewed and agreed upon, and that thereafter serves as the basis for further activities that can be changed only through the formal change management procedures. A configuration baseline can be obtained for most assets through a "snapshot" of their CIs at a particular moment. This may be done manually if the number of assets is small, but this quickly becomes unmanageable, so that the asset discovery tools described earlier may be needed in order to display the different CIs.

Special mention needs to be made for endpoints (laptops, PCs, tablets and smartphones). These, if company-issued are also managed by the company, and as such, it is the desire of IT that they all have the same deployments and configuration. Whenever new units are procured, these should be deployed with their corresponding baseline configuration before issuance. As such, it is the task of the US group to regularly update these baseline configurations so as to ensure that new issuances are updated with the latest patches and versions of the software. Before these are made part of the new baseline configuration, they may need to be tested so that no issues occur to the users as shown in the diagram of Fig. 4.13.

A similar yet more limited approach may now also be undertaken for servers, thanks to virtualization technology, allowing for the fast provisioning of servers.

Let us now go back to the switch example used in the previous Configuration Item section. For the CMDB, the switch, its brand, ID, model, firmware version, O/S version are important and should be captured, together with the specific configuration of the switch. At the same time, the relationship with each server, including the port in which it is connected and the characteristics of the port (number, speed, etc.) should also be captured. Any modification of the switch from this baseline shall call for the change management procedure.

Fig. 4.13 Endpoint baseline configuration deployment workflow

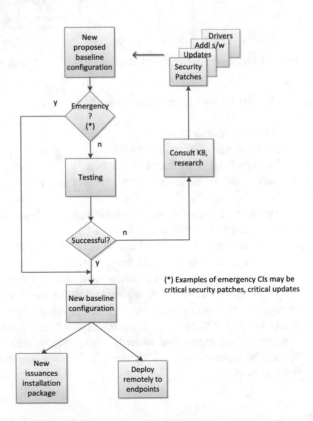

Service Assets refers to different tangible and intangible resources and capabilities that the IT organization owns and uses in delivering the different IT services. They are the value the IT organization possesses in creating a greater value (IT service).

IT Assets may be of differing forms:

- Management
- Organization
- Process
- Knowledge
- People
- Information
- Applications
- Infrastructure
- Financial Capital.

Configuration Management (Watts 2011) is a subset of release management that delivers a model of the services, assets and infrastructure by recording the information about components (Configuration Items), the relationship between these items, and how these will change based on the release. This enables other processes to access valuable information, such as the impact of proposed changes.

The main asset or system for this purpose is the so-called Configuration Management Database or CMDB.

4.4.3.1   Release Approval

Part of the approval may also involve determination on the right moment to release. In some organizations, specific weekly or monthly windows for releases may have been defined, especially if there is downtime or risk of conflict.

Regardless of whether such a window exists or not, the planning should take into account the timing for the release:

- Downtime (if any) for the release, and how this will affect the users
- Locking-out of certain users and transactions, if necessary
- Transactions that may "hang" due to the old process not being accessible or possible after the change. It is important to identify the best time to release, so that the number of "hanging" transactions is minimized. It is also important to identify what the proper procedure for the hanged transactions should be, whether:

  - These may be left hanging
  - These need to be deleted, and by whom (system administrator?)
  - Needs direct configuration into the DB (very risky! Should be minimized)
  - Needs a special procedure
  - Need to be manually canceled by the user, and re-created again after the release of the change

To illustrate the situation of a hanged transaction, take for example a self-service HR system in which employees file their leave requests. Because of a change in the leave request process, all the old requests pending approval or cancelation before the release result to be hanging, and do not proceed for approval in the system. As such, users need to be advised on what will be the effect and action to take. For example, they may need to refile all these leave requests that remain pending approval after the release. To fix this, a typical procedure may be:

- System administrator cancels old transaction
- HR informing the users to recreate
- HR informing the approvers to re-approve

Depending on the release, if it affects many users, this may necessitate a cut-over plan taking into account:

- Testing and even pilot release (if applicable)
- Advisory to affected users
- FAQ to Service Desk for easy and speedy resolution of queries and incidents
- Training (if any)
- Hand-holding for special users
- Back out procedure

In a way, this is a mini version of the cut-over activities during project deployment as described in Chap. 6.

The manner of the release is dependent on the type of application and what type of release management it supports, as each has its own release strategy, and may vary from the primitive to the sophisticated. Different ways releases are managed from one environment to another are (in accordance with what the application itself supports):

- **Manual**. Such that changes made in one environment need to be manually configured in the one being deployed to.
- **Copy of the configuration file** from the current to the deployed environment. This is for example used by MS Dynamics 2011.
- **Releases are deployed by means of a tool** within the system to the target environment without generally causing any downtime. Example of this is SAP.

Furthermore, some releases necessarily need to be done manually (many technical items, for example, as well as some master data in some systems), so the possible impact of the release needs to be assessed well before undertaking. A more exhaustive explanation of release management is in Sect. 7.9 as explained under projects.

4.4.3.2   Documentation and Knowledge Base (KB)

All releases need to be properly documented in terms of what they are, how they have been undertaken, and the reason for the change, among other details. Two types of releases:

- AM-related releases which refers to CIs of the applications
- TM-related releases which refers to CIs for the infrastructure

Each has its own type of documentation. The knowledge base documentation for AM-related changes would generally comprise of two components:

- **Business requirements document**: describes the user's requirement that triggers the change request. This document will be needed only when the user's request contains some degree of complexity which necessitates a document describing these requirements with some degree of depth, otherwise, a simple description in the body of the ticket will suffice. This document needs to be signed off physically or electronically by the requesting user before proceeding with a more detailed analysis.
- **Request for Change Functional specification**: this is a mandatory document which among other things contains:

  - Translation of business requirements into a language that the BA understands in order to configure, rationale for the change, as well as other relevant information. [*]
  - Would contain specific fields describing how it has to be undertaken, depending on whether this is a:
    - Report
    - Interface
  - Technical specifications
    - System affected
    - Module involved
    - Program or object name affected
    - Description of program or object name
    - Type, such as:
      - Java
      - ABAP

.net

Others

New/modification

- Configuration description, including code affected, parameters and description
- Database modification, including:

Table name

Fields affected

Details on the changes or configuration on the fields

- Data modification: this is if there is a direct data modification that needs to be undertaken
- Should include screenshots and other information that describes the issue, limitation, or other information that needs to be addressed. [*]
- Registry of effort involved in undertaking the change
- Signatories[*]

- Release to production information form [*]. Shall reference:

- Release code (if any) for audit trail purposes
- Ticket information
- Date
- Other relevant information for the release to be tracked

- Test plan and test scripts with results[*]

Those marked above with (*) are mandatory, the rest are dependent on the type of change being requested.

For TM-related changes, three general types:

- Incidents
- Problems
- Requests

In all cases, if the configuration needed is simple, then an explanation in the ticket itself of what is to be done is enough. For more complex requests, a Work Instruction level procedure needs to be produced describing how the change is to be executed.

For simple incidence resolution, description of the resolution in the ticket may be sufficient. On the other hand, for complex issues and for problems, several actions may be tested before the final resolution is attained. As such, all these attempts and work-arounds need to be documented at the work instruction level into the knowledge base. All incidences related to the same issue will then be referenced to the problem ticket and the Knowledge Base (KB) document, which should also contain the list of other incidences related to it that were raised.

4.5   Maintenance Phase

The maintenance phase refers to the day-to-day activities that are conducted in order to meet the defined Service Levels. This normally means:

- Managing the infrastructure so that it is performing according to its required service level
- Running the different batch programs that are needed in order to produce the intended outputs
- Receiving and processing any requests for changes
- Analyzing and proactively managing events detected
- Managing and resolving any incidences detected/reported

For infrastructure, the following specific aspects also need to be addressed:

- Capacity management
- Availability management
- IT Service Continuity Management
- Information Security Management

These are explained in detail the next sections.

Normal service operations need also to take into account the following processes:

- Event Management
- Request Fulfillment
- Incident Management
- Problem Management
- Access Management

Let us now discuss each of these separately.

4.5.1   Event Management

Events refer to some condition which require attention, and may also be called alert. It may be generated by an IT Service, Configuration Item or Monitoring tool. It is not yet an incident, but may lead to one, and thus, a request ticket may be opened to address this, or a request ticket must be raised for investigation of the event.

Examples of events are:

- Disk has reached 80 % threshold—the capacity management monitoring tool for the disk determines that the disk will reach full capacity in 3 months; it thus raises an alert so that it is properly addressed.
- A batch process failed to finish within the usual 3–4 h runtime, though it did finish without incidence in 6 h. The IT Operations Management team may raise this for investigation, as this could repeat, or worse, further deteriorate.
- The configuration of a server was detected by TM to be incorrect. The data being downloaded is being written into c: drive, which is normally reserved for the operating system. This is not causing any issue at the moment, but is an event that can eventually cause issues in terms of capacity management.

Events, once detected, need to be investigated and/or addressed by the corresponding team. Root cause of the problem needs to be evaluated, and the team will subsequently release a request for change to address the issue. Thus, an investigation ticket or a change request ticket may thus be raised to analyze or address the event, as the case may be.

Events, if they cannot be addressed immediately, may also form the basis for the continual service improvement, so that they be eventually addressed.

4.5.2 Incident Management

Incidences are events that actually disrupt a service from normal operation and service level. Incidences may be raised by different entities:

- Users when they detect the issue
- Any member of the operations team as well, when detected
- IT Project members that report an issue that is already under operations' responsibility

Incidences that are reported should be resolved within the timeframe as specified by the SLA. These may be treated generically (all type of incidences) or specific (depending on the type of incidence). The most immediate concern when an issue is opened is in restoring the service to its original level. This means that if the root cause may take time to be identified, work-arounds can be applied in order to do this, while the root cause is still being sought for. All these actions need to be necessarily recorded in the knowledge base (see later section), so that it be a clear reference on what were the actions taken, including work-arounds, what the root cause is, and the final resolution. Incidence tickets should not be closed until the proper knowledge base document has been produced. Take note that if the incidence's root cause cannot be identified, a problem ticket may need to be opened, as is discussed later. This allows for an in-depth analysis of the root cause, as problem tickets are not time-bound till resolution. All incidences related to the same problem ticket will be tagged as such, so that the problem ticket references all the associated incidence tickets.

> Take an example of a reported incident from a user which cannot log on to the different corporate applications as the login via Active Directory does not work for him. As these cases were encountered before, SD instructs the user to lock his screen, and after a few seconds attempt to login again. If this fails, he is then instructed to restart his PC, which again fails to resolve the issue. It then becomes a problem, as this situation has not been encountered before and needs further investigation to pinpoint the underlying issue. As the user however, cannot be kept hanging without his access, a work-around is effectuated, in which his PC is whitelisted in the Active Directory, allowing him access to all the different systems. In this case the incident ticket is closed, but the problem ticket remains until root cause is identified.

Incidence tickets normally carry different weights depending on their severity, major incidences are those that:

- Have a high potential business impact
- High urgency
- Impairs many business units

This is also explained under the Service Desk section. Severity should be identified at the point of reporting, which is normally Service Desk, major tickets would have a higher priority for resolution. Service Desk will also collapse several reported incidences into a same one if they are in fact one and the same, but reported by different users.

Incidence tickets will then be routed using their pre-defined escalation procedure to the correct Service Team for analysis and resolution. All incidences will remain open until such time they are resolved (totally or by means of a work-around), or if canceled. Cancelation of incidences may be due to the realization from the user that it is not a true incidence (he undertook the wrong procedure, for example), may have been discovered by the service team to be due to wrong procedure or data, or simply that the service was restored to its normal condition without any action (as it sometimes mysteriously happens! However, this is usually due to wrong user procedure being used).

4.5.3   Problem Management

Problem tickets are always the result of an incident or several incidences. In other words, an incidence is first detected and attempted to resolve, but then a problem ticket is created when:

- Many incident tickets of *differing* nature result, but are due to the same underlying root cause. For example, a network problem related to a faulty switch causes different type of incidences including slow response time, unstable network and unreachable servers.
- The root cause is not known beforehand nor is it resolvable within a reasonable period of time due to its complexity (it does not appear in the Knowledge Base)
- May require the analysis, involvement and participation of many of the service lines, not only one.

Problem tickets may be opened by any service team that is in charge of the original incidence ticket(s), and this will be automatically assigned to the team creating the problem ticket. Though the service team may require involvement and assistance from other units, principal responsibility still resides with the team handling the original incidences. Several steps may be taken from this point forward:

- Attempt to recreate the problem. Sometimes the most difficult incidences are due to the fact that they appear randomly or in circumstances that occur infrequently. If there is a sandbox environment, the team may attempt at recreating the incidence and then analyze logs, variables, etc., to try and identify the root cause.
- If the problem is related to a customized CI, then most likely this is due to the way the customization was done, so the first step is to analyze this CI's programming and related configuration.
- Consultation of internal knowledge base. This is to ensure that no similar incidence occurred in the past, which may give clues to the current problem.
- Consultation with the supplier's knowledge base and forums. To check if such issue was encountered before, and as to resolve faster.
- An incidence ticket may be raised to the hardware or software provider. It may be determined that the root cause is due to a bug or faults from the provider, so that once enough information is collected, it is then escalated to the provider's technical helpdesk for analysis and resolution. The Service team may also be unsure if it is indeed due to the provider, but reasonable suspicion warrants the raising of such a ticket to them at the earliest possible time.
- If still there seems to be no resolution after the steps above, a more lengthy analysis may be needed. If the problem ticket is of certain importance, the operations team may invoke the involvement of specialists, either from the provider or from external consultants, so as to resolve the issue.

Once the possible resolution has been identified, this shall undergo the regular change management procedure including testing and identification of roll-back procedures.

As explained for incident management, problem management needs to first and foremost address the issue of restoring service to its normal level. This means that while the root cause is being identified and addressed, a series of work-arounds may be applied in the meantime. It must be ensured, however, that such work-arounds do not mask the issue from being resolved permanently, or in other words, does not hamper the investigation into the final root cause of the problem. Common work-arounds are

- Restarting of the server or router (an all-time favorite of IT teams)
- Restarting of a service
- Rerun
- Rerouting of network switch
- Roll-back of a change
- Work-around procedure to address the issue
- Data modification

Again, it must be emphasized that these are only work-arounds and should not be abused. Restarting of a server is really a very bad way to address an underlying issue because it just temporarily defers the issue. Take for example the case in which the server is swamped with transactions that eat-up its resources, causing it to eventually fail or slow down to unacceptable levels. Of course resetting the server frees-up the server's resources, but only temporarily as it has terminated all processes handled. The root cause may actually be insufficient capacity or the incorrect utilization of the server by an application.

It is important that all work-arounds, successful or not, be recorded in detail in the Knowledge Base for future reference. If a similar incident occurs again in the future, it will then be easy to know and apply known good work-arounds, while avoiding those that are known not to work. All errors which have been resolved and are recorded in the Knowledge Base are referred to as Known Errors.

4.5.4   Request Fulfillment

Requests are tickets that are also filed through the Service desk, but unlike incidences and problems, are not considered issues, but form part of normal operations. Requests will have their own SLA, distinct from that of an incident. Generally speaking, not all requests will be treated equally in terms of priority (see Service Desk section) but will depend on the type of user, type of request, and as will be discussed here, the service line affected.

Requests related to TM, ITOM, US are usually straightforward to fulfill and can be met relatively fast (unless requiring field work), requests for information should also be straightforward, however, requests related to Application Management can be quite complicated in nature, especially if this involves the request for a totally new configuration or functionality in a particular service. Such requests will typically give rise to a request for change, which, as it may need sufficient man-days of work, will need a fulfillment date that is agreed upon with the requestor. Typical steps for fulfillment are:

- **Pre-analysis of the request**. Will be determined by the corresponding AM business analyst. Will first determine if the request cannot be met by any existing function or procedure, and whether it warrants opening a request for change. The business analyst will also determine whether the request needs to go through CAB or ECAB, as per IT policy. Depending on the gravity (urgency), it may already be raised to ECAB for approval, even without full documentation of the requirements.
- **Analysis of the request**. Once validated, the business analyst shall proceed with the detailed analysis and design of the request. He shall coordinate with the user in filling-out the design specifications documentation to ensure that the request's scope and details are captured correctly and entirely. This may entail:

  - Request for further information from the user by email
  - May require a sit-down meeting with the user
  - Once the design document is filled-up, a sign-off will be needed from the user. This signifies the correct capture of his requirements. This document will also contain details such as man-days estimate and resources required, tables, fields and objects used, as well as details on the customization (if any). Nothing should proceed after this unless sign-off is obtained.
  - CAB approval if required. If not, this will follow the normal ticketing procedure for approval process.

- **Execution/Build**
- **Testing**
- **Deployment**

These are the normal procedures for release management (see pertinent Sect. 4.4).

Some examples of different type of requests and their escalation and approval level are:

- Request for internet: approved by user's Department head
- Request for installation of a software existing in IT's catalog: pre-approved
- Request for transfer of files from old laptop to new laptop: pre-approved
- Request for access to the ERP: approved by his Department head/Business Process Owner or both
- Request to install a new trial software: approved by the II Head
- Request for a project: approval by the CIO

These approval levels are best configured inside the Service Desk, so that depending on the category, the ticket is escalated to the correct approver automatically.

More of this is explained in the next section.

4.5.5   Access Management

Access management is the process of granting authorized users the right to use a Service (including data or an asset), while preventing access to non-authorized users. Access management may be grouped into two general categories:

- **Pre-approved**: in which access can be granted to the requestor immediately by the Service Desk due to his position or role, as the access being requested is pre-approved as per IT policy.
- **Requires approval**: again, the basis is policy. Approval may not only be from IT, but may also require approval from the line organization to which the user may be reporting to.

> As an example of the first, say that company policy is to grant email utilization to any company employee, as such, a call from an employee requesting for email service is automatically granted by the SD. The SD then creates a ticket which is routed to the corresponding service team that will physically create the account. Supposing now that company policy is to restrict use of social networks unless properly justified and approved by the user's department head. An employee filing a request for the use of twitter would therefore have to seek his department head's approval before the request proceeds.

Some services may be quite complex and authorization on their use may not be apparent. This may be the case for example when requests for certain functions or roles in an ERP or a CRM system. Data may be confidential and should only be accessible to personnel with certain roles. As a best practice, there should be Business Process Owners (BPOs) defined for each major process, and these should be the ones to determine whether authorization should be granted or not. A Business Process Owner (BPO) is a role given to certain key users in the organization, their duty is that of caretakers of a process(es) which they are accustomed to as they normally either execute this process or are the managers of people who are the ones executing these processes. He is expected to know the process very well, including its intricacies, limitations, and find ways of improving it. In effect, IT is the entity that implements the process, but the relevance and use of the process is something the BPO is in charge of. These persons should regularly coordinate and meet, together with IT, to see what more can be done to improve the efficiencies of the processes; they are also in charge of the data that these processes produce.

As an example, take the head of Customer Service who is the identified BPO in charge of the CRM's customer data. A request from a user within the organization to access customer data in the CRM may only be authorized by the BPO after careful justification. The justification may be apparent, as for example, due to the position or role of the requesting user, but in cases it is not, he may have to explain why and what data he needs access to.

4.5.6   Capacity Management

This refers to the ability of the different components of a service to have sufficient capacity to deliver a service with the agreed performance as defined in the SLA. This is commonly thought of for infrastructure, but also holds true for human resources. Capacity management as a process refers to the continuous planning, monitoring and adjustment of available capacity in order to meet the overall SLA now and in the future.

- **Planning**—refers to the initial definition and allocation of resources needed for the service. Common type of infrastructure capacity applies to servers, their memory, CPUs, as well as disk size, network bandwidth required, as well as particular skills (people) needed to keep the service running. Capacity planning may be initially designed on a per service requirement, and then rolled-up to a total which will define the total capacity needed by the organization.
- **Provisioning**—in which specific assets and services are assigned specific resources.
- **Monitoring**—in which the different resources' utilization are observed during normal and peak operations in order to detect if any saturation occurs, which may impair performance.
- **Tuning**—in which additional resources may be added and configured until the desired performance is attained
- **Procurement**—in case no additional resources are readily available, then the procurement or availing of additional resources from external suppliers triggered. Alternately, resources may be reallocated from services or assets, if possible.

Capacity management used to be a difficult endeavor in the past, but due to the rapid advancement of current tools, work has been made easier:

- **Capacity management analysis tools**—these is a wide array of tools available to analyze allocated resources versus current performance. These monitor CPU, memory, network, and disk storage utilization. Some of the more advanced tools also have predictive capabilities, in which they predict when certain resources will fall short based on current trends (for example, hard disk based on current growth).
- **Virtualization**—previous to virtualization, hardware resources were all physical, nowadays, with the advent of virtualization and cloud technologies, resources can be allocated on-the-fly as the need arises, without the need to wait for the lengthy procurement and delivery processes to finish.

Capacity management reviews should also be called for regularly, so as not to be caught unaware on the capacity situation, and pre-empt requirements and procure additional assets if necessary.

4.5.7   Availability Management

Availability is the ability of an IT asset or IT Service to perform its agreed Function whenever called for. It refers to a general indicator of the % of time it is available for use versus total time. Take note that when we refer to available for use, it does not mean actually used. Also, the total time to be used in the denominator of availability refers to the total time DESIGNED for use.

As an example, take a certain service which is to be up and running 8×5. Thus, during the week hours of every working day, it should be up and running for use, even if it is not actually used. If there is downtime during the weekend, this does not matter, and is not counted against its availability because it was not designed for use in the weekend.

As such, it is of no use to overcommit on the availability (and thus, overcommit on resources), if it is not actually needed, resources are to be allocated only according to the expected service levels as per their availability metrics, which should in turn reflect reality and expectations for the service using them.

Though it may be obvious, availability must also factor-in downtime required for maintenance and upgrade, and this includes time needed for patch updates, DB and OS upgrades, application upgrades, etc.

Additional metrics that may be relevant are:

- **Reliability**—refers to the ability for a service or IT asset to perform without interruption. This can be measured by the Mean Time Between Failure (MTBF) or Mean Time Between Service Interruption (MTBSI). Depending on the case, this measure may also be important, and not just availability, as the service may be so critical that it needs a guaranteed reliability measure. As an example, take a particular service, say an ftp server that is expected to be up 99 % of the time (availability) which is actually met. However, this service has repeated disruptions, each of which lasts very few seconds so that the even if the total availability is met, its reliability is very low. Because of the frequent disruptions, very large file copy transactions to the server are disrupted and do not finish, so that these need to be restarted again. In this case, poor reliability has a direct effect on the service.
- **Maintainability**—A measure of how quickly and effectively an IT asset or Service can be restored to normal working condition after a Failure. This is commonly measured using Mean Time to Restore Service (MTRS).

Availability and related metrics in general depend on a number of factors

- **Adequacy of resources allocated to the different CIs**—say for example, memory, CPU, network bandwidth and hard disk must be sufficient for a server to conduct its functions correctly. Incorrect sizing will degrade the performance of the server to levels making it slow and eventually, unavailable. The same holds true for human resources, in which sufficient levels (number of man-hours) of properly skilled resources should be applied to keep it running. For example, Database Administrator (DBA) hours needed for tuning the DB, as well as time for applying patches to the applications as required.
- **Redundancy**—This may be used to increase the availability of the CI and service. Common practical redundancy measures includes clustering, having redundant application servers, redundant network path links and switches, and a multi-skilled workforce.
- **Spares**—in general, having spares is a second level approach needed to meet the availability requirements. By having spares, maintainability in the form of MTRS will be relatively lower (versus redundancy). Again, with today's virtualization technologies spare servers can be restored in a very fast fashion. With cloud technologies restoration is not only fast, but also at a fraction of the cost of having procured the spare altogether.
- **Backup**—is also a second level approach, which ensures if something goes dramatically wrong, the application and data can be restored in the fastest time possible. Backups can be done in a variety of ways, and is explained further in 4.5.10
- **Third party High-availability spares**—is a 3rd level approach, in which, instead of having the spares on hand and having procured them, a service contract is signed with an external third party for them to provide the spares on an as-need basis, in which the third party guarantees its particular availability of spares and time to restore. These third parties are either resellers/distributors of the product, or companies specializing in these kinds of services, and normally charge a percentage of the actual cost of the spare. Spares may be new or refurbished the last especially true for outdated technologies.
- **Security**—security breaches may cause downtime, some of them significant, so that security must be properly addressed. More of this is discussed in Sect. 4.5.9.

Poor availability is usually the first sign of poor IT practices, and the most obvious shortfall from a user's perspective, and yet, if bad practices have been running for a long time, it is also difficult to address, requiring cultural change and time for them to take effect.

4.5.8   IT Service Continuity Management

This refers to the management of risks that could seriously impact and impair IT Services. In other words, it refers to the ways and means to reduce risks due to force majeure (usually natural calamities) that could impact severely on the ability to provide the required services. Some important related concepts need to be kept in mind:

- **Business Continuity**—Overall business needs to ensure continuity of service in case of disaster or security breach. Since IT is well and part of the normal operation of a business, it needs to be aligned with the business requirements. As an example, if the priority of the business is to be able to keep invoicing even if in times of disruption, but it is acceptable for functions related to human resources to be impaired somewhat, then the IT services must take this into account. It is of no use to over allocate and over meet the overall expected service level, as this has a cost implication. IT's SLA must be aligned and support the overall service level of the business. The diagram of Fig. 4.14 shows an example of an interrelationship between the overall business service level and IT's in case of a disaster.

As you can see from the above diagram, the IT portion is just part of the overall business continuity plan (shaded globe) but an important component to meet the overall (impaired) SLA.

- **Risk Analysis**—a risk analysis should be made for the purpose of identifying possible impact the risks may have, and the probability of the risk. This should again be done preferably at the corporate level first in order to identify what its perceived risks are, and then perform this same exercise at the IT level. At the business level, not all the risks that are relevant at the IT level may have been identified, so that these necessarily have to be again identified using a more detailed analysis for IT. Please refer to Sect. 5.1.7 for more details on risk

Fig. 4.14 Example illustrating relationship between corporate Business Continuity and IT service continuity

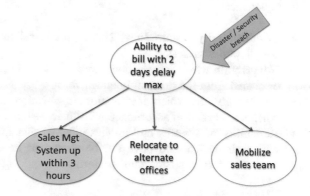

management. Risks will be mitigated in a variety of ways, and some risks which cannot be totally eliminated and are still significant need to be addressed by means of concrete actions in the service continuity plan.

- **Plan**—this is part of Planning and Design phase in which the different Services, their SLA during the Disaster are determined, and the corresponding mitigation actions identified. This should include a very detailed Disaster Recovery plan which should go all the way up to the transactional level of what steps need to be executed upon the trigger of a major disaster. The basic principle guiding it is the restoration of services within time so that it complies with the Business Continuity SLAs

- **Business Continuity SLAs**—when disaster strikes, the regular IT SLAs normally cannot be met. As such, a different set of SLAs takes effect until final recovery from Disaster.

- **Disaster Recovery Site**—fires, tornadoes, typhoons, and most especially earthquakes and floods are local in nature but may affect a large area. As such, it is best practice to have the standby infrastructure in a location far from the main location of the servers, normally 30 km or more. In case of total failure of the main data center, the DR site is to enter into production.

As a plan is best when it is tested, the IT Service Continuity Plan should be executed by simulating a disaster. By executing the plan, the different steps that are to be undertaken are followed and the times to execute measured. At the end-of-the exercise, things that were not accounted for or that can be improved are then used to refine the plan further. This disaster simulation should be done at least once a year, and should be selected at a date and time that minimizes possible impact to production.

4.5.9   Information Security Management

This is a whole topic just by itself due to the very fast and changing nature of the threats to which IT systems are exposed to.

Information Security refers to policy, execution, applications, and infrastructure that guarantee:

- **Confidentiality of data**. In which only personnel authorized to access such data are allowed to access it.
- **Integrity**. In which information, applications and systems remain unadulterated or altered from the original intended form.
- **Availability**. In which information, applications and systems can be used whenever needed in accordance with their design.
- **Reliability** of systems and applications, so that these perform in accordance with their design, and have not be altered or unadulterated by unauthorized personnel compromising their performance.

Information Security relies on many different components for it to be attained:

- **Policies** which determine the do's and don'ts, as well as the how to go about requesting and executing aspects which have an impact on information system security.
- **Guidelines and procedures** which determine at the working (operational) level how these policies are to be executed. While policies apply to the general populace including users and IT personnel, guidelines and procedures will be specific depending on the type of personnel, whether a user, or to which specific team in operations the guidelines will apply.
- **Configuration Items** which apply the different security settings in the assets so as to guarantee that the security aspects are addressed. Examples of these are patches, security upgrades, as well as settings in the application related to security (password lockout on the third try, for example)
- **Architecture of the network**. As there are best practices in terms of designing the network architecture so as to ensure its security.
- **Security infrastructure**. May be both at the network level, as well as on the server side. This may include security appliances (Intrusion Prevention Systems), firewalls, and the like.
- **Security software** that addresses particular security concerns, these may be at the server side, at the endpoint, or in-between at the network level as well. Includes anti-viruses software, whitelisting software, among others.
- **Code**. That is in accordance with policy and procedures, which should in turn be in accordance with global best practices in ensuring secure code.

Information Security management implies the proper application and management of all of the above. It is not enough to just focus in one area, all these need to be in sync and continuously monitored and adjusted so as to ensure that they address the changing landscape of security threats. Forgetting one of its components can result in serious consequences. As an example, having good network architecture, proper policies, as well as advanced security applications and appliances may not be good enough if the proper work-level implementation of security procedures is forgotten.

Although commonly thought of just as technical threats and vulnerabilities, most successful security breaches also carry some social component, such as:

- **Phishing**—in which a user voluntarily gives out personal or company information by being made to believe that the requestor is legitimate. These include emails which supposedly come from legitimate sources and request you to perform an action the user would normally not do so (such as entering his admin account and password in a false website).
- **Social Engineering**—refers to psychological manipulation of people into performing actions or divulging confidential information. For example, by befriending the person and extracting the information needed during conversation or by accessing his/her personal laptop.

- **Physical access**—to servers, switches, or other devices which normally would be physically isolated and protected from access.

Breaches in Information Security have several possible implications:

- Access and use of confidential systems and data.

  - This is especially critical in a financial, retail environment where financial information is kept. A breach may mean that the hacker can now reuse this information to conduct financial transactions using customer's details.
  - Sometimes the data may not have financial value directly, but may be used to blackmail the user or may be sold to others that may have a use for this information, including competitors.
  - Espionage and intellectual property theft.

- Destruction of data. In which the user or company is blackmailed if he refuses to accede to certain demands, which may be monetary or of other nature. Destruction of data may also be used to undermine a company or individual.
- Disruption of operations–either by destruction, denial of a service or decreasing dramatically the reliability or response time of an application. This is commonly found in internet-facing applications which are inherently exposed.
- Destruction of machinery. This is especially true for applications used in controlling machinery. If the application is made to control the machinery in a manner that causes it hazard, then it can actually destroy the machinery or the production it is handling.
- Taking over of the machine. This is when a server or endpoint is compromised so that it comes under the control of a remote, unauthorized user. This is usually the first step in using the machine for further intrusion within a company's network, or its use to launch attacks through the internet. By using a third person's machine, the originator of the attack can remain anonymous.

4.5.10   Backup

Backup policy will be determined by IT in accordance with the application, as well as backup resources available for that task. Backup may be undertaken by ITOM or TM, but policy should be determined primarily by TM. Backup policy should ensure that all systems and data be regularly and properly backed-up. Take note that there are diverse ways of backing up, and that the strategy will again depend on the type of application, data, and tools available.

Aside from the regular backup, policy should dictate that a special backup be expressly requested before any major change is released, so that in case of failure, restoration to the original configuration can easily be done.

Backups should also take into account physical location of the backup media, so that if for example a disaster occurs (fire, earthquake, etc.) the media is not in the same location as the servers backed-up, so the backup media does not get destroyed, or it becomes a time-consuming endeavor to retrieve the backup media. Media may be rotated physically (by getting a copy of the tapes) or may be means of a "hot" or "warm" replica offsite.

Backups may be incremental for a certain period of time (say a week), after which a full backup is performed. Incremental backups are much faster than full backups to execute, however, regular full backups are needed in order to ensure that the whole system can be restored to in case media becomes corrupted (in one of the incremental backups, for example).

4.6 Retirement Phase

At some point in time, services may become obsolete for a variety of reasons:

- An alternative technology has replaced it
- The business process it is supposed to address is obsolete and no longer used

When such circumstances occur, then the service will be flagged for retirement. Normally, retirement of a service is discussed long before it is actually undertaken, most especially with the end-users, so that their transition to the new system is as seamless as possible. A normal procedure for retirement would be:

- Advisory to all concerned users on the retirement of the service
- Final backup of the complete application, just in case there is a need to revert, for whatever the reason
- Decommissioning of the application and related software and infrastructure components.

4.7 IT Strategy

The main role of strategy is to update the service catalog with new services relevant to the business, as well as finding ways of improving the service levels and reducing the costs in delivering these services. IT Strategy provides the guidance on how to design, develop, implement and improve service management, aligning it with overall company strategy.

The overall aim of IT strategy is to ensure that IT services are strategic in nature and are aligned and contribute to the overall company direction and objectives. Mainly, the roles of IT strategy are:

- Identify the market for new IT services (for external customers)
- Design and develop these new IT services
- Guide on the service management improvement process so that it better fits and is aligned to company strategy. This includes reducing costs, having better service, and increased efficiencies. Such improvements may be significant, especially if the IT clients (whether internal or external) need to pay for these services. By making the services more cost effective, these will in turn be more attractive.
- Develop policies, guidelines and processes that will assist in the above.

Designing new services has a direct relationship with portfolio management. The portfolio manager will have a series of projects under his responsibility, which may also include O&M. Oftentimes this portfolio manager is the CIO himself, who continuously aligns the different portfolio components with the overall company strategy (see Chaps. 7 and 9). One of these portfolio components is in fact Operations itself. It is thus the duty of the Operations Head to inform the portfolio manager (i.e., CIO) of his perceived needs, so that the portfolio manager can prioritize on the different improvement actions and projects to design. At the same time, the portfolio manager must also inform the Operations Head on the company's strategy and how this needs to be operationalized.

Take a few examples:

Example 1: Improved collections

During the last management committee meeting, it was determined that the accounts receivables have been bloating to unsustainable levels. Upon analysis, this was due to several factors, but one being the lack of collection agencies accredited by the company for the payment by customers of their regular bills. As such, the commercial department initiated a program of accrediting new agencies, and this in turn requires that IT expand its coverage to integrate these agencies, as well as reduce the collection clearing process from the current 8 to 2 hours.

In this example, there is a practical and direct effect of what company strategy and direction requires from the portfolio, affecting all the way down to operations. For operations, this means having to find ways of improving the collection process in terms of performance. After some analysis, it appears that the program for posting the collections into the system is not optimized, plus a higher priority needs to be assigned to this batch process in the application server. In this case, there is a direct improvement on one of the SLA's KPIs, that of posting collections, and it was determined that the Operations team is able to address the above by opening a pair of tickets, assigning the optimization of the posting program to AM (and subsequently to a developer), and then to TM and ITOM for the prioritization of the batch process.

Example 2: online collections

Along the lines of the above issue that affects company strategy, imagine another scenario in which it was decided to come up with an app that allows for real-time, online payment which will now link with the backend. It was determined by the portfolio manager that this requires a payment gateway to be setup, with all the different validations, before sending the collection information to the backend. In this case, this payment gateway needs to be developed from scratch and was launched as a new project.

As you can see from the two examples, a change in company strategy may result in a modification for Operations strategy, or in a new project, depending on the scope and nature of the solution. More of this discussed in later in this section.

For operations, IT strategy is one of the main roles of the Operations Head, as well as the Portfolio Manager handling the operations, and if the latter is not the CIO, for the CIO as well. As you can see above, it is important that the strategy at each level be aligned, because otherwise, the effort becomes useless. A service may be improved way beyond its SLA, but if not required, it does little to contribute to the company's general strategy and objectives as well as its business.

IT strategy is also linked to continuous service improvement, in that it can also set the direction and guidance for the service improvement. Along these lines, projects may also be defined for the benefit of operations. This means that projects may also be put in motion for the specific purpose of improving operations, and consequently, operations' SLA. This may altogether be different from the project defined in example 2, as the project in this example was to provide a new service altogether. Operations' projects do not usually result in a new service, but rather, the improvement of an existing service. Take the following example

Example 3: automated testing of collections' posting processes

It was also identified that one of the more time-consuming aspects of integrating new collection agencies is the testing of their batch collection data and testing for the correctness of their algorithm. As such, a new project was put in motion to automate the testing of the entire posting process, and it involved the installation and setup of a test tool, definition of the test scripts to be used, and the automation of these. The testing effort was thus reduced from an average of 3 days to just 20 min.

As you can see, the installation of the test tool and deployment for the collections' posting did not create a new service, but rather, improved on the delivery of an already existing service. It thus improved operations.

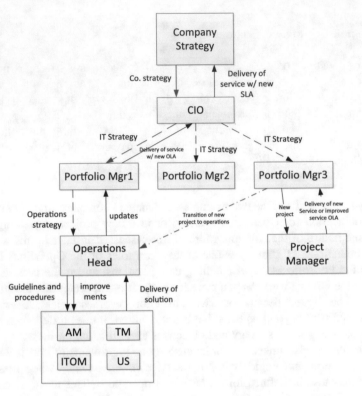

Fig. 4.15 Relationship between IT strategy, operations, and projects

Linking it all together, Fig. 4.15 represents a typical interrelationship between projects, portfolio and Operations with company and IT strategy:

What Fig. 4.15 shows is the typical process that would be involved in cascading strategy throughout the IT organization. Company strategy, usually defined in business terms, needs to be translated by the CIO into IT strategy and objectives. These are then cascaded as IT's strategy and direction to the different portfolio managers. As portfolio managers are continuously realigning their portfolio to meet company and IT strategy, they take this into account to create one of either two:

- An updated operations strategy which will further be refined by the Operations Head into new or updated guidelines and procedures. In turn, as there may be work that needs to be done to align operations to the new strategy, a set of improvements may be identified for execution by the O&M team. Once this is finished, it results in either a new service, or most likely, an improvement over an existing service. This improvement may be internal and thus requires only an update on the OLA, or may go up all the way to an improvement in a service's SLA. In case of the latter, this is then cascaded by the CIO as an update to the whole organization.

- A new project is identified by the portfolio manager. This new project may be:

  - An improvement for operations, thus enhancing its OLA (example 3 earlier); or
  - A totally new service (example 2)

In any case, the project is then assigned to a corresponding project manager to handle. Once the project is completed, the new service is updated into the service catalog, and the OLA and (if applicable) SLA updated, together with the transition of the service into operations (as shown by the dotted line in the figure).

In other words, new strategy may translate into additional operational improvements or changes, or into a new project which will eventually be phased into operations.

4.8   Continual Service Improvement

Continual Service Improvement is also referred to as the PDCA (Pyzdek, 2003) cycle, which stands for:

- **Plan** for the improvement
- **Do** the action
- **Check** the results
- **Act** to adjust the plan based on the results

It is referred to as a cycle because improvement is continuous and never stops, and may be represented by a diagram such that shown in Fig. 4.16.

Applied to operations, this is the process that leads to its continuous improvement. Normally, and in order to institute continuous improvement, this would have several phases, depending on the maturity of the organization:

Fig. 4.16 The PDCA cycle

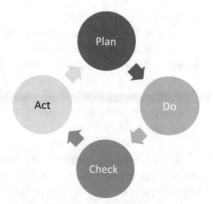

- **Phase 1, Stabilization**: the day-to-day operations must first be stabilized. One cannot think of strategy and strategic improvements if the basics are not yet addressed. A person firefighting cannot possibly devote time to more beyond to resolving his immediate problems.
- **Phase 2, Top-down driven improvements**: in which the more senior personnel (CIO or Head for Operations) identifies the areas for improvement, designs the actions and delegates his team for the execution of the improvements.
- **Phase 3, Collegial body improvements**: in which every person in the operations organization proposes new ideas for possible incorporation as an improvement. This is the final objective, in that all the employees devote time to think of ways and means to improve, and work in an open ambiance in which they can suggest ideas without fear of retribution.

The reason why the last is ideal is

- That it opens up a plethora of possible improvements because it is not just 1 or 2 people thinking of improvements but a whole team
- The best suggestions on what to do are from the people directly exposed to the work they do, because they are able to perceive of better ways of doing these.
- Using a top-down approach eventually stifles innovation and creativity because people have no room for expressing themselves as they believe the boss will always be the one to address and resolve the problem
- Ownership. In which people own the ideas, believe in what they do and execute it till the very end.

PDCA sessions when trying to achieve the most advanced stage should be formulated in such a way that there is open discussion, in which no idea is bad and should therefore not be shut down. People need to keep an open mind about ideas and not make pre-judgements. An improvement idea may contain several phases, so it is important that not only the end result is measured, but most importantly, the actions leading to the expected improvement are also measured in terms of progress. Each of these can be measured by means of indicators. Two types exist:

- **Lag indicators**—these are the RESULTS from applying an action. These are usually simpler to measure as they can easily be quantified. Samples are cost reduction, increase in revenues, capturing of more clients, etc.
- **Lead indicators**—these are the indicators (i.e., actions) that are really within the control of the person executing the plan, and these actions should lead to the improvements that will be seen in the lag indicators. They are generally more qualitative than lag indicators, but they must be executed for the final results to be achieved.

A good way to measure the progress of the continual service improvement mechanism is to use a scorecard. This scorecard will contain a mix of both lead and lag indicators so that they can be monitored in terms of their progress. Lag indicators need to be represented as these are really the actions within the control of the team. These need to be reported on a regular basis, until the final objective is achieved.

As a general rule, indicators chosen must be

- Specific
- Measureable
- Achievable
- Realistic
- Time-bound

Actions should be measured as they go through different phases of execution so that progress can be measured. Thus, for example, if the action consists of coming up with a new program that shall reduce the calculation time of a complex problem from 5 to 1 h, its different phases may look like that shown in Table 4.2.

As an idea is discussed by the team and accepted as the next improvement to focus on, a follow-through must be done. This means that its progress is to be monitored as it is executed until final results obtained. It is thus important that these initiatives be reported regularly, and the best way to report them is by means of visuals: graphs, displays, dashboard or color codes which shows the progress of the scorecard. Samples of these are shown in Fig. 4.17.

Simple use of colors such as red-yellow-green show the progress in the attainment of the initiative, or alternatively these can be represented by means of a signal light, a speedometer, or other eye-catching visuals. It is best to display these visuals in a location in which all involved employees can see them, and appreciate the progress being made.

A session for discussing these initiatives needs to be conducted regularly (weekly, every 2 weeks, etc.) and the initiative presented and discussed. The initiative should be aligned towards what the company's overall direction and objective is, or if this is too abstract, then at least to IT's specific objectives and strategy. These change from time to time, so that it is the CIO's task to give direction and indicate what is the updated strategy, and what are IT's priorities. When initiatives are presented, these should be analyzed for relevance by the group, and if the decision is to pursue them, then the regular meetings should indicate the follow-through progress. These meetings are also a chance to involve different departments, especially if help and/or collaboration are needed from them, so that it can be formally requested from them. In this sense, this discussion of initiatives involves the whole group, so that accountability is not only to the direct boss, but also to one's peers.

Table 4.2 Example of Lag versus Lead indicators

Lag	Lead
Optimized service rate calculation program (calculation time reduced from 5 to 1 h)	Analysis and design
	Coding
	Testing
	Deployment

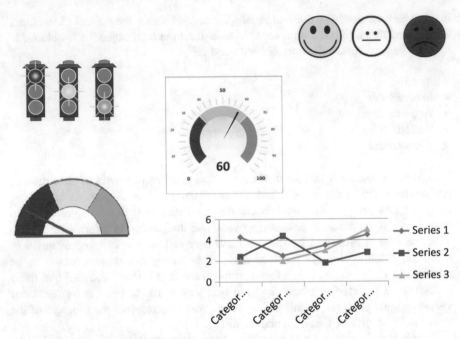

Fig. 4.17 Sample of dashboard display items

The regular Continuous Improvement Plans meetings should be brief and concise, discussing what new initiatives have been thought of, what are the steps in executing these, and what assistance is needed from other groups. Regular meetings discussions should update on what was done in the last time period, what will be done in the next time period, as well as any issues faced, and an acknowledgement on help received from another group in resolving the issue. This meeting should not turn into an operations meeting, and needs to be focused, hence a short time allotment of 5 min will be given for each person to discuss her particular initiatives. Too long a meeting will make it boring and will make other people drift from the meeting.

Take note that an initiative may take a long time period to attain its objective because of its complexity or number of tasks involved. It is not expected that the initiative be finished in the next time period, but it is expected that it be broken up into chunks of actions of which progress can be reported regularly. This is aligned to the expectation that all actions and initiatives be measureable.

Another important aspect is that indicators be realistic and achievable. It makes absolutely no sense to target initiatives which are way beyond comprehension, capability, capacity or responsibility for one to undertake. Continual improvement means taking small but successive steps for improving the performance or efficiency of IT's services, but given time, and as a whole, they make a big impact on the overall performance. Time-bound means that whenever a target is identified, there must a commitment by when this will be attained, and should be kept as such.

Lastly, we differentiated between lead and lag indicators. As lag indicators are those which are the result of the lead, they give evident benefits to the organization because they can be measured in ways that directly impact the service level: faster by, reduced cost by, reduced manpower by, increased revenue by, improved customer satisfaction, are some of the sample measures that can be used. As these, however, are the result of several lead indicators, they are not directly controllable. It is the lead indicators that are controllable, and usually, these are the ones being reported by the line during the continuous improvement meetings. Figure 4.18 shows a sample report with initiatives.

Fig. 4.18 Sample report of improvement plan showing initiatives

TECHNICAL MANAGEMENT

MEASURE	WIG (LAG)	LEAD	STATUS
97% (7175/7425) 28 for deletion 22 waiting user input	Update tag description for technical datawarehouse by 1st week of Feb (completeness of documentation)	List down all point sources of tags	
		Request from the owners to update tag description (Waiting for 2 more)	
		Consolidation	
		Updating	X
4/127	Firmware/patch upgrade for all switches by March (reliability)	Identify switches with latest upgrades	
		Application of script in switches of automatic patch update	X
		Implementation	X

APPLICATION MANAGEMENT

MEASURE	WIG (LAG)		STATUS
2/7 TBOM	Build up of HR processes in Solution Manager by Feb2015 (faster testing)	Inventory of HCM processes (still compiling existing blueprints) 7/7 pending Training and Events Management	√
		Build up of process structure 7/7	√
		TBOM creation (2/7)	
		Update configuration details	X
		Update program details	X
79/79	ETL (Business Intelligence) table verification by EO November (with BI) *New timeline: EO 2/18/2015* (address incidence)	Analysis and Documentation (79/79)	√
		Development (3 weeks for all tables) (79/79) MCF	√
		UAT (2 weeks; 1st week - report generation/testing. 2nd week - testing) SAP to staging extraction tables and Daily Jobs	√
		Implementation (per report) 2/18/2015	

If there is an initiative which merits a lengthy analysis and/or discussion, this can be taken up in a separate meeting with the concerned parties, so as not to unnecessarily burden the whole group discussing details not relevant to them.

Continuous improvement guarantees that the organization dynamically adapts to the changing environment scenario, including changing strategies and focus.

References

Axelos, 2011. *ITIL Service Lifecycle Publication Suite.* 2011: Axelos.
ISACA, 2015. http://www.isaca.org/COBIT/Pages/default.aspx. [Online].
ISO, 2011. *IOS/IEC 20000-1 International Standard.* Switzerland: ISO.
Microsoft Corporation, 2008. *microsoft.com/technet/SolutionAccelerators.* [Online].

Further Reading

Cavalleri, A., Manara M., 2012. *100 Things You Should Know About Authorizations in SAP.* 1st ed. Boston (MA): Galileo Press.
Burges, J., 1984. *Dseign Assurance for Engineers and Managers.* 1st ed.: CRC.
CompTIA, inc, 2013. *CompTIA Network+.* 1.1 ed. Rochester (NY): Logical Operations.
Hinde, D., 2012. *PRINCE2 Study Guide.* 1st ed. Wiley.
Knapp, D., 2010. *The ITSM Process Design Guide: Developing, Reengineering, and Improving IT Service Management.* J. Ross Publishing, Inc.
Kunas, M., 2012. *Implementing Service Quality based on ISO/IEC 20000.* 3rd ed. IT Governance Publishing.
Mora, M., Raisinghani M., O'Connor, R., Gomez, J.M., Gelman, O., 2014. An Extensive Review of IT Service Design in Seven International ITSM Processes Frameworks: Part I. *International Journal of Information Technologies and Systems Approach,* 7(2), pp. 83–107.
Brenner, M., Garschhammer, M., Sailer, M., Schaaf T., 2006. CMDB – Yet Another MIB? On Reusing Management Model Concepts in ITIL Configuration Management. In: S. v. d. M., D. O. T. P. Radu State, ed. *Large Scale Management of Distributed Systems.* Springer Berlin Heidelberg, pp. 269–280.
Chemuturi, M., Cagley Jr, T.M., 2010. *Mastering Software Project Management.*: J. Ross Publishing.
Pyzdek, T., 2003. *Quality Engineering Handbook (Quality and Reliability).* 2nd ed. CRC Press.
Schiesser, R., 2001. *IT Systems Management: Designing, Implementing, and Managing World-Class Infrastructures.* 1st ed. Prentice Hall.
Thejendra B.S, 2014. *Practical IT Service Management - A Concise Guide for Busy Executives.* 2nd ed. IT Governance Publishing.
Rogers, T., Esposito, A., 2013. *Ten Steps to ISM Success.* IT Governance Publishing.
Watts, F., 2011. *Engineering Documentation Control Handbook, Fourth Edition: Configuration Management and Product Lifecycle Management.* 4th ed. William Andrew.

Managing Projects

5

5.1 Project Management Principles

Much of terminology used here is based on the PMP standard as described in the Project Management Book of Knowledge (PMBOK) (Project Management Institute 2013). This terminology is widely accepted in the project management field, but as it is generic across all industries, we elaborate on the specific project management methods that are used in the IT field. All of this is based on a waterfall methodology approach and discusses techniques that I used and refined after many years of experience of working in this field.

5.1.1 Basic Principles and Characteristics of Projects

As already indicated in the introduction, projects have distinct properties as compared to operations, perhaps the most important being that projects have a very distinct start and finish, while operations are continuous in nature. As such, IT projects have distinct phases which can be described:

- Mobilization
- Analysis and Design
- Build
- Post-implementation support (which may or may not be part of O&M)
- Closure
- Monitoring and Control

Although these phases typically overlap, they can be distinctly identified as the tasks being undertaken are different for each phase. In general, these phases may be represented by a graph as shown in Fig. 5.1.

© Springer International Publishing Switzerland 2016
F. Castillo, *Managing Information Technology*,
DOI 10.1007/978-3-319-38891-5_5

Fig. 5.1 Graph showing the
typical phases in an IT project

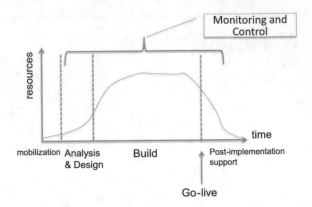

Below we explain each of these phases:

- **Mobilization**—typically this consists of the preparation activities for the project, and includes preparation and signing of contract, mobilization and readying
  of the resources, procurement of necessary software and hardware, preparation
  and on-boarding of team members, provisioning of resources, etc. This may also
  include a more detailed analysis of the customer's environment, needs, and may
  be accompanied by some interviews so as to quickly refine the project plan and
  some of the ambiguities in the scope of work.
- **Analysis and Design**—During this phase, a detailed analysis of the user
  requirements is initiated with the objective of having a full and complete design
  signed off by the users by the end of the phase. The idea here is that no
  configuration or coding work should start until concurrence from the users is
  received, in the form of the corresponding signed-off design documents.
  Installation and setting up of the O/S, DBs, environments, and applications may
  be part of this phase, however, only after the corresponding technical architecture document is also signed off by the users. Among the activities undertaken in this phase are:

  - **Project kickoff presentation**: in which a presentation is given to all those
    involved in the project, from both the vendor and the client organization to
    get concurrence and agreement. It usually contains the following:

    Table of Organization: in which the roles and responsibilities are
    defined including that of the vendor's project team, involvement, and role
    of identified counterparties from the customer organization (typically,
    counterpart project manager, business experts, users, etc.), as well as their
    concrete role in the project. This can be represented in a RACI
    (Responsibility Assignment Matrix) chart, if appropriate.
    Project plan: this should be a more refined version of the project timeline
    and tasks that will be undertaken for the project based on interviews as

well as more details obtained during the initiating phase, which allows the project manager to have a clearer grasp of the scope, current situation and environment in which the customer operates.

Project scope: even before the start of the project, the project scope should be clear to both parties, otherwise this may cause misunderstandings, costly change requests, and/or nonagreements which are detrimental to the project timeline and cost, not to mention the relationship between the customer and the vendor. However, there will always be gray areas which need to be further clarified, and the sooner these are clarified and an agreement is struck, the better. Remember, the later the change request comes in, the more costly overall to the project in terms of time, cost, and quality. Thus, the kickoff presentation and all related meetings should serve to tie down any loose ends that may remain. If these cannot be totally cleared, they should be flagged as such for further, early clarification and agreement.

Deliverables and acceptance criteria: same as with scope, this is the right moment to make it completely clear (if not yet clear) to both parties what are the exact deliverables and acceptance criteria for the project.

Communication plan: when, how, and who will be communicated what. This is further explained in the communication management section of this chapter. What is important is that this be discussed and accepted by all parties at this early stage, including the end users. It may be hard to get the end users' presence and acceptance at any other time, so this is the moment to do so.

– **On-boarding session**. This is a session conducted between the two Project Managers (PMs), as well as the lead personnel from the vendor's side. It serves as a discussion of important points for the project and normally includes the following:

Review of policies and guidelines. The project team is updated by the customer PM on the customer's guidelines, policies, and procedures to which the project must adhere to. This would include release management procedures, security guidelines, procedures for raising requests, procedures for raising change requests, among others.

Deliverable checklist. The deliverables should have been indicated in the Terms of Reference (TOR) at the time of tendering, however, every project and every application are different, so that there also needs to be an agreement on what deliverables are applicable for the project (more of this discussed in 7.3). This will not only include documentation, but also trainings, workshops, major sessions, and other "outputs" expected from the project. A checklist is the final list of deliverables agreed by both parties.

Documentation format: Part of the discussion during agreement on the deliverables checklist is the format of the documentation to be used. Again, typically, the customer will have its own formats, but because each application has its own intricacies, adoption of vendor's format or tweaking of existing documentation may be needed.

Authorized signatories. This should have been discussed with the users during the kickoff; however now with the customer PM, the signatories for each deliverable will be identified. This is because aside from the users, there are documents which only IT needs to sign-off (such as technical architecture, technical documentation, code documentation), so it must be clear for each deliverable who and up to what level should these be signed off.

Escalation procedure. This may have been touched briefly during the kickoff, but will now be discussed in detail. It is important that the procedure be clear from the very start so as to avoid dragging of the issues affecting both time and cost.

Change Request (CR) procedure. Again, may have been touched during the kickoff, but since IT is normally the party that has to shoulder any additional costs, there should be a discussion on how CRs should be raised and approved.

- **Requirement gathering meetings**. These meetings with the end users are for the project team to gather the specific requirements from them and successively define and refine the specifications until these are finally drafted in the form of design documents. Design documents are then drafted and presented to the users for their sign-off, signifying that the project team has been able to correctly capture their requirements. This is probably the most important part of the project, as mistakes here result in loss of time and effort, so the documents used specifically in this task are explained in more detail in Sect. 5.2.
- **Design Sign-off**: Needless to say, in order to proceed with execution, all of the design documents need to be acknowledged by the different parties as being final and binding. This works both ways, it is binding to the vendor in his commitment in producing what has been signed off, and it also means that any divergence from what has been signed off is a Change Request (CR) regardless of whether it has a cost implication or not. It is both the PMs' duty to manage and control CRs so that they do not become a cause for project creep which will cause further delays and possible cost overruns.

- **Execution (Build)**—in IT projects, execution can further be subdivided into subphases, these typically are (using a waterfall project management methodology):

  - **Build**: Once the analysis and design documents have been signed off, the build phase commences, this is where the configuration of the systems, and programming (if any) is undertaken. This is the technical part, undertaken mainly by the vendor that now translates functional requirements into technical specifications which are to be put into the application. Here the customer PM takes a more relaxed mode, and will just check from time to time the progress of the build phase versus schedule and inquire whether any issues have been encountered.

- **Testing**. Testing is composed of many different types of testing as explained in Sect. 5.5. In its most basic form, unit testing and integration testing are first conducted by the vendor team to check everything is working correctly. After this has been confirmed, then the end users are called for their validation, in the form of UAT (User Acceptance Test). Several UAT iterations are usually needed (2–3 typically) before the application is threshed out of errors and can proceed to go live.

- **Go live**: refers to the transfer of the application from the project environment (development and testing) and into production so that the users can start accessing and transacting with the system. This is the most critical in terms of impact, user's perception and acceptance of the application. Most critical here is proper cutover, for which we have a whole chapter devoted to it, but here is a brief description:

  - **Cutover**: refers to the activities required before, sometimes during and shortly after going live in order to guarantee a painless transition from legacy to the new system. It includes technical and nontechnical aspects, and is usually the most risky phase in a project. Examples of activities include data migration, familiarity of the users with the new process, training, manner in which old transactions in the old process will be moved to the new process (if not automatic), etc.

- **Post-implementation support**: once the project goes live, there are typically a large number of incidences, technical, functional, and user-related which need to be addressed as soon as possible. During this phase, both the project team and O&M need to be on standby furnishing first- and second-level support (who is in charge of which support level is discussed further in Sect. 6.7). This phase is one also commonly underestimated and requires careful planning and foresight. Good testing always minimizes the need for more post-implementation support, but it can never be eliminated.
- **Monitoring and Control**: this occurs during the whole duration of the project, principally the project managers (customer and vendor side), to ensure that the project is within scope, time, cost, and quality. This again requires extensive discussion, so that we have devoted an entire section to it.
- **Closure**: signifying formal project end. Formal closure is done after all reported project incidences detected under the warranty period have been resolved, all deliverables submitted and accepted, as well as training and documentation submitted.

Effort exerted by the customer side differs considerably from that of the vendor; if we were to represent the effort from both sides in a chart it would look like that shown in Fig. 5.2.

Fig. 5.2 Graph showing resource allocation per phase of a typical IT project

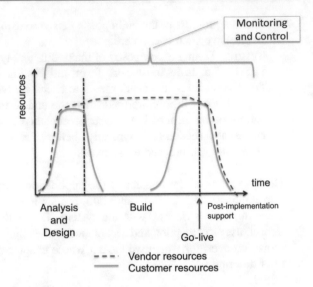

What this graph shows is the typical involvement in terms of resources. As is apparent, vendor resources peak and plateau during the build phase, as all the work defined during the analysis and design are to be implemented. On the other hand, customer resources have two distinct peaks: one during the analysis and design phase, the other right before going live during the cutover phase. The first is due to the deep involvement from the customer side, typically end users and business experts, in defining clearly the detailed design of the system that will be built. During cutover, the typically heavy involvement from the end users is testing (which should be done by them), and in some instances, additional cutover activities (please see relevant section in this chapter) that are needed for a successful go live. Examples of the latter are data preparation, recreation of live data in the new system from the legacy system, etc.

Projects have distinct characteristics if compared to operations as shown in Table 5.1.

One of the distinct ironies in projects is that they evolve from a less to more defined state in terms of scope definition, while at the same time, the ability for the

Table 5.1 Projects versus Operations

Projects	Operations
• Creates its own charter, organization, and goals	• Semipermanent charter, organization, and goals
• Purpose of change	• Purpose of status quo
• Unique product or service	• Predefined and approved product or service
• Heterogeneous team	• Homogeneous teams
• Definite start–definite end	• Ongoing (continuous)
• Progressively elaborated process deliverables	• Fully known process deliverables

project manager to direct the course of the project (and thus, its success) goes from high at the start of the project, to low toward the end, as the project takes its own course. This means that the project manager's ability to direct the project is in fact highest when his knowledge of the project's scope is lowest!

Uncertainty (and therefore risk) is also high at the start of the project, and tends to decrease as the project progresses due to proper monitoring and control. If properly managed, risk decreases with time, while the cost of any change increases dramatically as the project progresses. Changes are more costly as the project approaches the go live, as any change means additional scope which needs to be reanalyzed, built, and tested, and may have a high impact on the other project components.

One common mistake made by organizations in their IT structure is to mix resources from operations to handle projects. Though in principle it would seem to be logical (make a person handling the operations of a particular application handle projects which have a direct relevance to that of the application she is handling), it is in fact one common reason why projects are dysfunctional. Project management is a distinct methodology from operations management, and as such, a special team should be trained to become acquainted with them and have the discipline in applying and executing these. If IT personnel are to handle both, then there will be confusion as to what to prioritize, and even what methodology should be followed. Is the ticket an operations ticket? Request for a project? If there is a conflict, which should be prioritized? How do I assign my personnel? Who should handle the operations incidence tickets and who to work on the long-term fix that the project addresses? It is just but to be expected that urgency (short term) will always be prioritized over long term, and that usually means that incidence tickets will absorb the team's time, to the detriment of the project.

In the next sections, we take a look at all the different important dimensions and aspects in IT project management, many of these dimensions were patterned after the terminology used in PMP (Project Management Institute 2013), which is a very good standard for project management, though in this chapter we focus to project management dimensions which are specific to IT Projects and how these need to be handled (unlike in PMP which is generic for all fields).

5.1.2   Scope Management

Perhaps one of the most important features of IT projects is that the scope is not 100 % clear during the project start. This is especially more true for IT software projects because they in fact have a lot of intangibles (software process is in itself, an intangible). This means that scope is in fact successively defined during the progress of the project. This poses some distinct dangers and risks, first and foremost, since scope is not completely clear during the project start, it may lead to assumptions which may not be true or acceptable to the customer, there may be a mismatch between what the software can actually do and what the customer desires, and further down the project implementation, this ambiguity in the scope may lead to a protracted argument and discussion as to whether a particular scope is part or not of the project in the first place.

As a general rule, the more detailed the scope at the start of the project, the better. Incomplete, incorrect scope is perhaps the single biggest cause for project failure, as there is no alignment between vendor, customer, business users and sometimes top management, in terms of what should actually be the outcome of the project. In order to address this, several techniques can be used:

- **Have a clear-cut understanding of what the project is to deliver**. Needless to say, this takes time to develop, as it may need the vendor's IT organization to interview the business users as to what they need. Many times, the business users have a hazy idea of what they want, so it requires a major effort to translate these into writable specifications that can be attached to the terms of reference. Ideally, the requirements shall appear in a clear, objective, written list of requirements which vendors shall have to answer comply/noncomply, and which shall be contractually binding.
- **Research and vendor presentations**. As stated above, requirements gathering is an iterative process. It thus requires a lot of work before the actual tendering takes place. Research via Internet, reviews, and publications from research companies, as well as vendor presentations to both IT and the business organization are of great help in further developing these specifications.
- **Gap analysis**. Helps in defining current state versus to-be state as desired by the business organization. Gap analyses may be conducted in-house or contracted to a specialist consulting company.
- **Contracting of design specifications**. With this approach, the analysis and design phase is contracted separately from the main "build" part of the project. This has its advantages and also disadvantages, and may not always be applicable. Advantages are:

  - **No ambiguity**. As the detailed design specifications shall be the main output, the build phase need only to comply with a very detailed scope of work.
  - **Cost**. Once the detailed design is out, this may be used in tendering the build phase separately. As less assumptions are to be made, and less risk (which means less cost buffers) are to be covered for by the bidders, this should typically result in a more competitive price.

  Disadvantages however include:

- **Disconnect with the software**. If the analysis and design has been contracted out without specifying the software that will eventually be used in implementing the project, there is a major risk that the design becomes too theoretical, and may not be supported by the software.
- **Capabilities of the consulting firm**. As analysis and design without actual implementation carries little risk from the vendor's viewpoint (unless of course the customer organization already has a deep understanding of the processes

being designed, as well as the software product being implemented), the vendor may not put its best resources in this endeavor, may not exert all the necessary effort, or may not even have the necessary skills to actually conduct the work on hand. There is very little risk of exposure because their contract would end before actual realization of the project, so there is no good way of checking if their design is accurate and of quality.

– **Involvement during the build phase**. As stated earlier, if the consulting firm involved in the design is not involved in the actual build, the customer actually may be getting a very poor design. One way to overcome this is to let the organization that designed it bid and participate as well during the build phase. This may or may not be acceptable, depending on the procurement policy of the customer organization. If allowed, it also follows that the vendor that formulated the design is in fact in the best position to conduct the build phase, as they have the most complete information on the situation of the customer, need to make less assumptions, and would already have a very clear idea as to how much effort the build phase would entail. Again, this may or may not be acceptable to the customer organization.

As mentioned during the introduction, as a project progresses:

- Uncertainties decrease
- Scope certainty increases
- Cost of any change increases
- Stakeholder influence decrease

In summary, the dilemma may be summarized as "As the project progresses, scope becomes clearer and there are less uncertainties, but the ability to influence its direction decreases, and any wanted change in the project increases dramatically in overall cost." As the ability to influence and direct the project is greater during the beginning of the project, and it is also during this time that risks are highest and cost in changes in scope are lowest, it is best to devote the most time to properly define scope at the beginning of the project. This may seem obvious but is shortcut many times in the interest of expediting the project, which actually produces the opposite effect. Any man-day (and $) invested in the beginning of the project ultimately means savings in man-days and costs further down the project timeline.

During the analysis and design phases, previously agreed-upon design documents should be used to capture these. Discussion on analysis and design documentation is discussed further in Sect. 5.2.

During the course of the project, milestones which properly narrow down and detail the scope should be signed off before the next related task is initiated. This is especially true for analysis documents that lead to design, and design documents which lead to build tasks, test design documents before user acceptance testing, and so forth. It is a waste of time to progress to the next dependent tasks if acceptance has not taken place for the documents which specify HOW these tasks are to be undertaken.

Risks to project scope are many and varied, and they may come from many different sources. Some common ones include:

- End user changing his/her mind
- A senior executive having different ideas on what should be done
- Project creep—in which small incremental changes are accepted due to the small nature of the change, however, due to the many small changes, these add up to become a significant change
- Person approving is not the right person to approve (or does not understand the actual needs)—a key user which may be approving design documents and deliverables turns out to be the incorrect person due to many possible factors including his role being wrongly assumed by the customer's PM, inability to understand what is being discussed, or even having no credibility with the rest of the users (even though he/she may possess the formal title)
- Unruly behavior by the end users—includes nonstandardization of processes, such that obtaining approval to standardize design and process across the business organization becomes difficult or is iteratively changed by the users.
- Supplier starts development work without getting a sign-off from the users.

From the above list, it is clear that the only person capable of identifying and managing these risks and the overall scope is in fact the project manager, highlighting once more his important role.

Take an example of an executive changing his mind causing the project to delay. During the discussion on the procurement process to be implemented in an ERP, it was decided that Purchase Requests (PR) once created by the different authorized division heads, would immediately proceed to procurement for processing and eventual release of the Purchase Order, this was presented and agreed at in the steering committee meetings. At a later phase however and well into the development stage, a key executive in the organization decided that an additional approval was needed even at the PR level before proceeding to procurement, so that the development had to be redone and retested altogether.

5.1.3 Procurement Management and Contracting

The procurement and contracting of IT projects is quite different from that of other goods and services for the same reason as that of scope management: IT almost always deals with intangibles, and even when there are tangible assets involved, the intangible component (firmware, software, configurations) is just as important as the main asset itself.

What this really means in practical terms is that there must be a considerable effort to define and pin down requirements before tendering. Failure to do so will result in gray areas open to interpretation from both the customer and the contractor's side. The most important document here being the Terms of Reference (TOR) which is the main document used in requesting for proposals from the vendor, regardless if the tendering procedure is an open bid, price quotation only, or any other form. The TOR must be written in clear and concise wording, specifying what is required from the vendor, and asking that they comply with them, or if unable to comply, to indicate the approach they will take in addressing the requirement.

An example of a TOR is presented in Appendix A: Sample Terms of Reference (TOR). The best TORs are those in which the vendor is to answer "yes" or "no" in terms of their ability to comply with the requirement, leaving no room for ambiguity. As such, aside from the main TOR body which explains the requirements and explains the background of the project, it is recommended that it can be accompanied with a tabular list of requirements, a sample of which is also shown in Appendix A: Sample Terms of Reference (TOR). This list shall generally contain the following main sections:

- **Functional specifications**: which describe the functions the solution provided by the vendor must adhere to. This shall be answered by the vendor with a simple "yes," "no," or "work-around provided" to the table which asks whether they comply or not to the requirement. Under remarks, they are to fill this up with details on how they address the requirement, and if addressed by a work-around, how the work-around will address it. Optionally, the customer may opt to indicate in a column the importance of the requirement with a Mandatory/Optional indication or if one wishes, High/Medium/Low categorization.
- **Technical specifications**: describing the technical requirements for the solution. This would usually include technical specifications for standard software and hardware currently being used by the customer, which you would like that the vendor adhere to, typically:

  - O/S and its version
  - DB and its version
  - Preferred programming language
  - Virtualization software and version
  - Servers
  - Use of LDAP or Active Directory
  - Network Switch brands and acceptable models
  - Required environments (DEV, QA, PROD) and their recommended server sizes (RAM, CPUs, disk)
  - Warranty period required for the hardware
  - Software license support period required for the software

  Filling up of the technical requirements shall be the same as that of the functional requirements.

- **Other requirements**: usually pertaining to particular training, testing, or other aspects the vendor should take into account.
- **Curriculum vitae**: one commonly forgotten aspect is that services are the make or break for a successful project, the hardware and software components being only half the story. Thus, one may require a minimum compliance on the resources being assigned to the project, or if left open, vendor should include the CVs of key personnel with enough details for the customer to evaluate their adequacy.

It is also worth noting how different IT items affect tendering:

- **Procurement of commodity items**: includes laptops, PCs, printers, servers, memory, Microsoft licenses, etc. In this case the TOR indicates the desired specifications and the vendor replies whether he can comply. Award goes to the lowest complying bidder.
- **Tendering for a new hardware or application project**: in this case, the specifications for the required hardware and software are indicated in the TOR, however, due to the nature of the project, this is not just equipment delivery, as these components require a significant services component in order to be set up for the hardware and/or software to deliver the desired functionalities, working condition. In such cases, both the product and the services should be evaluated for compliance.
- **Consulting services tender**: in this scenario either the software application licenses have already been procured, are procured in a separate tender, or are not necessary. Desired here from the vendor are just pure services to implement a particular configuration or provide advisory services. In this case, the customer specifies exactly what he wants and the vendors must comply with the scope. Only CVs, methodology, and references are then evaluated in this scenario. The vendor may have a chance to propose an alternative approach to the vendor, but it is at the customer's discretion to accept such an alternative.

As mentioned before, good TORs take time and effort to build, and oftentimes the customer may not be fully aware of what is in the market, nor what exactly the end users want. Similarly, the end users may not really know how current technology can address some of their needs and they look up to IT for guidance. One way to build an effective TOR is by means of a Request For Information (RFI), as well as through research as shown in Fig. 5.3.

In the above flowchart, a Request for Information is used to get nonbinding proposals from vendors given some very generic requirements. This can be followed up by presentations from these vendors. Other sources of information are the Internet, research, analyst reviews, as well as by means of attending seminars, workshops, and presentations on the topic. Of course, essential to all of this are the end user requirements, which need to be captured by IT and put into a document. An RFI may help the users if followed up by presentations from the vendors in

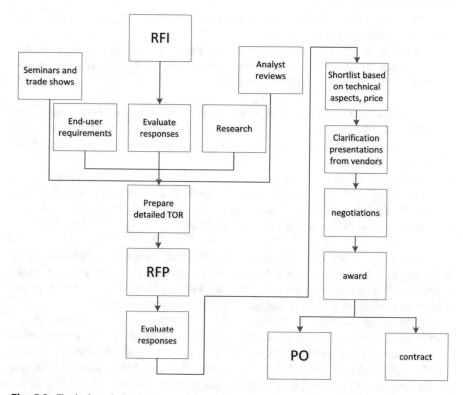

Fig. 5.3 Typical tendering process

which the users are part of the audience. This gives them insight and ideas on possible functionalities and approaches to their desired goal.

If the requirements can be interpreted directly by IT from the users and complemented by research, then the RFI may be omitted to save time and the TOR drafted directly. The TOR may then be validated with the users for concurrence before tendering.

Once tendered (Request for Proposal: RFP), the vendors are given a chance to submit their technical and commercial proposal, by answering to the TOR requirements. It is typical for vendors to stretch the truth in answering to the TOR requirements and be tempted to answer "comply" to all. In order to avoid this situation, a best practice is to make this proposal and answers to the TOR contractually binding, by including them as part of the contract. Nonadherence to their proposal can then be cause for cancelation of the contract, as well as application of penalties.

Evaluation of proposals can take many different forms, depending on the procurement policy of the company; however, one commonality is that any vendor considered for award must pass at least the minimum technical requirements specified in the TOR before any commercial consideration. Commercial terms must never be discussed by IT without procurement's presence, and it is always the last aspect to be discussed with any vendor.

First and foremost, IT has to select the vendors that meet the technical criteria, and to do this, it will usually seek clarification from the vendors or ask for presentations from them. Two approaches exist:

- **Start from the lowest priced bidder**. Ask for clarifications and presentations to ensure that his proposal meets the technical specifications and all aspects are clear and covered. If he results to a complying bid, then proceed with negotiations (with procurement) leading to award.
- **Shortlist all those technically complying bidders**. Request for clarifications from all bidders to ensure that they really do meet the specifications before they are shortlisted. Once shortlisted, open the commercial proposal and start negotiations with the lowest complying bidder.

In both cases above, if there is no agreement during negotiations, be that due to some technical aspect which they do not want to agree to, the terms and conditions of the contract, or due to commercial reasons, then one must then proceed with the next lowest complying bidder, and so forth, until award is attained.

The advantage of the first method is that it is much faster; you only ask for clarifications from the lowest priced bidder and move up. Its disadvantage is that there is always some room for favoritism from IT personnel, as they can already clearly see the pricing. It is however recommended for complex projects where lots of clarifications are essential before award due to the nature and complexity of the project.

Negotiations should always be led by procurement; IT will then support it with technical information and validation in the negotiations, in order to make these much more effective. As an example, supposing that a certain level of discount is being pressed for by procurement, and upon inspection, IT saw that the vendor was proposing 24×7 warranty support for the whole project when only 8×5 support is in fact necessary, the customer then used this fact to seek further price reduction by having the vendor commit to a much less stricter support framework. Such discounts would have not been detected if procurement acted alone without IT's involvement.

It must again be emphasized that commercial (price) negotiations should always be left for last, it is important to be totally satisfied with the technical proposal being offered before talking of price or any discounts. If during the course of clarifications IT detects points which may be used as a leverage for price negotiations (such as in the example above), then these are noted and then brought out during the price negotiations, but not before.

Concurrence and agreement during price negotiations lead to the award. It is important that all points raised during the presentations and technical clarification meetings are not be forgotten. As such, these minutes of meeting should also be binding and made part of the contract, and should supersede the vendor's original proposal in case of conflict. With these, the vendor cannot escape with empty promises in which he fails to deliver later on.

Lastly, it is important to note when to use a standard Purchase Order (PO) and when to use a full contract in awarding to a vendor. Purchase Orders are contractually binding documents which place an order to a vendor. They carry a standard, albeit simple set of Terms and Conditions, usually the expected time of delivery of the goods, payment terms, general corporate quality guidelines, and the like. They are appropriate for the procurement of equipment and software which require minimal services component, as the delivery of the goods in good state are enough for payment to be released. For projects which have a significant service component, the terms and conditions of a contract are very important, and thus, these would always require a contract to be signed by both counterparties (and not just a PO).

Two general types of services and project contract exist:

- **Turnkey projects**. In which the total project is of a fixed amount and vendor gets paid a % of the total whenever a specific milestone is attained; and
- **Time and Material (T&M) contracts**. In which the vendor proposes hourly or daily rates for different types of resources to be assigned to the client, and gets paid according to the number of days work they perform for the client. Additional expenses may also be reimbursed from the client such as airfares, hotel, taxis, per diem, etc.

As is apparent, T&M contracts are much more risky for the client than turnkey, so that turnkey projects should be preferred by the client. Of course, turnkey projects necessitate a very detailed level of scope so that vendors can cost their proposals effectively. T&M contracts are appropriate only when:

- **The scope is too difficult or impossible to define exactly**. Take for example a problematic system which produces downtime, the customer has no clue whatsoever as to what is the underlying problem and decides to hire an external expert organization to help it troubleshoot, it is therefore impossible to know beforehand if the work entails a few days or several weeks.
- **Consulting projects** in which it is difficult to know beforehand how much work will actually be devoted to the endeavor.
- **Support contracts which will be based on the actual number of work hours or days utilized**. It may be that actual support days may be zero or little, so it is also in the customer's interest to use a T&M contract.

Of course, in order for the billing not to bloat without limit, it may be wise to place a cap on the amount approved for the T&M and/or place checks and balances such that any work that is to be performed by the vendor must be estimated in man-days and preapproved by the customer PM before proceeding.

Sometimes in the desire to limit risk, the opposite is sometimes achieved. Take as an example a particular government-owned corporation wherein all major projects would have to be tendered and the lowest priced complying bidder awarded, including that for consulting services. In this particular case, this organization was to implement its first ERP system, and following government procurement rules, required that the consulting for the design of the ERP would come first before the procurement and setup of the ERP itself. This meant that the consulting design would have to be made generic, without actually knowing what product would actually be implemented. The award and work proceeded for the consulting work, was finished and became the blueprint specifications for the ERP. The result was disastrous as the design did not take into account particularities of the ERP application itself, so much so that certain designs were not implementable off-the-shelf and required extensive customization, and led to a protracted fight between the customer and implementer as to the manner in proceeding with the implementation.

5.1.4   Time Management

Project time management can be undertaken in many ways, however, due to the availability of many project management software, these can now be used, making it much more effortless than doing this with excel sheets or the like. These softwares allow interdependencies between tasks to be defined, and adjust automatically in accordance with precedence and interrelationship rules, which would otherwise need to be handled manually. A very useful technique for drawing project dependencies is the use of the Precedence Diagramming Method (PDM) (Fondahl 1987), which can be entered into these softwares, or reproduced from a Gantt chart, which is usually easier to enter. Many of the other measures we will discuss in the succeeding sections can also be automatically handled and calculated by PM software. It is however very useful to have at least a basic understanding of the theory behind the use of PDMs, so we shall be discussing this thoroughly in this section.

A PDM is a graphical representation of project tasks wherein:

- Activities are represented by a Node in the form of a RECTANGLE
- Dependency is represented by an ARROW

In the example shown in Fig. 5.4, tasks A to H are represented by their corresponding nodes.

As is evidenced by the arrows, task H is dependent on task G finishing first, which in turn depends on both tasks D and F finishing. While task D depends on task B finishing, and task F depends on task C. Both tasks B and C depend on task A. By means of this diagram, one can easily appreciate dependencies between tasks.

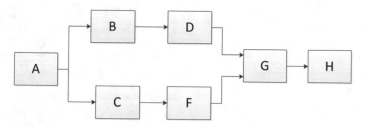

Fig. 5.4 PDM diagram

Fig. 5.5 Components of a
node in a PDM

Early Start	Duration	Early Finish
	Name of Activity	
Late Start	Float	Late Finish

In order to appreciate the power of PDM further, we first need to understand some more concepts. First, we can represent inside each node the amount of time it takes for that particular task to be executed. This shall be represented by a number in the duration side of the node's box (upper middle portion) as shown in Fig. 5.5.

The duration is expressed in number of standard time units, in accordance with that used for the project (hours, days, weeks…). The other numbers will be explained in a short while.

In some cases, though a task is dependent on a previous one, it may not be necessary for the previous task to finish completely before starting the new task, as it may in fact start a bit earlier. Or it may be the opposite; a previous task needs a certain "rest" period before the next dependent task is started. In order to account for such cases, a number is added on top of the arrow with a (-) minus sign if it is a lead precedence, meaning, it can start early by the number of units expressed above the arrow, or if a (+) positive sign is used, then it is a lag precedence, which means the dependent task can only start after the previous task has ended, plus an additional such time units. Take Fig. 5.6 as an example, in the diagram task D can start 2 time units even before task C has ended, while for task F, it must wait 2 time units after task E has ended before starting.

Let us now take an example and build the PDM, given the tasks and precedence defined in Table 5.2.

The resulting PDM would look like that of Fig. 5.7.

We now conduct a series of calculations:

- **Forward Pass**—Starting at the beginning (left) of the network develop early start and early finish dates for each task, progressing to end (rightmost box) of the network.

Fig. 5.6 Lead and Lag
delays between activities

LEAD
Lead indicates subsequent activity can be started early

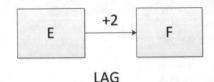

LAG
Lag indicates subsequent activity should be started late

Table 5.2 Sample activities
with their duration and
preceding activity

Activity	Duration (days)	Precedent activities
A	2	–
B	1	A
C	2	–
D	2	B, C
E	3	D with 2 days lag
F	4	D
G	3	E
H	2	F
I	1	H, G with 2 days lead

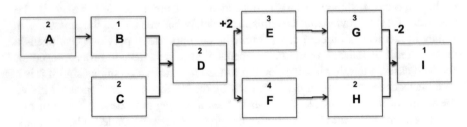

Fig. 5.7 Resulting PDM from the example in Table 5.2

- **Early Start Date (upper left number)**—Earliest possible point in time an
  activity can start, based on the network logic and any scheduled constraint. In
  other words, for each activity, determine if it has a predecessor, if none, the early
  start date is 0. If it has a predecessor, then get the preceding activity's early
  finish and add the lag/lead that is in the path, to determine the early start date. If
  the activity has several predecessors, then do the calculation for each path, the
  early start date then will be the greater (latest) among all those calculated along
  different paths (as all preceding activities must finish before it can start).

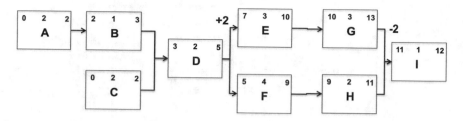

Fig. 5.8 PDM with forward pass applied

- **Early Finish (upper right number)**—Earliest possible time an activity can finish, which is calculated by adding the early start date to the duration of the activity.

For the sample example, and applying the forward pass then Fig. 5.8 will result. A similar calculation is then made but in the opposite direction, starting from the rightmost activity toward the left, this is called the backward pass:

- **Backward Pass**: Calculate late start and late finish dates starting at project completion, using finish times and working backwards.
- **Late Finish (Lower Right number)**: Latest point in time a task may be completed without delaying that activity's successor. In this case, and starting from the rightmost node, we annotate the late finish in the lower right-hand side of the activity node. If the activity has no succeeding one, then its late finish is equal to its early finish. If it does have a succeeding activity, then its late finish will be equal to the succeeding activity's late start plus the lag/lead delay in the path. Take note that this time the sign of the lead/lag is inverted with respect to the forward pass' calculation, such that if there is a lag delay (+ in sign), we subtract to obtain the late finish, but if the relationship between activities has a lead delay (− in sign), then we add to the late start of the succeeding activity to obtain the late finish. Once more, if there are several activities that are succeeding it, we then calculate the possible late finish using all different paths, but select that which is smallest (earliest).
- **Late Start Date (lower left number)**: refers to the latest point in time that an activity may begin without delaying that activity's successor. This is calculated by subtracting within an activity, the activity's duration from its late finish.

If we apply the backward pass to our example, this results in that of Fig. 5.9. Lastly, we can calculate the float (Martino 1968) (lower middle number) by:

Float = Late Start − Early Start

For each activity, and annotating these where there are X's in the boxes above. The resulting diagram is then shown in Fig. 5.10.

Float gives a lot of interesting information about the project activities. First, it is defined as the amount of time a task may be delayed from its earliest start date without delaying the project finish date. Any activity which has a nonzero float has

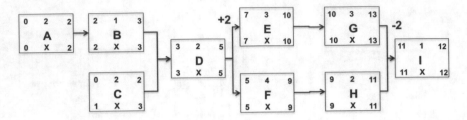

Fig. 5.9 PDM example with backward pass applied

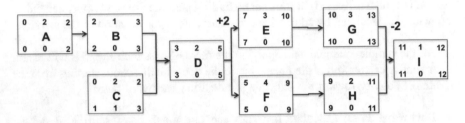

Fig. 5.10 PDM example with float calculated

a certain "slack," which may be used in the project as will be discussed later on. In the example above, only task C has a nonzero float, of 1 week. This means that instead of starting task C on week 0, we may actually opt to delay it for a week and start on week 1, and it will still not cause any delay on the overall project timeline. How can this be used for practical purposes? Well, if for example, task C demands the use of a resource which cannot be easily obtained from the very start of the project, his involvement can be delayed by 1 week without causing any negative impact. Many other possibilities can be evaluated for different project situations and resource situations. In cases where slack is significant and there is a commonality of resources, resources that are in activities with slack can be assigned to do other activities first instead of those with slack, as a delay in these activities need not affect the overall project timeline.

This brings us to the concept of critical path (Weaver 2014). Critical path are those activities which when delayed, will cause a delay to the whole project timeline. Activities in the critical path are those with 0 float, and so, these are the activities which should be given more attention by the PM due to their (pardon the redundancy) criticality. To define it formally:

Critical path is the successive list of activities (path) which affect the overall finish date of the project if any of those activities delay.

In our PDM earlier, the critical paths are both A-B-D-E-G-I and A-B-D-F-H-I. From the point of view of risk management, it makes more sense usually to devote resources to critical path activities (vs. other activities), as these will have more impact overall.

Some other important terminology to take into account is:

- **Duration**: Number of work periods, *excluding* holidays or other nonworking periods, required to complete the activity, expressed as workdays or workweeks
- **Elapsed time**: Number of work periods, *including* holidays or nonworking periods required to complete the activity, expressed as workdays or workweeks

Again, one of the big advantages of using a software project management tool is that Early Start, Early Finish, Late Start, Late Finish, slack and even the critical path are all automatically determined. This automates the mechanical and redundant work, and let the PM concentrate on more analytical tasks. Furthermore, any changes in the project baseline will automatically adjust all activities and calculations.

There are many more functionalities in these Project Management tools which are of great use to the PM, however, we shall restrict ourselves to the basics, and let each reader explore these by herself.

5.1.5 Time-Cost-Quality Management

For a defined project scope, there are three dimensions that are at the PM's disposal as shown in Fig. 5.11.

What this means is that for any defined scope, there is a fixed time-quality-cost relationship which cannot be broken given a fixed amount of assets and resources. The PM may increase or decrease any of these dimensions, but if the scope is to remain constant, this will in turn affect at least one, maybe two of the other dimensions.

If delivery time for the project is to be reduced, for example, then either the quality suffers as a consequence of maintaining the same cost, or more cost (resources usually) are to be added in order for quality not to suffer. The same is true for quality, if it is to be increased, then either the time to deliver is extended or more cost is to be put into the project. Of all three, time is usually the most inflexible and hardest to control. Putting in more time into the project usually also affects cost, due to the prolongation of resources' stay into the project and may not necessarily result in an increase in quality.

Fig. 5.11 Scope and the time, quality and cost dimensions

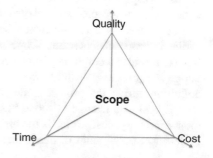

All three dimensions however, should be monitored and controlled by the PM, as otherwise these may get out of control, or worse, fail the project.

5.1.6 Monitoring and Control

It is often said that the Project Manager is the person in the project that does nothing, and yet, if there was a single person most influential to the outcome and success of the project, it is the PM. This seems ironic, and yet it is true. The PM "does nothing" in the sense that he/she does not actually execute any of the concrete tasks defined in the project plan, these are all specialized team members that undertake them. The role of the project manager is to coordinate, make sure the tasks as being undertaken correctly, resolve if there are issues, monitor using the appropriate tools, and control the scope, quality, time, resources, and cost assigned to the project. To some extent, he also has the ability to propose, design, and utilize the appropriate tools needed for proper monitoring and control of the project.

It is essential that proper tools be used for the monitoring and control of the project. The proper use of these tools will lessen the dependency on the project on individual initiatives and personality of the project manager, and instead leverage on best practices. Poor tools and governance result in poor results. These tools are also not static, but should be improved iteratively as more projects are handled, more experience gathered, and more knowledge acquired. Usually, this is the responsibility of the Portfolio Manager that conducts review and improvements on project governance, together with his project managers (see Chap. 9).

In concept, the principles of IT project monitoring and control are simple, they are to monitor the most fundamental dimensions of a project:

- Cost
- Resources—these also have an impact on cost
- Time
- Scope—to ensure adherence
- Quality

Of all, the most difficult to measure is quality due to its intangible nature, followed by scope, all others can be quantified. Quality and scope are the usual points of dispute between the customer and the vendor, and the biggest reason why a project is not accepted and delayed, affecting in turn the other project dimensions.

Let us discuss each dimension separately, starting with scope. As discussed earlier in scope management, scope is usually the single biggest source of project failure. It is also a common point of contention, and is very much related to quality. Scope is a joint responsibility from parties, customer, and vendor, as a poor scope definition during the project tender is very hard to resolve once the project has started, and as a change in scope has a direct effect on the other dimensions, and most especially, cost, which is the biggest concern for the vendor. There is always a trade-off in the amount of detail that the scope should carry during the tendering process. Too much, and it will take time to prepare the tender; Too little, and it leaves room for ambiguity and discord. In any case, from a project manager's point of view, the more detail, the better. For the Project Manager (PM), the ideal scope is that which can be enumerated in the form of a table and checked for during the monitoring and control process. This leaves little room for ambiguity.

Milestones defined throughout the project lifecycle are a tool for the PM to check the effective status and progress of a project. Concretely, they show how the project scope has progressed up to that point in time. It is recommended to have deliverable milestones defined throughout the project timeline, and not only milestones which flag payment. Milestones are the "yes/no" signal on whether the project has progressed to that point, and in order for them to be effective, some guidelines need to be followed. Milestones should be

- **Nonambiguous**: Project progress needs to be objective, in order for it to be so, a milestone must signal completion/noncompletion. Avoid partially completed milestones as it again, makes it open to interpretation. Good examples of milestones are

  - Deliverable of XXX document
  - Acceptance of XXX document
  - Installation of software
  - Acceptance of blueprint design
  - Completion of training
  - Completion of workshop
  - Submission of first wave draft reports

- **Easily checked** by both parties. Again, this is to minimize misinterpretations, ambiguity, and "sugar coating."
- **Spread** out throughout the project. So that the PMs can effectively monitor the project, if there is a lag of several months between milestones, monitoring between those months is a guess at best.
- **Practical**. The best milestones are those that are actually needed for the project as part of its deliverables, and not made just for the purpose of monitoring and control, as it may be a considerable effort just to prepare that milestone deliverable.

Time utilized for the project is of course monitored by annotating the current time, and where the project is at now. This gives you the % completion of the project. Unfortunately, this measure when used by itself has several flaws. For one, if not used in conjunction with proper milestones, it gives you an untrue picture of where the project is really at. How many of us have encountered projects that seem to be on time, and reported as so, only to find that the last 10 % of the project takes double the time as the rest of the project. Not only is this a ruinous project, but the PM may have no clue on why this has actually happened. Take another example in which the "build" part of the project (which is also the hardest to monitor) reports progressive achievements, and yet fails miserably during the testing portion of the project. This of course is related to the quality of the monitoring, which we will discuss later, but it also shows the importance of building in nonambiguous milestones throughout the project lifecycle.

The second big reason on why % completeness is a bad measure is that it tells you nothing on how advanced or delayed the project is with respect to the baseline. The project may be 50 % complete to date, but it should actually have been 70 % complete by this time, and that is not captured by this indicator alone. If the project is run on a time and materials basis (and not turnkey) then the cost overruns (savings) versus the cost baseline is also not apparent. It is for this reason that two complementary indicators taken from Earned Value standards (Devaux 2014) may also be used, at the very least:

- SPI (Scheduled Performance Index) which gives you an indication of how the project is faring in terms of time versus baseline project time duration; and
- CPI (Cost Performance Index) which gives you a similar measure but in terms of cost.

In order for these indicators to be well understood, however, some basic theory needs to be explained first, including the concept of Earned Value.

Earned Value (Stamatis 1997; US Department of Energy 2008) refers to the value of the work done up to a particular moment in time. This is different from cost. Earned Value reflects how the customer values that amount of work in terms of its value to him as an intangible, and not how much it has actually cost him in terms of paying the vendor for it, which is totally different. Take for example, a construction project in which a 4-storey building is to be constructed for a total amount of US$40million, or to simplify the example, a fully proportional, US $10million per floor, to be built in 8 months, or 2 months per floor as per project plan (baseline). Suppose also (even if not a very good project management practice!) that the building is being built using time and materials costing, as invoiced regularly by the vendor. From the point of view of the customer, the number of floors actually finished reflects the value of the project to him, which is different from how much he has actually paid the vendor so far. Thus, take into account the following example:

Four months into the project, you have paid the vendor US$30million but only 1 floor has been completed by the contractor.

The Actual Cost (AC) of the project is thus US$30million, corresponding to what was paid, however, the Earned Value (EV) of the project is only US $10million. The planned value (PV) at month 4 is actually US$20million, meaning, by this time, two floors should have been completed worth US $10million each. The project not only has cost overruns, it is also way behind schedule!

Let us now define formally:

Earned Value (EV)	= The sum of the approved cost estimates for the physical work that was actually accomplished on the project and the authorized budget for activities or portions of activities that have been completed. This is also called Budgeted Cost of Work Performed (BCWP)
Planned Value (PV)	= is the physical work that was scheduled or planned to be performed and the authorized budget to accomplish this scheduled work. This is also called Budgeted Cost of Work Scheduled (BCWS)
Actual Cost (AC)	= the total cost actually incurred in accomplishing the work that was completed

We can now define appropriate indicators based on the above:

Schedule Variance = EV − PV. Is a Measure of schedule performance on a project, it indicates project schedule status versus baseline schedule;

Cost Variance = EV − AC. This is a measure of cost performance on a project. It indicates the relationship of physical performance to the costs spent; and

Cost Performance Index (CPI) = EV/AC (%). Is a measure of the value of work completed compared to the actual cost vs. progress made on the project so far.

Schedule Performance Index (SPI) = EV/PV (%). This is a measure of progress achieved compared to progress planned on a project.

For CPI, if it is <1 then the project is having cost overruns, if =1 it is mark-on to budget, and if >1 then it is running below budget.

For SPI, a value <1 means the project is delayed, if =1 then it is just on time, and if >1 then it is actually advanced versus its baseline schedule.

By making use of CPI, SPI, and % completeness, a project manager has a very powerful tool on hand because it marries scope, time, and cost into a single report. Nowadays, with the advanced use of project management tools, these indicators can be calculated automatically based on the project task % completion, giving the PM an unambiguous, objective view of how the project is actually doing.

Let us look at some further examples that illustrate the concept. For example, take an IT project which has defined deliverables and a corresponding PV as shown in the y-axis of the graph in Fig. 5.12.

At time = t5, the planned work was to have module 1 tested, with a value worth US$400k. However, at time = t5 we spent US$600k, but actual work done was up to functional design only, with a value of only US$200k, so the EV = US$200k only. Therefore,

- Project is above budget
- And behind schedule

The power of earned value is that it translates scope into a value translatable into monetary terms. It is thus easier for top management to appreciate, as it usually prefers to talk of costs and monetary impact.

Fig. 5.12 Example showing EV, PV, and AC

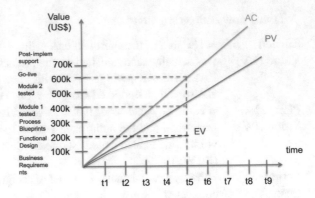

By having a chart with cumulative value versus time, and plotting AC, EV, and PV in the charts, we get the so-called S-curves which can quickly show how the project is doing. There are four possible scenarios as shown in Figs. 5.13, 5.14, 5.15 and 5.16.

Fig. 5.13 Project ahead of schedule and under budget

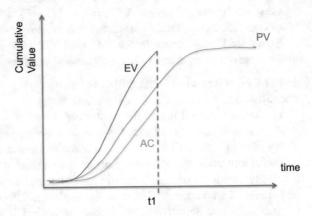

Fig. 5.14 Project with cost overruns and behind schedule

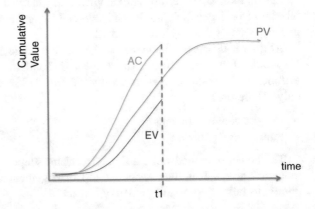

Fig. 5.15 Project behind schedule but underutilizing budget

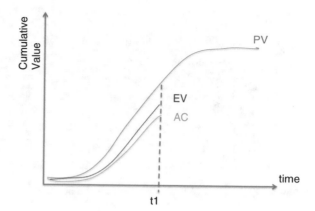

Fig. 5.16 Project ahead of schedule but overrunning budget

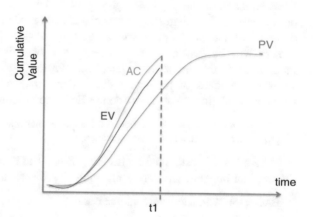

Figure 5.13: Project ahead of time schedule and under budget (which I think is mainly theoretical and belongs to science fiction!).

Figure 5.14: Project overrunning costs and behind schedule (probably a more usual scenario to many of our readers).

Figure 5.15: Project behind schedule but under budget.

Figure 5.16: And project ahead of schedule but overrunning budget.

Of course, Actual Cost and CPI have no real meaning to the project if the project is fixed cost (turnkey). In that case, only EV and SPI have relevance.

Scope, time, cost have been discussed, how can all these be put together into a meaningful monitoring and control tool? Advanced tools nowadays allow you to monitor these in very efficient ways, so that by plotting the different tasks with their interdependencies, and estimated duration, the baseline of the project is obtained. If the project is turnkey, a fixed amount is attached to this baseline, which is the cost of the project. Deliverables are also identified in the project plan (Fig. 5.17).

As the project progresses, the % completion of the task is input by the project manager, and the EV, SPI can then be calculated automatically by the project

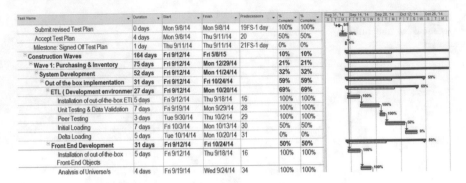

Task Name	Duration	Start	Finish	Predecessors	% Complete	% Complete
Submit revised Test Plan	0 days	Mon 9/8/14	Mon 9/8/14	19FS-1 day	100%	100%
Accept Test Plan	4 days	Mon 9/8/14	Thu 9/11/14	20	50%	50%
Milestone: Signed Off Test Plan	1 day	Thu 9/11/14	Thu 9/11/14	21FS-1 day	0%	0%
Construction Waves	164 days	Fri 9/12/14	Fri 5/8/15		10%	10%
Wave 1: Purchasing & Inventory	75 days	Fri 9/12/14	Mon 12/29/14		21%	21%
System Development	52 days	Fri 9/12/14	Mon 11/24/14		32%	32%
Out of the box implementation	31 days	Fri 9/12/14	Fri 10/24/14		59%	59%
ETL (Development environment	27 days	Fri 9/12/14	Mon 10/20/14		69%	69%
Installation of out-of-the-box ETL	5 days	Fri 9/12/14	Thu 9/18/14	16	100%	100%
Unit Testing & Data Validation	7 days	Fri 9/19/14	Mon 9/29/14	28	100%	100%
Peer Testing	3 days	Tue 9/30/14	Thu 10/2/14	29	100%	100%
Initial Loading	7 days	Fri 10/3/14	Mon 10/13/14	30	50%	50%
Delta Loading	5 days	Tue 10/14/14	Mon 10/20/14	31	0%	0%
Front End Development	31 days	Fri 9/12/14	Fri 10/24/14		50%	50%
Installation of out-of-the-box Front-End Objects	5 days	Fri 9/12/14	Thu 9/18/14	16	100%	100%
Analysis of Universe/s	4 days	Fri 9/19/14	Wed 9/24/14	34	100%	100%

Fig. 5.17 Sample project plan with tasks and milestones

management tool and displayed, giving the PM an easy way to understand how his project is actually going. Projections can also be made for costs and time, using the current CPI and SPI to project what the total costs and total time to complete the project will be, assuming the current rates of efficiency (or inefficiency) are maintained till the end of the project. PMP (Project Management Institute 2013) has several techniques of projecting these. For our discussion, we merely take the simpler calculation. First, let us define Estimate at Completion (EAC):

EAC = An Estimate At Completion, is a forecast of most likely total project costs based on project performance and risk quantification

Where EAC is estimated by dividing Budget at completion (BAC), which was the original budget used during planning at project end, by the CPI:

EAC = BAC/CPI (cumulative till data date)

Assumption here is what the project has experienced to date can be expected to continue in the future (same CPI throughout the project).

The same estimation can be made for the time component:

Estimated Duration = Baseline duration/SPI
Estimated Finish = Baseline Start + Estimated Duration

What this means is that using your current project (in) efficiency, based on SPI, we can project when the project will actually finish.

Resources can also be captured by such tools, such that assigning specific resources to tasks allow you to monitor % and utilization of your resources, as well as cost for the use of such resources. If the project is time and materials, you can also calculate Actual Cost based on the rates of these resources.

These tools also allow you to view project information in a variety of ways including Gantt charts, table formats, predefined reports for specific uses (resource usage, cost report, efficiency reports, etc.), and calendar views, among others.

We have reserved the most difficult and contentious for last, Quality, how do we ensure it? The challenge with quality is that unlike cost, time, and even scope, quality is very much project-dependent, customer-dependent, and can be very subjective. The key therefore is to make it as objective as possible, illicit agreement on it, so that all parties are aware of what is required of them, what needs to be attained, and ultimately, how they will be measured, and the project accepted. Let us face the reality, not all customers demand the same amount of quality. Some customers are obsessed with cost, and though they may say otherwise, are willing to accept low-quality work for as long as it meets a low budget. This is precisely an intangible that is factored-in during the sales process by the vendor if he is sufficiently acquainted with the customer. If the vendor knows beforehand that the customer demands a high standard of quality, it will factor that in with a certain premium, as that is what is necessary in order to achieve the desired quality level acceptable by the client.

Ok, all that is well and good, but how can we really measure quality and ensure that it is being met? Main components to this are

- Detailed scope
- Standards
- Documentation

Detailing the scope describes the concrete quality that is to be delivered by the project. Take as an example a scope requirement defined during the tender process:

- Software must be able to generate the bills for 100,000 customers

As compared to a more detailed requirement:

- Software must be able to generate the bills for 100,000 customers,

  - Must be generated within a 2 h batch window,
  - Must be generated in pdf format,
  - Output format must be user flexible, with the ability to add graphs, pie charts, historical billing data,
  - Must be able to print in full color, etc.

It is of course a major effort to define the quality components of a project, but is absolutely necessary if one is to ensure their delivery. As discussed earlier under scope management, not all aspects of the scope can be defined during the tender process stage, so it is a reality that scope is successively defined and refined as the project progresses, but once it has reached the end of the design phase, all its aspects must be fully defined, clear, and agreed upon. Successive definition of scope components should be reasonable and agreed to by both vendor and customer, and not go against the content nor spirit of the tender documents; otherwise, this should be treated as an additional scope, and thus, a change request.

The second leg toward guaranteeing quality refers to the use of international standards and documentation. Standards such as CMMI, ISO20,000, ISO9,001, ITIL, PMP, Prince, may be required from the vendor, as a way to guarantee that at least awareness of international best practices exists, but of course, there is no guarantee that they will actually be used correctly. Standards will also exist in the customer organization which has learnt from the many years of experience running operations and projects. This may include coding and configuration standards as well as policies which should be given to the vendor for compliance. Standards set a general framework, but do not indicate the specifics that are to be used, which brings us to the third component, documentation.

Software is an intangible, and most hardware is intangible as well today. Think of it, hardware performance depends more and more today on the way it has been configured, set up, and architected, which are intangibles again and are not captured by the hardware technical specifications. Hardware specs tell us nothing on these, and yet today, these intangibles are the make or break for how hardware performs. The conclusion therefore is that the quality of software and hardware depends on what and how services are performed on them, and this, being the ultimate intangible, can only be defined, monitored, and controlled by means of proper documentation describing what is to be done or how it has been done.

Documentation type differs per project type (please see Sect. 5.2 for an extensive discussion of the documents), and this is a valued Intellectual Property in each organization. It is the PM's duty to define what is the relevant documentation for the project and use available ready-made standards, which may either be the customer's or the vendor's, a combination of both, as agreed upon. If due to the type of project some additional documentation needs to be made or modified, then this is to be discussed between both parties and agreed upon. All relevant documentation should appear as deliverables in the project plan part of the deliverables checklist as discussed in Sect. 7.3, and monitored for compliance, content, and completeness. Nonacceptance of the documentation means the milestone has not been attained due to nonattainment of the desired QUALITY. Only when the project milestone is accepted, the project has progressed with the necessary quality. It is of course the duty of the PM to understand the content of this document, to read it thoroughly, and if not completely in the know, to consult other colleagues in his organization for verification.

A quick way for the project manager to monitor the quality of the project is by means of an issue registry, as well as a deliverables checklist. These are explained in more detail in Sect. 7.3, but in essence the issue registry is a project management document which registers any issue encountered during any moment in time in the project. The issue reflects here until it is resolved or canceled (becomes nonrelevant). The deliverables checklist is a list of all deliverables, documents, workshops, trainings, and the like that are part of the project; it complements the project management tool. All deliverables to be produced are registered in this sheet, and updated as they are submitted, approved, or pending.

5.1.7   Risk Management

Risk management is the ability to foresee how events or circumstances can affect a project before they actually occur. It is thus important because by focusing on what may happen, one can proactively plan and develop a mitigation plan for them, instead of just reacting, thus reducing or mitigating their negative effect.

We commonly think of risks as being negative, however, positive risks exist too. For the former, we mitigate, eliminate, or transfer the risk, but for the latter we enhance and promote its probability of occurrence. Positive risks have an overall positive effect on the project in terms of time, cost, quality, or all. Risk management is an inherent function in IT operations (and operations in general), but for the project manager, it is focused toward the outcome of the project.

Risks may further be classified according to certainty (Cleden 2009):

- Known–Known
- Known–Unknown: partially known
- Unknown–Unknown: totally unknown

For the first two risk types, project reserves (buffers) should be allocated. This really means that if they occur, these will have an effect on time, cost, quality, or on all of these dimensions. Time extensions can be mitigated by adding additional time buffers into the project plan baseline, which actually translates to cost as well, while quality impacts usually need to be addressed by rework, additional time to fix, or additional resources into the project, which again translates to cost. For this reason, buffers to be added to the project will usually be in the form of both time and cost, as these will cover for the occurrence of potential risks.

Unknown–unknown risks cannot be accounted for in any way, and so including it in project reserves to mitigate them would be extremely expensive for the project. For this reason, management reserves are usually allocated for this type of risks, meaning it is the management that allocates for these additional costs at a corporate or portfolio level. These can be in the form of emergency funds, insurance, or expert resources that may be on standby for such purposes.

Risk management is not a one-time activity, but rather, a project-long activity which is continuously undertaken, much like the monitoring and control of the project. Risk analysis is best conducted having the different stakeholders in the project to participate in brainstorming sessions to identify risks, as each will have his/her own perspective of what are the significant risks. Risks also change as the project moves along its different phases, so that risks identified during the analysis stage may be different from those at the design stage, and may be different from those at the testing phase. Risks may move in terms of relevance, some being totally eliminated, others increasing in probability, while others still ceasing to be relevant. As mentioned during the start of this chapter, risks are greater at the start of the project, yet are hardest to identify at that point in time. It is however when the PM has greatest influence and time to actually mitigate or enhance a risk. It is therefore recommended that risk analysis starts early in the project, otherwise risks may be more easily identified in the later course of the project, but with very little possibility of actually mitigating them. Risks are also cheaper to address at the start, because they may require less rework if work has not advanced too much into the project.

Risk analysis may be qualitative or quantitative. Different projects will require deeper and more or less effort in terms of risk management. If the project is inherently risky, then more time and effort should be devoted. Typically risky projects are those that affect business process across a wide number of departments, and which have a large user change management component. Technical projects, unless these are relatively untested technologies, typically carry the least risk.

In order to better understand how risks may affect a project, risks should be classified for probability and impact. Both probability and impact may be classified as High, Medium, or Low (or any other alternative scoring system may be used). By sorting risks on their overall ranking, high-high risks, meaning risks that have a high probability of occurring and a high impact on the project should be the first to be addressed for mitigation. At the other end of the spectrum are the low-low risks. Please take note that in all this discussion, we focus on negative risks, but the same technique is applicable to positive risks, save that they are to be enhanced rather than mitigated. A sample risk registry (Low 1994) template can look like that of Table 5.3.

Fields in this sheet are a description of the risk, its probability, its impact, mitigation identified, person or team responsible for the risk mitigation, as well as the date identified. In the example above, the phase of the project was identified as well, so that specific risks are identified per project phase. After that phase has passed, most of the risks associated with it become irrelevant, either because they were mitigated, accepted, or simply occurred. Risks can be acted upon in several possible ways:

- Accepted: meaning, no action is taken
- Mitigated: an action that will either enhance (for positive risks) or decrease (for negative risks) its influence
- Transferred: by transferring the risk to another party that is better prepared to deal with it

Generally, only low-low risks can be accepted, all others should warrant action in order to deal with them, and definitely high-high risks need mitigation action, or a transfer. Mitigation also needs to be well thought of, and is not the responsibility solely of the PM. He/she is the person that needs to call for a risk assessment meeting, but each and every party and stakeholder are to participate in this endeavor, as it enriches the discussion and gives many different views for the same project. Risks can be of any nature, they may be technical, project management related, task related, change management, training, logistics, and others. No risk identified should be discarded, in fact, discussion should be encouraged so that all

Table 5.3 Sample risk registry

No.	Project phase	Risk	Probability	Impact	Mitigation	Date	Assigned To	Affects
1a	Training Planning	Poor Quality of Trainors	M	H	Training on Presentation Skills; Get feedback from HR on the Profile of Trainers (Quality); Core Team	29-Jul	Homer	Quality of training
1b		Quality of Training Materials	L	H	Review of Training Materials: Training Deck; Addition of Talking Points to the Training Deck Update as of July 9 > Talking points submitted as of July 9. For review and update of Noel and Joan		Homer	Quality of training
1c		Availability of Trainees	L	M	Additional Trainings to be provided (as Buffer); Promoting Project to the Business Users so the Dept Heads can push this proactively		HR; Francesc	Project acceptance
1d		Availability of Trainors	L	M	Promoting Project to the Business Users so the Dept Heads can push this proactively		Francesc	Project acceptance
1e		Retention of Basic Computer Knowledge	L	L	Retraining of Basic Computer Knowledge; For those trainees attending without enough computer knowledge, they will have to be advised to retrain first then be pooled for the Additional Training sessions		HR	Project acceptance

(continued)

Table 5.3 (continued)

No.	Project phase	Risk	Probability	Impact	Mitigation	Date	Assigned To	Affects
1f		Lack of Training Equipments (Computers)	L	L	Sir Noel to monitor the delivery of the 12 additional computers for Training		Noel	timeline
1 g		Retention of WMS Training	M	H	Users Access to QA System' Contractor to load the data Update as of July 9: > UAT Testers were given access during the UAT		Contractor (Julia)	
2	Change Management	Resistance of Process from Users during Training	L	H	Roadshow for Business Units Update as of Sept 20	August 6–9 (Before)	Francesc	
2a	Data Conversion	SAP: Accounts, Contacts, MRU, Zone—Quality of data like Duplicates, Inconsistent Data	L	H	Julia to provide Homer the list of errors during import of data to dev (06/27/2013);		Julia/Homer	

risks identified by the team are to be enumerated, afterward, these are then revisited one by one and their corresponding probability and impact updated in the registry. Very low-low risks can be discarded altogether. It is for this reason that the risk analysis and issuance of the risk registry cannot be done mechanically, as the discussion itself is probably of greater value even than the output of the above table, as it makes everyone on the team aware of risks that they probably would not have been aware of in the first place.

5.1.8 Knowledge Management

Knowledge management refers to the activities leading to the buildup of a knowledge base that can be used not only for the project, but more often, used for subsequent projects as well. It is a repository of "lessons learned" so to speak, so that subsequent projects be guided to avoid identified pitfalls, learn to leverage on positive aspects, as well as refine the tools used to manage the project (project governance). Knowledge Management is of primordial importance if project management is to be a core competency of the organization practicing it.

Knowledge base, or the capture of this knowledge, can be in many forms. For IT projects, it comes primarily in the form of:

- Documentation—as described in Sect. 5.2
- Project Management tools—in terms of templates, configuration, and utilization of these tools
- Methodology—which refers to the manner in which the project is executed and managed

One of the most immediate and apparent benefits of knowledge management is the recording of how project issues were resolved. These details, once accessed by the Operations team upon turnover will help them in not repeating past mistakes, as well as giving them information on the resolution of issues which may reoccur.

Documentation, project management tools, and methodology are all existing knowledge assets in the organization, but by further refining these after every project, they are further sharpened and improved, capturing the lessons learned from each project.

Modern document management system (DMS) tools help incredibly in the management of one's Knowledge Base (KB). Modern DMS not only allow manage different permissions over documentation such as ability to read, print, view, upload, and approve, but they also incorporate powerful search capabilities which allow users to search through the KB by providing keywords and terms, the DMS presenting the best matches. Thus, for issues encountered before, a user may search through all the material to get most relevant KB documents by indicating the type of issue or key word description of what he wants to search for.

5.1.9   Communication Management

Let us revisit some of the risks identified during the scope management section. We enumerated samples of factors that can affect scope in terms of risks that can lead to a change in scope in the middle of a project:

- End user changing his/her mind
- A senior executive having different ideas on what should be done
- Project creep
- Person approving is not the right person to approve (or does not understand the actual needs)
- Unruly behavior by the end users
- Supplier starts development work without getting a sign-off from the users

If you look at this list above, there is little one can do to mitigate these but to properly communicate to the different stakeholders so as to avoid having these risks. This example was used to emphasize the importance of communications, which although often cited, it is sometimes forgotten to be a key component of project management.

Oftentimes, communication management is something that comes naturally to the Project Manager, without having to undertake an explicit communications management plan. In many instances, this may be sufficient, but for large, complex projects with many stakeholders involved, a more planned and coordinated effort may be needed. It is not just who needs to be informed, but the frequency and medium in which the information is to be disseminated identified as well. One approach is to conduct a communication matrix, which describes how communication is to be conducted, as shown in Table 5.4.

Next is how to inform the stakeholders, there are many different media which may be used:

- **Project meetings**—these are regularly defined meetings which involve those stakeholders most directly involved in the project, usually the key business users, project managers, as well as the key IT personnel involved in the project. Additional stakeholders may be invited if the topic is of concern to them. This meeting is to regularly update the team on the progress, discuss next steps, ask for involvement, and resolve arising issues. The risk registry may also be discussed and updated in this meeting, together with the project plan, issue, and request registry.
- **Steering committee meetings**—steering committee meetings may be preset in schedule, or may be called for as the need arises. The main purpose of the steering committee meetings is usually to inform the top management stakeholders of the progress of the project, seek approval for major decision points

Table 5.4 Sample communication matrix

Stakeholder	Content	Frequency	Manner
Project Manager	Project Updates	Weekly	Physical meeting
Steering Committee	Updates and key points for resolution	As-need basis	Physical meeting
Key users involved in project	Project Updates	As-need basis	Physical meeting
	Weekly project updates	Weekly	Portal
Project sponsor	Project Status	Monthly	Physical meeting
HR	Change Management and changes in Table of Organization, roles, and responsibilities	• After blueprint • before go live	Physical meeting
Finance	Discussion on change of financial report contents	After blueprint	• email blueprints • meeting if required
General users	General advice on the project	Before go live	• email blast • details in portal

which need to be made at their level, or to ask for guidance and resolution in case of contention.

- **Project reports**—which may be distributed to those identified as "need to know." Project reports may contain a summary of the key indicators, % completion, SPI, CPI, project plan updates, risks, issues, requests and identified next steps, including those needed to address the risks and issues encountered/identified.
- **Email**—can be used to disseminate in a simple way the project reports and other information, without having to call for a meeting.
- **Portal**—can be used to upload all the documentation and give access to relevant parties.
- **Scorecard**—can be a summary of project performance based on predefined metrics which can be used by higher management to monitor project progress. This can be loaded into the portal, emailed, or an online reporting tool used where it may be accessed by the different parties.
- **Roadshows**—one important aspect in user change management is to keep users informed, involved, and make them feel they have a stake in the project being rolled out. Roadshows are one way to inform users in a relaxed manner, where the project highlights are presented, their involvement highlighted, and their questions and concerns answered.
- **Posters, magazines, and handouts**—to drum up awareness and support to the project, highlighting the benefits the project will deliver to the organization and to individual departments and users.

It may seem apparent as well, but different contents, level of details, and media need to be used for different type of stakeholders. This is commonly ignored, to the detriment of the communication message's effectivity. As a general rule, the higher up one goes into the management organization, the lesser the details and the shorter the messages should be. The main focus to upper management should be related to aspects related to the overall business, as top management is busy with running the business, so its attention span is short if they cannot relate it to the main business and its bottom line. Messages should be concise, direct, and the petition for guidance or decision clearly defined.

On the other end of the spectrum, users will be more concerned about how the project will affect them personally in the way they conduct their business. Will it make their work easier? Will I have to learn how to use a new application? Is there a new procedure? Why was it designed that way? Will I have a job at the end of the project? Will my job responsibilities change? These aspects should not be taken lightly as end users have much influence in the success or failure of the project.

As such, the message contents should be changed according to the intended audience. As a guide, some sample audiences are:

- key executives
- key users
- general users
- suppliers
- project team

This details who should be informed, through what means, how often, and the key content that should be included or highlighted. It may seem obvious, but it is important that whenever a meeting is called for, the agenda for the meeting be clearly stated, so that the stakeholder knows whether he has to devote his valuable time for it, or if he can delegate it to someone from his team.

One part of communications management involves that of identifying stakeholders, which may by itself be a challenge because though most stakeholders may be apparent, some may not be, and may have a major impact and influence over the project. Stakeholders can come in many different forms:

- Senior Management (in general)
- Department Heads whose process the project touches on
- Project Sponsor
- Business Process Owners
- Key users
- General user populace
- Suppliers
- Project Team
- IT's O&M team
- IT's Senior Management
- Outside customers

Failure to identify a stakeholder may result in no (or scant) communication being made to the stakeholder, which may result in his negative reaction once he finds out that he should have been more involved and possibly consulted in the first place. Also, seniority may not be the only factor to qualify a person as a stakeholder. It is fairly common to find in many organizations a person without the formal title but still respected as an "expert" for particular processes, so that involving and consulting that person eases the whole project implementation. On the other hand, some senior manager may not have a direct influence over the process because it does not touch his department, yet for some other reason, may want to be involved and contribute to the project, so it also pays to take this person into account in the list of stakeholders. All this identification and planning on how to manage the stakeholders is usually done mentally by the PM, however, if the project spans across many departments and is quite complicated, the use of the communication plan may be called for.

One of the objectives in managing stakeholders is in proactively changing resistant and neutral stakeholders to supportive ones, and possibly bringing up key supportive stakeholders (especially if in senior management) to that of leading and sponsoring the project. One of the key factors is communication, and as explained above, communication styles vary according to the stakeholder in question. As all stakeholders are persons, it is important to be aware of their personal stake in the project, and try to align this to the overall objective of the project. Generally speaking, the more senior a stakeholder is, the more his concern will be toward the general company's benefit, while the lower management ranks would focus more on his own personal well-being, this is represented in a diagram in Fig. 5.18.

As such, the communication delivered to each stakeholder should also take into account that mix of company benefit–personal well-being. At the CEO level, little concern would be given (usually) to the personal stake of each employee (of course, for as long as the expectations are within a reasonable level), but more toward what efficiencies, revenues, and cost reductions the company can achieve. On the other hand of the spectrum, a rank and file employee would be eager to know how this

Fig. 5.18 Stakeholders' seniority versus stake

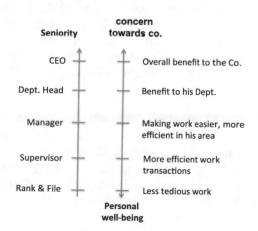

project will actually simplify and make his work less tedious. Thus, when explaining to each party in his particular venue, messages should be delivered accordingly, keeping in mind the audience at hand.

5.2 Project Documentation

Generally speaking, the type of documentation to be prepared for each project depends to a large extent on the type of project and software (if any) to be implemented. Purely technical projects are simpler to document and manage, as they do not involve business process design, and the users are commonly restricted to IT personnel. On the other end of the spectrum are software implementations that touch core business processes needed in the day-to-day operations of the business and whose processes span across several departments.

We have subdivided the type of documentation depending on the phase of the project: analysis, design, build, and cutover.

5.2.1 Analysis

Analysis refers to the phase in which the vendor is getting sufficient information from the customer organization's users and IT, in order to come up with a proper design. Typical documentation at this stage includes:

- Minutes of meetings—in which the discussions are transcript
- User requirements document—which summarizes in an organized manner, the requirements from the user, usually arranged by process or main functionality, and explains in narrative format these requirements, and enumerates them.

In the analysis phase, it may be advantageous to create mock displays so as to give the users a better feel of how the resulting system may look like, especially if display outputs, report formats, and the like are important part of the deliverables. If the project entails a reporting system, a mock report in excel or dummy dashboard will also help the user understand how his results would look like, and critique these before actual development starts. For some other projects, a mock transactional display, the so-called Conference Room Pilot (CRP) may also be used.

5.2.2 Design

Business process may typically be captured using flowcharts which show the flow of the process as it progresses through different departments and users. It also identifies conditions, decision points, and outputs. Process flowcharts however, may be defined at differing levels of detail, so that a common understanding on what level of detail is required needs to be agreed upon at the project start. A sample classification on the level of detail to be used is:

- **Level 0**: a list of involved processes with a brief description
- **Level 1**: a diagram showing the highest level process interaction between different types of users shown in diagram form (see Fig. 5.19). This does not explain the chronological order of the process steps, but merely illustrates how the general philosophy of the entire process works.
- **Level 2**: process flowchart describing in sequence the tasks involved for each particular process. A single process is typically depicted in 1 process flowchart and may span across several pages, a sample of which is shown in Fig. 5.20.
- **Level 3**: a more detailed process flowchart in which each task defined by the level 2 flowchart is further broken down into transactions as undertaken in the system. Thus, as an example a Release Purchase Order task in level 2, which may be represented by a single function block is here further broken down into details such as, "Prepare Purchase Order"—"Approve Purchase Order"—"Release Purchase Order"—"Print Purchase Order." Figure 5.21 shows a sample with this level of detail (for SAP, this level would correspond to the T-code level).
- **Level 4**: Work Instruction level, is a step-by-step depiction of how a user is to transact. Typically includes screenshots and an explanation of the parameters and selections the user is to make in transacting. This documentation is usually prepared for the Testing and Training phases, and also in the User Manuals.

The process of designing and documenting the processes is typically an iterative one, in which each successive level is signed off before proceeding to a more detailed level, guaranteeing alignment.

Aside from process, a document should also be used for defining how the user interface (UI) will look like. This may be more or less important depending on the type of project. For reporting, billing, web interfaces, presentment, sales and marketing systems, this may be of primary importance, as the appearance is just as important as the content. For standard systems such as ERPs, in which the interface is more or less fixed, this is less important (and flexible), unless it is tied directly with productivity factors, such as how long it takes to transact. In such cases, mock displays should be presented to the user for sign-off, including content fields, color schemes, layout, and esthetics.

Some softwares may not be so heavy in terms of process; however, they conduct other functionalities which also need to be signed off by the customer. For example, document management systems, portals and the like, may carry very limited process flows, but functionalities such as functions made available to the users, search criteria, metadata, fields to be stored, selection menus, and others need to be agreed. A functional design document is used for this purpose. This document is seldom standard, as it is highly dependent on the type of software being utilized, but it essentially captures:

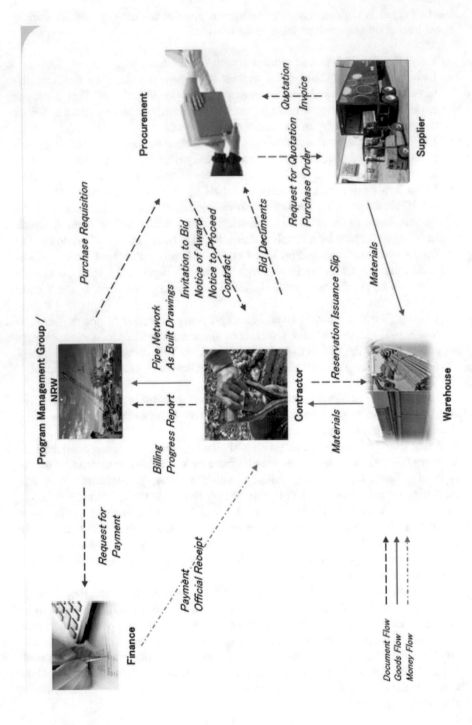

Fig. 5.19 Sample Level 1 process diagram showing a "Plan to Construct" typical process

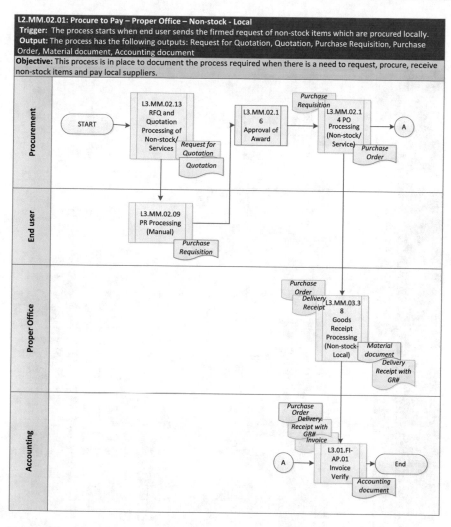

Fig. 5.20 Sample Level 2 process diagram

- Overall functional architecture: includes different modules to be used, as well as interfaces to/from other systems
- Functions, attributes, and forms to be used. This may go up to the level of describing each field to be used and their possible values.
- Process flowchart: if process is simple enough, it may already be included into this functional design document
- Layout of user screens (if possible)
- High-level description of interfaces used. Interfaces may then be detailed further in a separate document
- Roles and Permissions

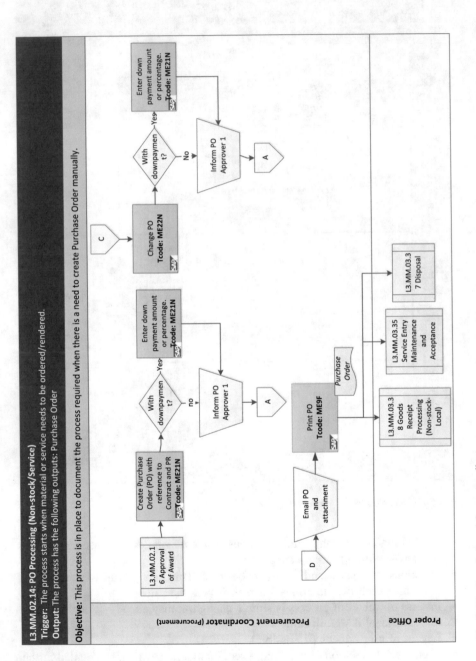

L3.MM.02.14: PO Processing (Non-stock/Service)
Trigger: The process starts when material or service needs to be ordered/rendered.
Output: The process has the following outputs: Purchase Order

Objective: This process is in place to document the process required when there is a need to create Purchase Order manually.

Fig. 5.21 Sample Level 3 process diagram

Its counterpart document is the technical design document, which captures all technical (infrastructure and technology components) setup information. This document is essentially reviewed by the IT personnel only, for conformance with the company's standards and policy, ensuring that the solution once implemented, will be in accordance with company IT standards. IT will also check for appropriateness of the infrastructure allocated, though this also needs to be in accordance with the software vendor's technical specifications. This document is also highly dependent on the solution and product being implemented, but typically contains:

- **Overall technical architecture**: a diagram showing the different software components, in what servers these sit, network components with their interconnections and configurations, description of the different type of servers needed (application server, database server, web server, management tool server, etc.), as well as any special components utilized (load balancing, high availability servers, etc.).
- **Description of the different environments to be used**: including Development server, QA/Testing server, Training server, Production server, whichever are applicable.

If this is a technical project relating to infrastructure, this document will be much more exhaustive and cover aspects such as:

- Configurations and rules implemented into the appliance
- Sizing calculations including basis and assumptions used for the calculations

For custom development programs (which are a subcomponent of the main project), a combined functional and technical design document is usual called for, in which:

- Descriptions of the functional requirements for the program are given. This entails an explanation of the data that is used, how it is to be processed, and the resulting output. It may also include a process flow, if relevant.
- Technical details of how the program code is to be executed. This will include data, table, and field details, objects, and functions called by the program. If there are custom tables that are created, these will also be described.
- Error and exception handling processes

For nontransactional systems, the design documentation is very different, as it does not describe process, but rather, how data is processed so as to produce the desired outputs (reports, dashboards, etc.). As such, several components need to be defined:

- **Architecture**—describes the different software components and how these interact. There are many ways of producing the outputs, so the overall architecture needs to describe these. Does it make use of Business Intelligence tools?

What type and how is data stored by these front-end tools? Does it have a data warehouse for storing data or is data extracted directly from the source systems without a database staging area? How does data flow from the source transactional systems to the outputs? Are ETL tools used? Where is metadata stored? Are there any other advanced functionalities/modules used such as data mining, sorting, or parsing tools? This document should give the reader a general idea on how the whole project is to be set up and will work.

- **Outputs**—description of the front-end screens which the user will be seeing, including reports, dashboards, and other displays. This should also include a functional and technical description of how these reports and front-end interfaces are stored in the system. As MOLAP and ROLAP structures differ considerably, the manner in which these reports and their corresponding data are stored shall differ, depending on the tool.
- **Datawarehouse data model**—a detailed description of tables, fields and what these represent, as well as the overall structure type of the data model (star, snowflake, etc.)
- **Data mapping**—a description of where data is sourced from, how it is transformed (processed), and where it is stored.
- **ETL or loading scripts**—description of the different scripts used in obtaining the data. Each script should be described functionally as what it does on the data.

Other types of projects will have their own particular documentation, and this should be agreed upon beforehand. The basic precept of the documentation is that *what will be done* should be described *before it is actually done*, so that there is no loss in effort during the build phase, by having the customer organization agree beforehand. Of course, detailed design documentation is in itself a lengthy process, so that the overall design should be first discussed and agreed upon. Thus, the general philosophy is to go from general documentation, and once this is accepted, move on to the details. Failure to do this may result in costly rework.

5.2.3   Cutover and Go Live Phase

Once the solution has been built (or nearly so), the focus now is on the different steps leading to the go live. Cutover requires special documentation and procedures by itself (see Chap. 6 which explains cutover). The exact documentation to be produced depends on the nature of the project, and thus, it is the project managers that need to come up with a cutover plan. Generally speaking, it should take into account the following:

- **Data migration plan**—describing how data will be migrated into the new system from the legacy system or other data sources
- **Test plan**—this is a document describing in high level how the new system will be tested, by whom, and how (high level). The basic precept of this document is

to answer, "How will the outputs of this system be confirmed as correct?" and "What are all the scenarios which I need to account for in accepting the system as correct?" It is a high-level document, meaning, no details will yet be given on what the actual test work instructions are, as it is constructed so as to confirm that the overall approach is correct and complete. Verification on how the outputs are correct necessarily needs to be identified in this document, so as not to leave it hanging till it is too late. Some typical ways of verification include:

- Comparison of output to a legacy system's output which is known to be correct
- Manual calculation of outputs
- Loading of dummy data with known output

- **Test scripts**—these are the details on the test plan, and indicate work instruction level of scenarios to be tested, which will then be executed by the testers.
- **User manuals**—these should be ready in time for the user acceptance testing and the subsequent training. For good user understanding, work instructions are necessary but not sufficient, as it is important for users to understand not only how to conduct transactions mechanically, but the reason why such transactions are being used in the first place, thus, an overview explanation of the process from the users' perspective is also necessary.
- **Operations manual**—this is usually a forgotten document which is necessary by the IT team that is to operate and run the system (ITOM). Typically, these are batch processes which need to be undertaken in order to produce the desired outputs. Examples of this are batch billing processes, batch interest rate calculations, regular report generation, as well as regular process monitoring functions.

5.2.4 Closure

Post-go live support kicks in the moment the system goes live. The structure and lines of support will of course depend on the setup established, as well as the contract between the vendor and the customer organization; many different forms are possible as explained in Sect. 6.7. In any case, the trigger on when the vendor's support role ceases and the criteria for such trigger should be clear upfront to both parties, and a formal document indicating the end of the post-implementation support, which usually goes hand in hand with the project, is then signed off.

5.3 FRICEW

Taking a page from a common definition used in SAP methodology is the term FRICEW (also called RICEFW or RICEF). These refer to customized components in an application and stand for:

- **Forms**: input screens for users
- **Reports**
- **Interfaces**
- **Conversion**
- **Enhancements**: these are particular to the application, but generally are modifications over standard code
- **Workflows**: in some applications, this may not be considered a customization, so it would depend on the application.

In SAP, these are the components customized using ABAP programming, or in other words, these are the typical components which are customized using code (vs. configuration of the application). Why do we make special mention of it here? Well, it is a good general strategy to minimize customizations and coding for several reasons:

- **Coding is error-prone**. This means that all components with customized code take time to develop, test, and thresh out all detected errors. Testing is particularly time-consuming, and there is always the big risk that not all scenarios have been tested so that bugs in fact show up once put into production.
- **Customizations are not supported during application upgrades**. This means that all custom code has a chance of not working once the core application is upgraded. What this means is that every upgrade would need exhaustive testing on the customized code before deployment to production. What this also means is that anything that does not work would need recoding (and hence, retesting), a patch from the application vendor to fix the issue, or a work-around. All these take time, so that this actually delays the release to production of the upgraded version.
- **No product support on custom coding**

FRICEW therefore needs to be monitored and minimized. One must be absolutely sure that the FRICEW proposed is: (1) really needed; and (2) not possible by means of configuration. The first means that the PM needs to rationalize requests from users (and consultant). There is a natural tendency for users to want a process that is exactly or close to what they are currently doing, but the question is if this is an industry best practice, and whether it really makes sense given that one is migrating to a standard package. The second aspect is really a limitation in the know-how of both the PMs and the team implementing the application. If they are not aware of how to execute using standard configuration, the tendency is always to customize. It is recommended to consult application support, public blogs, and even other alternate sources of support before making big decisions and conclusions to customize.

As such, it is important that any program FRICEW as well as any other additional customizations be reported by the customer PM to the portfolio manager and even the CIO, if required by the company IT policy, to seek approval for their undertaking. This highlights the importance of screening all customizations before undertaking them.

5.4 Implementation Strategy

The riskiest implementation strategy is of course the big bang approach, in which the solution is released into production for the general populace. For some projects, this may be the only possible way, as it may be impossible or impractical to have systems or two different processes working in parallel at the same time. This big bang approach is however, the most difficult (if not impossible) to rollback, and also, launches you into a state of immediate urgency as all incidences discovered after the go live need to be expedited, much faster than if the users would have an alternative environment to work in.

Incidences after a go live are normal, but that does not mean they cannot be minimized. There is no substitute for good, exhaustive testing. At the same time, the more contained the release is, the more room and time there is to detect issues, and the easier it is to resolve them.

If possible, alternate strategies to the big bang approach can be applied, for example, by having a pilot deployment before proceeding to the general populace. This pilot can be chosen in accordance with a geographical location or a concrete department first. Oftentimes, we may choose a guinea pig department to pilot, and IT is usually a good candidate for this due to its maturity in terms of computer knowledge.

A phased approach may also be employed, wherein the whole system is released to production, but only limited modules or functionalities are made available to the general public so as to ensure proper and smooth transition.

5.5 Testing

Testing involves the thorough examination of software, or its modules/components to check if it actually performs according to expectations. One the challenges of any IT project, is that the cost of a bug increases exponentially over time, so that the later in time it is detected, the more expensive it is to fix, and the more negative impact it has on the company's operations or project as shown in Fig. 5.22.

Cost of fixing the bug is even greater after going live as it now has a direct impairment on the company's operations. On the other hand, the ability to detect a bug is more difficult at the beginning, but decreases over time as the project progresses as shown in Fig. 5.23.

So that it is best to detect a bug early, yet it is more difficult at that point (also because specifications may not be completely clear and/or understood by the vendor), and is also least costly to address. As a general rule then, the earlier the testing and the more exhaustive, the better for the project and the least costly. Bugs detected only after go live will need an extension of all the resources involved in the

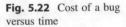

Fig. 5.22 Cost of a bug
versus time

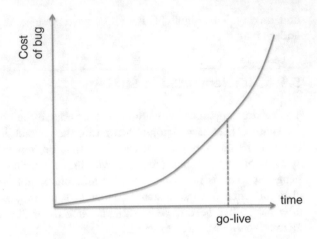

Fig. 5.23 Difficulty in
detecting a bug versus time

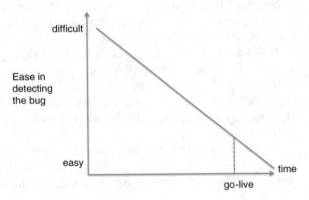

development of the module, and may require redoing many of the initial steps
(functional design, configuration, coding).

There are many types of testing, depending on the extent and manner in which
the testing is to be conducted. The type of testing to be undertaken shall depend on
the type of project, budget, and time. Some types of testing may be required and
made mandatory, as will be pointed out later in this section. Some typical types of
testing are:

- **Unit testing**: in which a software module is tested to ascertain that the function
  for which it was designed for is performed correctly.
- **Regression testing**: testing undertaken in which the new module
  implemented/enhanced is tested to verify that it does not cause faults within its
  module or in other parts of the software. It is also used whenever a new patch or
  fix is applied to resolve a known issue.
- **Integration testing**: In which the module is tested in conjunction with the other
  modules of the software to verify that it functions correctly as a whole.

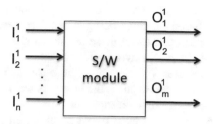

Fig. 5.24 Software module showing Inputs and Outputs

Testing is a topic all by itself which merits specific study and understanding. One of the challenges in testing is that given a software module with n distinct inputs and m outputs, all possible combinations of the inputs must be applied to ascertain that testing is comprehensively complete (assuming here that module has no memory retention, and is purely combinatorial) as shown diagrammatically in Fig. 5.24.

Now imagine that each input may be an integer value of $0 \ldots 9$, then to test the module exhaustively, we will need 10^n different combinations, so for a 10 input module, this would give 10 million combinations. For integers in the range of 256, the combination would balloon to more than 1,208 billion–trillion combinations. If the inputs would be text strings, then you can easily see that the number of combinations would indeed be intractable. The module above represents what occurs during unit testing. Now take a scenario in which integration testing is undertaken for three modules as shown in Fig. 5.25.

In this figure module 1 has up to n inputs, module 2 up to m inputs, and module 3 up to k inputs. Not all inputs for modules 2 and 3 are directly controlled by the user, as these proceed from previous modules' outputs. This complicates testing even more, due to the controllability of inputs to the modules, aside from the combinatorial issue on the possible inputs. A further issue is whether intermediate outputs (the O^1 and O^2 series) between modules are at all visible to the tester, for if they are not, any error occurring will only be detected in the outputs of the last module. If there are many modules which are being tested for integration, it can become quite complicated to detect which module is actually causing the error.

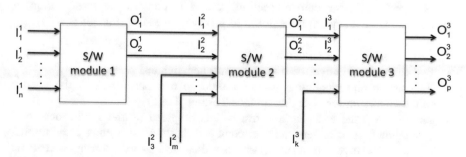

Fig. 5.25 Example for three cascaded modules

Due to the limited number of combinations that can practically be tested, the test scenarios are selected based on their being a good representation of the many possible combinations, such that using these test cases, they will most likely bring out errors in the modules (if any). Having said this, this is more of an art rather than a science and ideally, requires knowledge of the business processes and/or functions embedded in each module. As such, the best personnel to design the test cases are in fact the functional users of such modules.

Furthermore, two types of tests exist based on expected results:

- **Positive testing**: the most common, in which inputs are given to each module and the outputs are checked to ascertain that they result as expected.
- **Negative testing**: often forgotten, but very important. Testing a scenario in which the module is not to proceed normally. Testing is done so as to verify that it indeed does not proceed; it should trigger its exception handling procedure, which should log sufficient details for proper identification and handling of such exceptions.

As a very simple example of negative testing, take the preparation of a purchase order. One may test that it actually does not proceed with the release of the purchase order taking into account several scenarios, such as

- Person has no permission to generate the purchase order
- There is no Purchase Request approved for the PO
- There is insufficient budget

For positive testing:

- Purchase order proceeds in its generation under different scenarios
- Purchase Request approval actually proceeds to the generation of the PO

Negative testing is important as in actuality the software should really be able to handle all possible scenarios, not only the ideal ones that are thought out in a contained environment. Once more, the best personnel for designing negative test scenarios are the functional users of the system.

As explained in the cutover section, testing is perhaps the most important activity to ensure a smooth transition into production. A few guidelines:

- Test cases should be comprehensive
- Test cases should cover both positive and negative test scenarios
- Unit testing and integration testing should be first performed by the vendor before endorsing for User Acceptance Testing (UAT)
- During UAT, the test plan and test scripts prepared by the vendor acts as a guide, however, it is very much encouraged that the users think of additional scenarios (positive and negative) and test these to make the testing as realistic and exhaustive as possible

- The test plan is the first document to be reviewed for sign-off. This document is explained further below. The important aspect is that the test plan be comprehensive enough. For integration testing, it should clearly define what procedures will be used for testing end to end.
- Test scripts should be based on the test plan. Each test script document is a compendium of test cases.

A test plan is the first document that needs to be drafted. Ideally, it should be made early, even in the design phase, because it gives a clear idea on how outputs are to be considered correct (and incorrect). This may seem obvious, but it is not so. Additionally, it must state who will test, and using what data. Typically, the ways to validate software outputs during testing are:

- Comparison of outputs with that of a legacy system which is known to be correct. This however, is not always possible, even if such legacy system exist, as any change in the business process of the new system, however small, may result in differing outputs. It is very much applicable however if the project consists of a technology update/upgrade only, in which the business process and rules basically stay the same.
- Manually computed/defined outputs. Obviously, this may be tedious, but if there is no alternative, this will be the approach. Important is to define WHO will manually compute the expected outputs. Normally the best persons to do this are the end users, so it is important to get their participation and buy-in, as this is a time-consuming effort. Related to this, there are two further possibilities:

  - Preparation of manual test data: in which data specifically for the purpose of testing is prepared beforehand. Again, the data is designed and selected so that it covers as many scenarios as possible.
  - Slice copy of production data: normally, production data is copied into the QA/Test server shortly before the testing is undertaken, guaranteeing that up-to-date production data is used for the testing.

- Mock program. In which a program is created to emulate the function of the software to be tested, so that the input data is given to both in parallel and their outputs compared. This is normally done for programs that are quite critical to test, and that may have several complex rules to be tested which may be difficult to recreate manually. An example of this may be billing programs used in utilities, which have complex rules. Manual testing may not be exhaustive enough, and placing these in production with possible errors due to incomplete testing means too big a risk.

A sample test plan is shown in Fig. 5.26. Some aspects which need to be defined in the test plan include:

Definition of Test Scenarios

The test scenarios will be the list of functionalities in the Requirements Section of the User Requirement Document. These functionalities are stated below:

Ref#	Business Req. ID/s	Process	Scenarios to be Tested	Pass or Fail Criteria
TS003	DS-BUR-005	Data Load	Verify that Input Files are loaded from 1am to 3am	*Pass Criteria* – Bills Presentment started the batch job for data loading between 1am and 3am
TS004	DS-BUR-006	Data Load	Verify generation of .csv file for WMS Synchronization	*Pass Criteria* – Bills Presentment generated a .csv file and dump it to the agreed folder for WMS
TS005	BG-BUR-001	Bill Generation	Verify generation of eSOA has same format as the paper based counterpart	*Pass Criteria* – Customer's bill was generated with a look and feel of the printed bill from handhelds.
TS006	BG-BUR-002	Bill Generation	Verify generation of eSOA is available for Portal Presentment and Email Presentment	*Pass Criteria* – PDF file of eSOA was generated and available thru Email and Web Portal
TS007	BG-BUR-003 BG-BUR-004 BG-BUR-005	Bill Generation	Verify generation of eSOA for current bill and adjusted bill	*Pass Criteria* – PDF file of eSOA for current bill and adjusted bills were generated

Fig. 5.26 Sample test plan excerpt

- What will be tested, in terms of modules. It should also specify what integration testing will be done, so as to guarantee that the plan is complete and exhaustive
- Who will test
- Who will prepare the test scripts/test data. It may be understood that the vendor will do this, but any participation from any other party should be explicitly stated.
- How outputs will be validated (as explained above).
- Other relevant information (any dependencies, aspects that should be taken account, etc.)

Once the test plan is approved, this will form the basis for the test scripts. Test scripts are detailed transactional-level instructions of how the software modules are to be tested. They should be understandable by a user using the system for the first time, and so, should contain detailed step-by-step instructions, and if needed, screenshots as well.

A sample test script is shown in Fig. 5.27.

An additional type of testing is stress testing. This is used in order to simulate the handling of multiple parallel transactions by the system, which should be able to process the transactions in accordance with the design specifications' latency and throughput, or if an enhancement/upgrade to an existing system, should perform

Project: Bills Presentment System

Step No.	Action	Expected Results	Actual Results (w/ screen shot)	Pass / Fail
Objective:				
1.	Enter Username	N/A		☐ Pass ☐ Fail
2.	Enter Password	N/A		☐ Pass ☐ Fail
3.	Click LOG IN button	Redirect to *Lookup* Screen		☐ Pass ☐ Fail
4.	Enter CAN	N/A		☐ Pass ☐ Fail
5.	Click LOOKUP CUSTOMER button	Customer details will be displayed under Potential matches by.		☐ Pass ☐ Fail
6.	Click View / Assist	Redirect to *Un-Enrolled Customer Profile Update* Screen		☐ Pass ☐ Fail
7.	Enter Mobile Number	N/A		☐ Pass ☐ Fail
8.	Enter Alternate Mobile Number, if applicable	N/A		☐ Pass ☐ Fail
9.	Check "By sms" in Delivery Channel	N/A		☐ Pass ☐ Fail
10.	Click Update Profile button	Message will appear: *Profile update successful*		☐ Pass ☐ Fail
End of Test Script				

Fig. 5.27 Sample test script excerpt

equally well as the original system. Stress testing can be done by means of a specialized stress test tool, which simulates and generates all these transactions, and reports the results. Failure in passing the stress test may be functional in nature, technical, or both.

One of the basic precepts of testing is that the test environment should be as close as possible as that which will be during actual usage (Production environment). Some common pitfalls:

- Testing is done in the QA/Test environment using user profiles which are not identical to those that will be used afterward in actual production. A common situation here is when the testing is undertaken using a super user or administration account, which allows the user to access all modules and functions. Of course, problems due to authorization will not be apparent at this stage, but will come out once in production. Thus, the purpose of testing (flushing out issues before going live) has actually been defeated.

- Last minute changes are done in the configuration without undertaking a thorough integration testing. Typically, due to the rush, only unit testing is done, only to discover a much bigger problem later on.
- Test data. In this scenario, test data reflects an ideal world, which does not reflect the reality in terms of scope, nor in terms of data cleanliness (one must be realistic in knowing that not all data in the real environment will be clean, and this must be tested as well to see if the software handles these gracefully), nor in terms of depth (amount of scenarios).
- Test data and test scenarios used during User Acceptance Test are limited to those prepared by the vendor. Of course, if the vendor had previously tested these scenarios, they will pass the UAT! The only component that has practically changed is the persons executing them! Testing by the users has to be a combination of predefined scenarios, as well as ad hoc situations which are thought of by the users. The more ad hoc scenarios, the better and more complete the UAT will be.
- IT is the one to test the scenarios! This is a typical case of IT asking for trouble, as they will get the blame once the software fails. Remember, IT is not an expert in the business scenarios being tested, so it is no position to pass/fail them. Of course, it would be advantageous if IT does a first round of testing before endorsing to the users, but this is in no way a substitute for a proper UAT.
- Testers do not understand the overall process. Testers are made to sit in a room, given the test scripts, and asked to mechanically test each scenario. Again, this is similar to the aforementioned scenario where UAT is only using the vendor's prepared test scripts. Because the testers do not understand the process and the system, they will be incapable of launching additional test scenarios. It is important that the overall architecture, overall business process, software, and rationale for the processes are explained to the user before even delving on the test cases.
- Configurations are done directly into production! Need I say more? Well, aside from the obvious in that these configurations were not actually tested properly, there is also a very big issue in doing this, which is that both the DEV and QA/Test servers will not have these changes reflected, so these changes are essentially lost, which will also give problems to the next round of testing done in DEV and QA/Test environments because they do not reflect what has already gone into production. Of course, there are always configurations and data that may need to be applied manually, directly into the production environment (e.g., some Master Data), however, even if manually applied, they must first be manually applied in DEV, QA/Test, tested thoroughly there and thereafter manually entered in PROD.
- Testing in PROD. Is there anyone out there this stupid?
- No negative testing. We spoke extensively of negative testing, failure to include negative tests are obvious.
- No rollback procedure. Not strictly part of testing, but for every release, there has to be a possible rollback. Think that the release can go wrong even if thoroughly tested.

- No thorough testing of integrations. Yes, these are some of the most difficult to test because you need to conduct transactions in both ends of the integration points. In fact, the testing should not stop at the integration interface; it has to proceed all the way to the end. This means that if system A is interfaced to system B via integration program AB, then you must first test the sequence of transactions needed to trigger the interface to system B, but continue with the subsequent transactions in system B to verify that indeed the data taken-in by system B has been correctly recorded and that system B is able to utilize this data correctly.

Test documentation is also very important, each test script must be run, verified, and in the test results portion of the test script, a proof of correctness included. This may be a screenshot, or if you believe the tester, the output result, with a pass/fail field, comment, and tester's signature for the whole test script document indicates that whether it actually passed or failed.

5.6   Test Automation

Nowadays, new tools have emerged to facilitate in the automation of test scripts. This means that test scripts can be run by the tools, so that instead of manually entering all the inputs, these are placed in a file, from which the test scripts reads the input data, executes the different transactions, and compares the resulting output with the expected correct output (also available in a table), to mark it pass or failed. Tools of this sort have a lot of advantages, including:

- Faster test runtime
- No possible errors in interpreting results
- Automatic reports
- Easy tracking and managing of the tests
- Easy to rerun test scenarios once modification/fixes have been undertaken

Of course, one must be aware that the setting up of these tools exacts considerable effort because:

- All transactions and processes to be tested must follow a hierarchical structure (i.e., Technical Bill of Materials) which normally has a structure software-module-submodule-process-transaction. Just defining this hierarchy, if for the first time, takes considerable effort, and making sure all the necessary details are complete for each hierarchical level as well.
- Each test scenario must be prepared, including the data and the transactions (typically, these tools will "record" your every transaction, and then have a "playback" button)

- Expected outputs must also be recorded
- The structure of the test scripts and scenarios must be planned and structured beforehand

So in fact, these tools become quite useful for transactions and modules that will be tested frequently. Frequent testing may be due to modifications done regularly or master data regularly updated. Examples of commonly changed processes are

- Billing process in a utility company (due to the rates changing)
- Payroll (changing tax and regulations)
- Sales and Distribution processes (new sales processes and products)

5.7 People Change Management

This is referred to here as "people" change management to differentiate it from ITSM change management, which is related to changes in the Configuration Items. People change management as referred to here is the process of changing people's behavior toward an impending process and/or system change, and managing this properly so that the reaction is more positive than negative. One definition of people change management is

Change management is an approach to transitioning individuals, teams, and organizations to a desired future state

As discussed in Sect. 2.2, IT is generally composed of systems, processes, and people, the last component being the most difficult to manage. The reason for this is that people resist to change. Resistance is a natural defense mechanism by a person in minimizing risk to themselves. Change means the unknown, and it may mean for them (rationally or irrationally):

- More work
- More effort to learn the new processes
- No work (being laid off)

As such, managing change is a special skill, which, depending on the complexity and impact of the project, may require full-time or near full-time dedication. Some projects have change management agents embedded in the project, and these may be:

- **Internal**: normally mid-management personnel with a good understanding of the processes to be implemented and convinced of their benefits to their organization. She becomes a "champion" in convincing others on the need for the change. In other cases, HR may be the department to champion the changes, taking up the role of change manager.

- **External**: a highly credible specialist for that particular process. This person is normally not an IT consultant, but a domain expert familiar with industry best practices. Most importantly, he must be seen as an expert by the recipient organization, otherwise it becomes an impossible task to convince the users.

Change management is an important task that the CIO himself must partake in. In this sense, his role is primarily that of convincing higher management of the appropriateness of the change, so that management supports this endeavor (if it was not endorsed by them in the first place). Ideally, he should also find a champion within the higher management level so that the change not becomes only an IT change (which is dangerous), but a process or a business change toward a business goal.

Change management is an art, and it has both carrot and stick components which need to be balanced depending on the situation, but no matter what the case, proper communication management is very important (see Sect. 5.1.9). As change is inherently difficult, it needs to be explained well:

- **What are the benefits of the change?** As much as possible, these should be for each (if applicable) at the corporate, department, and personal levels. Eventual personal benefit will be beneficial for the employees and will result in more support for the change, while corporate- and department-level benefits will garner support at the mid- and upper levels of management.
- **Why do we need the change?** Explain current shortcomings, or how the market is evolving such that it warrants a change in the way things are being done.
- **What does the change mean for each and every employee?** Again, the change will mean something different to each user, depending on his role in the process, so that the message needs to be changed depending on the audience. Implementation of a new Enterprise Asset Management system means something different (and different tasks) to the maintenance engineer as compared to the plant manager, or to the finance department in charge of assets.
- **When and how will the change take effect?**
- **Elicit the support that you need from the users**. Be as concrete as possible in what you need from them, such as approval of process documents on time, sufficient dedication to testing activities, volunteers for Trainor's training, etc.

Change management is usually one of the most difficult tasks in making projects succeed, and requires very special skills. Communication may be maximized via a variety of channels; the idea in general is to buildup the tempo until the go live date:

- Presentations to the higher management. This should explain the points above: benefits, reason for the change, what the change means, and very important, one must be honest at to the possible difficulties and risks in applying the change, so as not to build false expectations. It is of no use as well to overstate the expected benefits, if these cannot realistically be met.
- Email blasts announcing the project and what this means for the employees

- Announcements and specials in the company's internal newsletter and/or magazine, explaining in laymen's terms the project.
- Banners, leaflets, and other materials
- Special feature in the company's portal
- Workshops in which management and key users are invited to present and discuss with a more general users' audience the implication of the project.
- Roadshows in which IT and other key departments reach out to the users by going to them

The manner in which change management is to be conducted depends to a large extent on the culture of the company, the maturity and profile of the users, as well as the credibility that IT has in the eyes of the users.

Typical challenges faced by the change management team include:

- **Little kingdoms**. Sometimes, certain departments do not want to share data or prefer to stay opaque so that their internal inefficiencies cannot be seen by others. The remedy to this situation is to force it open by means of the mandate handed down by senior management; there is usually no way to convince these middle managers by just discussing.
- **Nonstandardization**. Related to the first, processes may be differing in different geographic locations even if under the same department, for the mere reason that no implementation was previously done to standardize. In this case, users and managers may want to keep their old process merely due to familiarity. In some cases, they may be willing to change but the challenge here will be to get all the different units to agree to a common process. In this case, it becomes necessary to explain and have the necessary patience to get the buy-in of the users for the new process; however, if things get nowhere, it may be necessary to invoke senior management or the steering committee's direction and push.
- **Adherence to their known process (inertia)**. This will also require time and effort in explaining the new process and its benefits. Buy-in from key users is essential for the project to succeed, as imposition may result in a backlash when things divert from the ideal.
- **Wanting too much**. This is the opposite of the former, in which the users, having attended some seminars and workshops, want to implement a super-perfect process which may be unreasonable or impossible to implement at this moment in time due to the complexity, company culture, budget, etc. This again requires careful management of expectations and explanation to the key users. Part of the explanation may be to indicate how much complexity, risk, and cost this would entail, and a compromise may be to delay to a later phase, which will then be evaluated.
- **Users changing their mind**. This is very risky, as accepting this, even if a small change, may lead to further changes down the road, leading to project creep. One must weigh whether such changes are indeed warranted, and as a general rule changes should be discouraged as they introduce additional cost, risk, and

delay to a project. A possible compromise can be to evaluate these requests for a later phase (if possible and feasible) after the go live.

- **Senior management changing its mind**. This is very difficult to manage indeed. Most that can be done is to properly inform management on the implication of this change in terms of time, risk, and cost. A possible protection may be (if the request is only from one particular executive) to escalate this to the steering committee for decision.
- **Fear of getting fired**. If this is unjustified, this should be explained as such. If justified, then HR has a special role in ameliorating the situation by having designed the severance package for those affected, or having identified where personnel will be reallocated. This must have been discussed very early during the project, flagging HR on the possibility of such a downsizing resulting from the process change. In a highly unionized environment, a heads up must be given to the union so that they will not oppose and sabotage the project.
- **Fear of being irrelevant**. This again may be founded or unfounded. Oftentimes however, there is a misconception that when the process comes in and makes things more efficient, their clerical work now is not needed and they become irrelevant to the organization. It may be unfounded because their previous role, though not existing in the new process, may be replaced by a more sophisticated and analytical one. Of course, this may not be true for all, but sometimes the fear of change is so strong that even people who should not be wary of the change are swept by this sentiment. This may even be true for IT personnel, wherein the implementation of a new ERP system in place of the custom developed in-house application is seen by the old programmers as a threat to their existence, as they think that the new application will do everything they have been doing before. Again, this takes careful coordination with HR, and also assistance in leveling up and skilling up so that personnel can take on new roles.
- **Fear of losing power**. This is again similar to the "little kingdoms" syndrome explained above and again is usually nonnegotiable as users bearing this attitude will usually not be convinced no matter what, so there is no choice but to impose.
- **IT has no credibility**. "Here we go again…," "What did IT cook up this time…," and "Oh no, another one of this useless IT projects…" may be some of the comments heard. In this case, the IT organization has a serious credibility problem which will not be addressed by dialogue nor imposition using senior management's support. If the project is quite complex, it should not have started in the first place, but rather, it should have been postponed until such time that IT has enough credibility to succeed in the project. It may need to start with smaller projects and smaller wins before attempting the big one. This of course may not always be possible, take for example a new CIO given the task to push through with this big project. In such a case, he needs to ensure during the course of the project that things are running smoothly and not out of hand so that his credibility is enhanced during the project. He needs to get more involved in the project than usual.

- **Fear of technology**. Let us face it, some people, and especially the older generation, may fear technology. Because they do not know how to use it, they may reject it altogether. Within this group however, there are those who can learn, but also those in which trying to learn becomes an altogether useless endeavor. The ideal scenario here is to retrain the first and layoff the second. Again, the particularities of the organization will dictate if this is at all possible.

Senior management may also have expectations of reducing the headcount of the company by means of the project, so this necessitates heavy HR involvement in identifying the people affected, designing the retirement package, as well as communicating this properly to the employees. Redundancy should not be hid from the employees, but should also not be emphasized (unless of course, many of the affected employees have in fact a desire to leave the company). It will form part of the discussion on how job positions and roles will be affected.

References

Devaux, S. A., 2014. *Managing Projects as Investments: Earned Value to Business Value*. CRC press.

Project Management Institute, 2013. *Project Management Book of Knowledge*. 5th ed. Project Management Institute.

Further Reading

Beecham, R., 2011. *Project Governance - The Essentials*. IT Governance Publishing.

Cleden, D., 2009. *Managing project uncertainty*. 1st ed. Gower.

Fondahl, J., 1987. Precedence Diagramming Methods: Origins and Early Development. *Project Management Journal*, XVIII(2), pp. 33–36.

ISACA, 2012. *COBIT 5 Framework*. ISACA.

ISACA, 2015. http://www.isaca.org/COBIT/Pages/default.aspx. [Online].

Heldman, K., Heldman, W., 2010. *CompTIA Project+ Study Guide Authorized Courseware: Exam PK0-003*. Wiley.

Low, S. P., 1994. *Marketing Research for the Global Construction Industry*. 1st ed. Singapore University Press.

Schafer, M., Melich, M., 2012. *SAP Solution Manager*. 3rd ed. Boston (MA): Galieo Press, inc.

Helfen, M., Trauthwein, H.M., 2011. *Testing SAP Solutions*. 2nd ed. Boston (MA): Galileo Press, inc.

Martino, R., 1968. *Project Management*. MDI Publications.

Phillips, J., 2010. *IT Project Management: On Track from Start to Finish*. 3rd ed. McGrawHill.

Stamatis, D.H., 1997. *TQM Engineering Handbook (Quality and Reliability)*. 1st ed. CRC Press.

US Department of Energy, 2008. www.directives.doe.gov. [Online] Available at: www.directives. doe.gov [Accessed January 2016].

Weaver, P., 2014. A Brief History of Scheduling—Back to the Future. *PM World Journal*, III (VIII), pp. 1–27.

Cut-Over into Operations

6

One of the most crucial, risky, and yet an unavoidable stage is when projects are turned over to operations. Oftentimes, the team(s) handling the project is not the same as those handling operations (and is not even recommended), even if the IT project in question may be using a technology that is currently supported by the O&M team. In many cases, the team handling the project has been contracted from outside the organization, or may be a mix of in-house and contracted resources. Cut-over is crucial, as a proper hand-over guarantees long-term success of the project, as well as its proper long-term support, and yet is risky simply because the team handling the operations has not till this moment been exposed to the project, sometimes to the technology, and most probably also have little knowledge of the processes that are being implemented.

It has been my experience that even for applications where the O&M team is familiar with the application itself, a major change of business process may throw the O&M team in disarray as they are still thinking of the old processes that were in place.

As a real-world example, we implemented a reconfiguration of an ERP to introduce a different materials ordering and reservations process in the central warehouse. Previously, the materials were ordered and reserved by the different respective divisions until their full consumption by the division that ordered them. This resulted in inefficiencies when a different division would require the same materials but would not be able to withdraw as the materials were already reserved by the former division, even if not consumed immediately, resulting in an additional reordering and delay in the delivery of these additional materials. We decided to do away with this by centralizing materials into a "pool" anyone could request withdrawals from, even if they were not the division that had originally ordered, resulting in lesser idle inventory, increase availability and less delays. It was however not enough to have the O&M team (and the users for that matter) understand how to

© Springer International Publishing Switzerland 2016
F. Castillo, *Managing Information Technology*,
DOI 10.1007/978-3-319-38891-5_6

transact, this was a major change in the way the whole ordering and inventory philosophy was redesigned, and it was crucial that all the teams understand the differences, so not only did they train on the transactions, sufficient time was given to explain the overall philosophy and process, so that whenever an incidence would occur, they would have the capability to analyze and diagnose what the root cause could possibly be.

Needless to say, the earlier the O&M team is updated and is familiarized with the project, the better. The amount of details that the O&M team should be given however shall depend on where the project is, at that moment in time

- **Kick-off/inception**—if the project is closely interfaced or involves modifications or enhancements to existing systems and processes, it pays to involve the O&M team early and discuss the overall philosophy, architecture, and processes that the project will embody. The O&M team is in the best position to analyze, criticize, and give suggestions. This will also make them aware of when the project will come online, as well as what shall be expected of them (for example, if the O&M team is to develop new interfaces to systems currently in production), and at what point in time.
- **Architecting phase**—the technical management team should be involved here as the project shall need servers, storage, network, and other infrastructure requirements. The technical team should generally provision these and the corresponding environments (DEV, QA, Training, and Production). It is imperative that the technical team understand the requirements and suggest on best options (e.g., have a separate QA environment from the existing QA being used in operations, have a separate training environment from QA). Some specific items which will be further discussed should be taken up during this stage

  - Approval of the overall architecture
  - Approval of the different environments
  - Backup and restore procedures
  - Release management procedures (also with the application Management team)
  - Password change management: how?

To cite some other practical examples of the importance of having approval for the overall architecture let me refer to 2 projects. The first project involved the delivery of a Datawarehouse solution with several software components. The project team assumed that all these different components (ETL, front-end tools) would be installed in the same server, however, this was not the software vendor's recommendation and it resulted in very poor performance of the servers. This meant that a whole reinstallation had to be done, even after the project had started and already carried several configuration changes in the platform, which obviously had to be repeated manually, causing a significant delay in the project.

My other example is with regards to security. Nowadays mobility and internet access of applications is pervasive. When we implemented a new customer relationship application on the internet, we reviewed the different software components that had to be installed, the servers they would reside on, as well as the connectivity and network Access Control rules between all these components. Because internet-facing applications need to retrieve data from the back end which is in a secure area (intranet), this would need to be done in a secure manner. Internet-facing applications would reside in the DMZ while leaving no loopholes in terms of possible breaches in security and confidentiality to the back end. A risk review on possible security breach scenarios needs also to be conducted as there is no way to guarantee 100 % that security breaches would never occur.

In both cases, an early review and sign-off of the architecture is crucial in avoiding issues and delays.

- **Hand-over preparation**—as the go-live date comes near, the O&M team should be prepared by giving them more specific details on the project. This has to be timed correctly, giving details and training too early will mean that the team will forget once the actual go-live date approaches, too late and they may not have enough time to understand completely, or as it happens many times, the project team is too busy with the go-live preparations and fire-fighting activities to dedicate sufficient effort to this. Specific aspects need to be discussed during these sessions

  - **Solution overview**—involving TM, AM, ITOM, and SD. Here is the discussion of the objectives of the project, general architecture, the processes involved, end-user departments involved, and leaves the floor open to the different teams for Q&A. It is important to note their inputs, as they may be very valuable in avoiding issues down the road.
  - **Process discussion**—mainly for AM's benefit, is an in-depth discussion of the processes captured by the system, usually described in detail by the blueprints and functional requirement documents. This is a more detailed version of the solution overview but going into the details of the process that AM would care about. How does the new process fit in with the legacy? Are there modifications that need to be done in the current process? Will resources be needed by O&M for this?

As an example, when we implemented the updated Automatic Debit Agreement process for automatic payment of customer bills from their bank account, there were tweaks that were needed in the way the payment allocations were done to the accounts. The default process is allocating the full payment to the oldest outstanding amount, but this was found to be problematic as some arrears were historical and had to be written off, and customers advised of the fact before the allocation rules could be applied automatically. Otherwise, the customer might get surprised to find his bank account deducted with a tremendously huge amount!

- **IT Operations**—once the system is turned over, this will describe any day-to-day operations that will be handled by ITOM group. This usually includes data maintenance and cleanup activities, report generation, batch processes that need to be scheduled and run, error detection analyses, etc.

  As an example of this, the ITOM would be in charge of the daily generation of reports. Though the reports may be scheduled, they would still be monitoring the batch processes for proper completion, in some cases validating the outputs with the users before officiating the reports (as for example, finance personnel giving its go-signal on financial reports before release due to possible last minute reversals or adjustments that may have not been captured), as well as identifying the reasons for errors in the generation of the reports.

- **Technical discussion with TM:**

  - Final backup and restore procedures
  - Pre and post-go-live tasks that will be performed
  - Final Password change management procedure
  - Release Management (also with the AM team)

- **Frequently Asked Questions (FAQ)**—for the benefit of SD, questions that may be raised by the users, to enable the SD to immediately reply without having to escalate the ticket. The more comprehensive their understanding of the system and the FAQs, the more tickets that will be resolved under a First Call Resolution (FCR). Imagine a change in the configuration to access internet within a company in which the proxy is now disabled and goes to internet directly. If for some reason this change has not taken effect in an endpoint, the user will not be able to access the internet. Rather than SD escalating this ticket to TM for investigation, best is if they have sufficient information to

  - Determine if the proxy is still enabled in the endpoint's route (open your browser settings, check internet options, …)
  - If still enabled, the step-by-step instructions on how to disable it
  - Procedure on how to confirm that the issue has been resolved (please restart your browser; try to connect to this site…)

- **Configuration Management**—this is for the benefit of the AM group, will teach the team how the system is configured, meaning of the different configuration parameters, so that the team will be able to support and maintain the new application once requests or incidences are raised by the users.

This particular training is quite detailed and technical, as well as easily forgotten unless put into practice shortly after the training. In my experience, we have even had to conduct several repeat sessions for O&M for them to actually get a good grasp of what it entails (but are time well-spent). It is always complemented by the configuration manual, reference manuals, as well as training slides which can be returned to for reference.

- **Program code**—this will be turned over to both AM's Business Analysts and programmers that will be in charge of subsequent support. Needless to say, the programs must be properly documented according to the receiving organization's standards, and the program coded as well using its standards.
- **User Acceptance Testing (UAT)**—end users should ideally be involved during the User Acceptance Testing, in fact, the best users are those that will actually be transacting with the new system. It is also recommended that O&M either participate in the testing, or at least observe the testing so as to familiarize itself.

A common pitfall here is that although the end-users test, it is not the proper end users that do so. Sometimes this may be due to the real knowledgeable user not wanting to dedicate time, other times this is because due to the change in process, roles inside the organization change but is not apparent to the end-user departments.

- **End-user training (EUT)**—similar to UAT, the people trained will be those to actually use the systems, but it is also recommended that O&M be part of the training, or at least be involved and present during these for familiarity's sake.
- **End-user awareness campaigns**—the project may be perfect, but if it fails to generate acceptance by the users, it will ultimately fail. This of course cannot be addressed only during the cut-over period, users must have been involved from the very onset of the project (see earlier change management section), but of course, not all end users can be involved, especially if it involves a large number of users. Depending on the breadth and importance of the project, it may be important to drum-up awareness and support for the project, this can be done through several means, such as

  - Getting the buy-in from top executives: they can in turn be your best "salesmen"
  - Awareness posters, brochures, T-shirts, and information campaigns
  - Awareness Workshops
  - Publishing information in the company magazine and portal
  - Roadshows, if users are in dispersed geographical locations

- **Agreement on 1st, 2nd level support**: one of the most difficult decisions to make is how and who will render 1st level support upon going live. Right after going live, the number of project-related incidences shall jump, and it is of course preferred that these be acted upon as soon as possible. The tendency therefore is usually to assign the project team to be the one to render 1st level support until the warranty expires. The danger to this is that once the warranty period expires and the O&M team takes over, they are basically neophytes in handling the system. The warranty period is also the best time to learn on how the system is configured, familiarize oneself with its processes and learn how to troubleshoot. By taking over after the warranty period, there has been little adjustment and learning time, even if the O&M team was tasked to observe during this period. The trade-off is further discussed in the next sections, but what is important to mention at this point is that there has to be a formal agreement on how 1st level and 2nd level will be undertaken, the exact process (of how tickets will be escalated, closed, etc.) and who will be in charge of what.
- **Go-live**—this is the moment of truth, the next few days and weeks will oftentimes define the success or failure of the project, depending on the users' acceptance, the ability to address incidence tickets coming in, and fix these in a timely manner.
- **Post-go-live**—it is imperative during this crucial period that tickets be closely monitored. Incidence tickets should be given primary importance, and the root cause of the incidences identified. As such, incidences with a common root cause should be grouped, and depending on the urgency and severity, be prioritized for fixing.

In the next sections, we explain in detail some of the specifics of how a proper cut-over should be done.

6.1 Backup and Restore Procedures

This seems self-evident. For any application and system, a backup and restore procedure should be in place. The reason why I mention this explicitly is that there is no unique way of conducting backup and restore. It not only depends on the application, it also depends on the DB, the infrastructure used, as well as the type of backup, and what one wants to backup. Same goes for restoration.

And so, the worst situation possible is that you are ready to go-live, but before you do that, you wish to back up your QA and Production environments in case something goes wrong, only to find out that you do not have complete, detailed information on how this is to be done correctly. The project team will have its particular opinion on how backup and restore should be done and TM will have its own idea. It is important therefore that early in the project (during the architecting phase, which comes very early on), both teams have an agreement on how this shall actually be done. Actual execution however should be undertaken by the TM team.

Important aspects to take into account are (wherever it says backup, restore also applies here)

- Full back up or partial?
- How to backup specific portions of the system, for example, only the configuration, only the data. For the configuration, what are the different configuration files and what are their functions?
- How to make a fast backup (for example, a dump to disk)
- When to do which type of backup
- How do you know if backup completed successfully
- The detailed instructions on all of the above (this can be agreed upon before going live), including pre-backup and post-restore configurations that may need to be executed.

If possible, an actual backup and restore procedure should also be conducted for test purposes.

A typical mishap scenario here is that the backup and restore procedures are incomplete. Take an example in which the configuration is to be backed-up separately from the data for purpose of releases. This means that the backup is done not just by copying an image or dumping the entire contents of a server into a tape, but exporting a configuration file from the application and copying that into the backup media. It may be that the application has several configuration files that need to be backed-up, so that if one is forgotten, the recovery will be incomplete. It is also for this reason that a simulated recovery is always recommended as it ensures that nothing is forgotten.

6.2   Release Management Procedures

As discussed in the previous chapters, release management refers to the procedures on how a change that is made (normally starting in the development environment), is to be replicated into the QA/Testing environments, and subsequently to the Production environments. Release management procedures refer to the manner, the control, and authorizations around the release (Fig. 6.1).

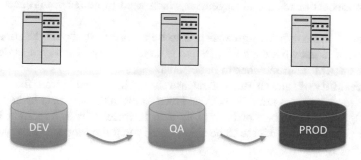

Fig. 6.1 Common release lifecycle

Fig. 6.2 Release by means
of copying a configuration file

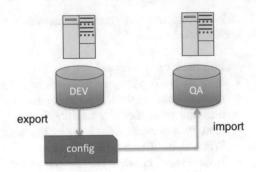

In its most primitive form, release management is done manually, meaning, that
a change (in the configuration, for example) is then replicated manually in the
subsequent environments by undertaking the same tasks as what was done in the
DEV environment. This, of course, is the *most primitive form*, and should be
avoided and not used if the application has a better way to undertake release
management. The reason why this method is not preferred is that it is error-prone, a
change undertaken in Development may not be fully reflected in the subsequent
environments, resulting in discrepancies between environments, possible errors or
incidences which may take time to troubleshoot.

Other manners in which release management procedures are typically undertaken are through export-import of configurations, in which the configuration is first
exported to a file, this is then copied to the next environment (say QA) and then
imported, taking effect in the new environment. This is shown in Fig. 6.2.

It is only the configuration that should be exported and imported; as otherwise,
the procedure is not feasible because production data (once released to the production environment) is overwritten, same concern as for the QA and testing
environment.

For some other systems release management is highly automated and efficient,
having been given due attention. As an example, SAP ECC has its so-called
"transport" procedure, which allows not only the whole configuration, but specific
configurations to be released, and can easily be reversed. This may also include
authorizations and user profiles.

Some aspects of release management which need to be taken into account are

- **Scope of the configuration which is to be released**: It should describe first in
  layman's terms what the configuration is, and then give the technical details on
  it for an AM team member to understand.
- **Traceability of the release**: The release should be traceable from the beginning
  of its journey (from DEV into QA and then to PROD), there may be an identifier
  (key), a ticket number, or both to be able to trace it. It is important for TM,
  which conducts the release to be able to verify that the proper release procedure
  is being followed.

- **Cancelation and reversal procedures should be clear**: In the worst case, this can be a restore from backup procedure (worst because it is usually the most lengthy to execute), in some applications, there is a release management system which allows you to roll back the release.
- **Whether releases can be made while the system is live**: More advanced applications allow this, however, for those that need to import-export the configuration files, this is generally not the case, and the system will require downtime.
- **Freeze**: Even if the system is live, are there transactions that require a "freeze," meaning, that they cannot be executed. This can be done by locking the transactions or locking out the users. The reason for the freeze is that the release will affect these transactions, and therefore will create a conflict if the release is done simultaneously with the affected transactions.
- **Order of the releases**: If the application allows for live releases, this means that the configurations are released piece-meal, so that if there is a lot of changes that need to be released, these will come in batches, and oftentimes, this batch of releases has a relative sequence, so that one release cannot be done before the other. This should be taken into account and explained correctly in the ticket.
- **Roles of different Operations teams in the release management:** Ideally, request for release will be done by AM, execution done by TM

In my experience as CIO, I have come across multiple bad practices from vendors:

- Configuration changes made directly into production: this is the worst possible practice; it results in very different configurations in PROD, DEV, and QA which are now hard to trace and reproduce back into DEV and QA, and need to be recreated manually. This is also a common reason why some IT departments require many personnel, because they are the "experts" in knowing what changes have been made to the production server while failing to document it, so that the organization becomes overly dependent on their knowledge, and unfortunately, bad practices, while they continuously configure things in Production.
- Development and/or configuration changes done directly in QA. In this case, DEV is not in sync with the changes in QA and PROD and when the next releases are made from DEV to QA and PROD, there is a chance that the changes become undone. This results in a lot of analysis and troubleshooting to detect what went wrong.
- Testing in DEV. DEV is a machine without practically any data (so not much to test), and with insufficient resources to conduct a thorough testing, which typically consumes a lot of resources and would require a bigger machine.
- QA environment not in sync with PROD. This means that even if a test passes in QA, it may still fail in PROD.
- QA data is very old, so that testing in QA passes but not when the actual data in PROD is encountered. This can be addressed by refreshing QA data with the latest PROD data.

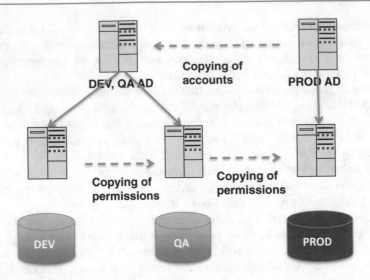

Fig. 6.3 Managing active directory accounts

- Insufficient testing (in QA), so that the errors come out when released to PROD!
- Testing in PROD! You will overwrite valid transactional data with garbage test data!

Special mention should be made on

- **Roles and permissions**: They should be the same across all environments as explained under testing. Thus, it is best that roles and permissions be made part of a release across all environments (also originating in DEV).
- **Active Directory and LDAP**: If the application is using LDAP and/or Active Directory in which a single sign-on is used, then it is also recommended that the actual LDAP/AD accounts for production also be defined during testing. This can be achieved by having a DEV/QA/Test AD server specific for the DEV, QA, and Test environments. In this case, the rights and permissions in the AD flow in the opposite direction, they are to be defined in the production AD server and copied into DEV/QA/test AD, guaranteeing that all environments are using the same account names, and guaranteeing that the testing will be undertaken under realistic conditions. This is illustrated in Fig. 6.3.

6.3   Business Process

As mentioned before, it is imperative that the O&M team understand the underlying processes of the new system. Understanding purely technical aspects of the solution is not enough. Business Process helps the team to understand the way things work, their rationales, how they are being undertaken by the system, and importantly, why they are being done in such manner. This will help during the analysis and troubleshooting, since O&M is able to grasp the intended outcome. For this purpose, the blueprints, functional design documents that were developed and finalized during the analysis and design phase of the project are commonly used, and are then explained by the project team during a sit-down interactive session with O&M.

6.4   Data Migration

Another commonly underestimated task refers to that of data migration. This refers to the process of importing into the new system, data that either resides in a legacy system that will now be supplanted, or in different sources which now need to be consolidated and uploaded into the new system. A data migration plan must be prepared well before the go-live date as part of the cut-over, and depending on the amount and complexity of the data, could range from a few weeks to months prior to the actual go-live. Data migration itself, if complex, may need its own plan, with its own go-live dates and milestones, which need not necessarily, coincide with the system go-live. For example

- Data may be migrated only shortly before going live; or
- The data may be too voluminous and complex to risk being uploaded only shortly before going live, so that a partial upload may be conducted for testing purposes well before the date

The source data may also vary

- Source data may be static or semi-static, in such case, a single upload shortly before the go-live may be sufficient or if not, a big time upload with a subsequent update will suffice; or
- Source data may come from another transactional system which changes every day, hour, etc. As such, the data migration needs to be carefully thought-out as the final data must reflect the complete source data for there not to be incongruences. In this case, a "freeze" period may need to be defined for the source transactional system, in which no new data is created while the final migration is taking place. Depending on the system (e.g., sales system), this may not be acceptable, so that the migration shall necessarily have to take place during a narrow window when no transactions take place, for example, during a weekend.

This brings me to the point that a data migration plan needs to be formulated well in advance so as to minimize mishaps! The plan may start as a very high-level document detailing the general philosophy of how the data is planned to be migrated, milestones, QA, etc. In general, it should contain

- A general plan and tasks set forth for doing the migration. If a calendar can be defined, so much the better
- Dependencies for the tasks
- HOW the data is to be migrated. This may take the form of extraction programs, upload programs or tools that will be used for this purpose. Take note that some of these programs and tools will have to be developed/conducted by the O&M team as it involves current systems in production, so their early involvement and understanding is crucial.
- Quality Assurance: How will the data be tested for correctness, basis for correctness, as well as the acceptable pass/fail criteria

6.5   Cut-Over of Transactions and Data Quality

Transaction cut-over may mean many things depending on the context. If a legacy system is to be replaced with a new system, it refers to all the procedures associated in ceasing to transact with the legacy system and having to transact with the new system. For systems that are being reconfigured while in use, it means having to deal with a new configuration which may not work with the legacy data, configuration, and setup. In both cases, there are a number of tasks that need to be done, and many of these are not IT's responsibility but the end users'. In spite of this, it is IT's responsibility to identify all these tasks, disseminate to the end users, conduct proper training and awareness, and monitor these before and after going live to ensure the new system encounters minimal hitches. This is of course simpler said than done, as many times it is hard for the users to fully grasp the implication of these procedures, and may be time consuming for them to perform.

Some examples of cut-over tasks are

- In implementing a new General Ledger chart of accounts, data should be mapped from the old GL to the new GL, these may be limited to end/beginning balances, however, the new account structure may necessitate that a mapping and recomputation of these be done so as to know which accounts are to be transferred to the new GL using what rules.
- New billing system: Similarly, a mapping for each customer's billing details needs to be done and data from the old system mapped to the new one. Questions will arise such as what level of detail should be carried over and in what specific fields should these be loaded. As the new billing system will work with different business rules versus the legacy, it is unrealistic to expect that all fields will map seamlessly, so that a decision

must likewise be made where and if to store certain information. For example, storing details on an installment plan that is being phased out.

As a practical experience to share, we implemented a new billing system in a large utility company, however, the management of the utility company did not entirely trust the new billing system, so that they required that both the old and the new system run in parallel and all discrepancies be cross-checked. Needless to say, this was a very tiring and expensive exercise, because as expected, many of the bills did not match, not because of errors, but because of data being processed differently, and because they did not have the same business process (otherwise, why replace?). It would have been much more efficient to test thoroughly the new system, and for the remaining errors that would still show, have a team analyze these and tweak the system accordingly. This parallel run was eventually dropped a few months after as management realized its futility.

- A new purchasing and inventory system: As purchases and deliveries cannot be stopped due to the continuous nature of the business, a conscious strategy must be thought-out on how to handle transactions that spill over from the old system up to the new one. As an example, take a purchase order that was released by the old system, and in which the goods have not yet been delivered (received). How these will be accepted by the new system needs to be clear, including

  - Should the Purchase Requests and Purchase Orders be recreated in the new system? How will these be traced to the old system?
  - Is there a budget implication? If these transactions referred to the old budget, should the budget now be adjusted accordingly?
  - What information needs to be disseminated to the suppliers? (i.e., reference new PO number that supersedes old, etc.)
  - Should an inventory count be done shortly before going live to make sure system stock reflects actual? Should there be a materials withdrawal freeze?
  - For withdrawals from warehouse, how are these tracked while the system is down due to migration to the new system? If manually recorded, how will these be reentered into the new system once it is up?

The list of activities will vary according to the type of project and specific situation on hand. As much as possible, data that can be migrated using special scripts and loading programs should be utilized so as to minimize manual intervention. These programs' mapping rules should be done in accordance with the users' inputs, the users that own the data. It is apparent from the above, however, that migrating ALL data automatically will be impossible, and that some transactions will need to be undertaken manually in preparation for the go-live, as well as during post-go-live. These must be carefully identified, and the correct procedures for conducting them discussed and finalized with the users. It is important to involve the users early so that they understand the need for the procedures, have a buy-in, and subsequently commit to undertaking their part of the tasks. Failure to do so may be disastrous, so that when things go wrong upon go-live, all the blame goes back to IT. If for whatever reason commitment from the users cannot be obtained, an analysis should be made on whether to postpone the go-live, and in any case, the situation should be escalated to higher management (typically the steering committee) so as to get their support, and subsequently, that from the line units.

All of this discussion in the end falls into the general category of data quality. No matter how good a system and its designed processes are, if the data is dirty, inaccurate or obsolete, the system will fail to deliver its function, and it is much less expensive to address data issues before implementation, rather than afterwards. Inventory systems with inaccurate inventory counts, billing systems with billing errors and reports with unreliable information are examples of such failures which no IT manager wishes to encounter, and yet, are all too common.

As an example of dirty data, and how it needs to be corrected, we implemented a new self-service HR application which did away with all the manual, email-based and paper-based processes for viewing pay slips, requesting for leaves, requesting for loans, overtimes, etc. The employee would now go to a self-service portal and have access to all these or initiate the request electronically. As such, it is essential that for the system to work correctly, the data should be clean. For example, data on who is the person's next approver should be correct, otherwise the request for approval (for a leave, for example) would be routed to the wrong person. As the information came from paper and was put into the system, it was expected that such errors would occur, which they did, and were corrected after the system went live. Take note that in this case HR's participation is essential for this cleanup to happen as IT has no knowledge whatsoever on the correct employee–approver relationship.

Nowadays, the relevance of Data Governance and Data Quality has taken new importance and new meaning, especially in the light of the mishaps that have occurred in the financial industry during the financial meltdown. Financial institutions failed (or did not want) to understand their own data in terms of products they were offering, and their relationship to the liabilities they would face if a sudden reversal of fortunes in the economy would happen. The "off-the-books" attitude they took in creating these new financial instruments basically hindered them in fully understanding the data underneath these products, its customers, the loans they were collateralizing, and most especially the underlying risk exposure. For this reason, regulators have started to come down hard on the industry and new ways of addressing data quality have taken renewed interest. Although this topic is way beyond the scope of this book, there is a bit that can be said with regards to data migration and data quality.

As an example, we developed a new set of comprehensive reports to conduct geographic and demographic analysis of our customers, however, when the address information was utilized, it became apparent that this information was "dirty" such that the address field which was a free-form field containing inaccuracies, inconsistencies, and omissions. We therefore embarked on an address-cleansing project which entailed structuring the address information in a standard, structured manner

Region-Municipality-District-Subdistrict-Street-House#-Block-Appartment-Door

This posed a major challenge because unlike in other countries, addresses in the Philippines do not follow a usual pattern. However, this was a necessary step in getting correct analysis reports. Cleansing also does not stop at cut-over, but is a continuous process.

In another example for a hotel, we found out that many of the essential data on the customer where left blank by the front-office personnel as they would hurriedly check in the customer by merely pressing <enter> or entering dummy data into the front-desk system for many of the required fields, in order to advance fast.

Data correctness is always easier to implement at the point of capture, and much more difficult to correct afterwards, as many of the banks are now realizing when dealing with "Know your client" and Anti-Money Laundering laws that are being enforced globally.

6.6   Interfaces

Interfaces are a common source of errors and malfunctions as these are commonly custom-developed in accordance with project-specific requirements, the systems being interfaced, as well as the data flow requirements between the systems. As with all custom-developed programs, these are usually the pieces that need most testing, and will commonly have some malfunctions slip through undetected. Due to this, interfaces need to be especially thoroughly tested. A test plan (see Chap. 5.5) should have been established first to make sure that the whole interface process is taken into account in the testing, and not only itself in isolation. This means the whole process from when the data is prepared in the source system, sent through the interface, accepted by the recipient system, and then consequently processed by the recipient system to produce the corresponding expected results. It must be emphasized that the testing should encompass the *whole process* from end to end. If just the interface program itself is tested, there is no assurance that it will actually give the expected results.

Some other special considerations when testing interfaces

1. **Completeness of test data**—the interface must be tested under different data scenarios.
2. **Negative testing**—testing for data scenarios in which the interface should not proceed. Negative testing should always form part of any test scenario, but is especially important in an interface.
3. **Log errors**—if an error occurs, this must be properly reported and logged so as to be able for the O&M team to debug. One must always assume that some failure will occur in the interface at one time or another, so it is important that this be detected and that enough information is given so that it can be traced. Errors may be due to unacceptable data ranges, wrong data format/type, one of the systems not be ready for the data transmission/reception, etc. The more explicit and more information logs give, the easier it shall be to debug later on.
4. **Invalid data transmission**—it may be that the interface worked correctly and data was transmitted to the recipient system, however, the data as received by the recipient system may be in inappropriate format for it to be meaningful, so that the recipient system cannot continue processing it. Proper testing would minimize such situations; however, it is again impossible to assume 0 % probability of this happening. As such, proper messaging and logs need to be produced by the interface (and related) programs, so if and when such situations occur, they can easily be detected and traced.
5. **Error-handling procedures**—again, it is important to assume that errors will occur, and so the interface must have had an error-handling procedure defined, so in case it happens, there is a clear operational procedure (not a project procedure) in terms of what should be done. If say, for example, the recipient system continuously accepts erroneous data, there must be a clear way to identify the problematic data, as well as a contingency plan on what to do with it. Failure to have come up with such procedures may affect operations permanently or for an extended duration of time, as there may be no way to identify the erroneous data, nor a clear way to clean it up.

Needless to say, interfaces should as much as possible use or be based on standard available interfaces. For SAP systems for example, these would be the BAPIs which can be further modified or embedded in other code. Use of standard interfaces minimizes customizations, as it means reusing previously tested interfaces.

A particular experience we undertook was in interfacing a CRM system with the back-end Customer billing system. The interface was designed to take into account the process needed for when a new customer would open an account. This was triggered in the CRM and would send the details to the customer billing system for the creation and setup of his entire account structure, including the initial payment for opening the account. This was tested and worked correctly, however, it was tested only up to the point of account creation in the billing system, but the billing system was not run for a complete cycle. It turned out that although all the details and account structure seemed correct, upon running the billing system, receivables were created where they should not have, an oversight in terms of not having conducted a complete end-to-end testing of the new process, for even if the billing system was legacy, the process was new and should have been completely tested.

6.7 Support Strategies and Structures

As mentioned during the introductory section of this chapter, there is a need to clearly define support roles and responsibilities. Generally speaking, there are a maximum of four entities types involved

- O&M Team—in charge of supporting the operation and maintenance of systems in production
- Project Team—in charge of the delivery of the new project being put into production
- Product support team 1st level—may or may not be part of the project team. May be part of a formal support team supporting all deployments of the product, and may be handled by the product reseller/distributor or the principal (product owner) itself.
- Product support team 2nd level—if the 1st level product support is handled by a reseller/distributor, then normally, a further support level is handled by the product owner itself, for tickets that cannot be resolved by the 1st level.

However, the above does not describe clearly the delineation of responsibilities for each team during a project. It is indispensable to define these before going live and preferably during the start of the project, as this may have contractual and monetary implications. If responsibilities for ticket handling and escalation are not clear, this may cause undue delay in the processing of tickets. Ticket escalation and handling may be a policy dictated company-wide or specific per project, and as explained in the introduction, requires careful thinking due to the trade-off between quick response time and the essential knowledge transfer from the project team to the O&M team. Table 6.1 is an example of a typical support matrix that can be utilized.

Needless to say, in ALL CASES (except for the pre-go-live period of the project), the first level call handling (and therefore, support) is really O&M's Service Desk (SD). As such, service desk personnel should be properly trained to try and resolve during the moment the incidence is reported without further escalation. In

Table 6.1 Sample support structure

	What it is	Unit handling the support level			
		Project before going live	Week 1-2 after going live	Project Warranty period (*)	Thereafter (covered by annual license maintenance)
1st level support	First to receive and handle incident tickets (after service desk)	Project team	Project team, shadowed by Operations team	Operations team	Operations team
2nd level support	Incidences that cannot be resolved by the 1st level support	Product support team: 1st level	Product support team: 1st level	Project team	Product support team: 1st level
3rd level support	Incidences that cannot be resolved by the 2nd level support	Product support team: 2nd level	Product support team: 2nd level	Product support team: 1st level	Product support team: 2nd level
4th level support	Incidences that cannot be resolved by the 3rd level support			Product support team: 2nd level	

(*) also called post-golive support

order for Service desk to be effective in this function (i.e., maximizing the number of first call resolutions), it must be properly trained and informed of commonly expected tickets. This can be done by

- Formulating an FAQ (Frequently Asked Questions) with a format of Question, Analysis steps and Possible Resolution detailed in laymen's terms so that the service desk can easily follow and apply these
- Conducting a session before the go-live between the project team, the rest of the O&M team and the service desk agents describing the application that will be going live, overview of the process it encompasses, and review of expected common issues. These issues may be of any type, such as

    - Settings (in the web browser, application, etc.)
    - Questions that may be typically asked for a user unfamiliar with the new application such as procedures
    - Where to find documents such as manuals and guides
    - Permissions and password-related inquiries
    - Errors that may be expected from improper usage of the system

- As a support, user manuals, PowerPoint presentations, and videos can be prepared before going live and placed in a portal for users to access in case they need assistance on the procedure for using the new application.

- One may assume the typical errors and inquiries that are to be expected; however, the reality may be different, so that shortly after going live (a few days) the tickets for the new application must be analyzed. A new version of the FAQs and a new discussion with the service desk personnel should take place so as to fine-tune the procedures.
- Although this may seem obvious, it is important for the service desk to know who to escalate tickets to, which will also be explained below.

Once the different support levels are clearly defined for the project, then the service desk ticketing system must be configured accordingly. Some questions need to be answered

- Will the project team be given direct access to the service desk system? If not, then who will handle the tickets escalated from the service desk in behalf of the project team?
- If the project team is given access, how many will have access and how will their responsibilities be delineated.
- Visibility over all the tickets. Typically, the O&M team should have this.
- How is the product support team to be contacted? The escalation procedure should be clear and ready for escalation.

Once having gone live, it is also important to see the trend of the incidence tickets, whether these are on the rise or declining. It is expected that shortly after going live the incidence tickets spike, but these should eventually decline. Failure to decline normally means that the root causes have not been addressed. Another important aspect is to check the rate in which the incidences are being resolved. If more incidences are being produced than being resolved, this means that incidences are accumulating, which may mean that either the root causes are not being addressed, the support manpower is insufficient, or both.

Typically, incidences will see a rise right after going live. This is typically 20–50 % more for a system affecting multiple divisions, and will stay there for the first 2 weeks to a few months if business process changes are significant. For technical upgrades and changes with few business process changes, this rise of tickets will typically last for just a week if properly implemented. It is important however to observe that by the 2nd week, the number of resolutions > the number of new opened incidences, otherwise the team will have a snowballing number of incidences to resolve. It is also important to

- Analyze if several incidence tickets are the same (collapse them).
- There are several incidences related to a problem. In this case, problem tickets typically take longer to resolve, so that it should be escalated to the more experienced, 2nd or even 3rd level support for investigation.

- Analyze those that are procedural (users not following procedure) or data-related (inconsistent or wrong data, usually also because of the users or legacy reasons). If these have been escalated to the AM support team, then an analysis should be done to see how the SD (or end-user department) can immediately resolve these so that they do not escalate. Typically, this is done by updating the FAQ and meeting between AM and SD (or end-user department) so that an understanding and explanation of the issues happens.
- Is there a technical issue? This needs to be addressed by TM.

If by the 3rd week tickets continue to escalate, then either the system was very complicated and the users failed to understand its usage, or you have a major issue on hand, meaning, there is a problem with the design and/or deployment. Emergency meetings should be called between the different relevant teams and the users to get to the root cause, work-arounds identified, new advisories sent, and if needed, additional training, while the root case is being addressed.

Some incidences do not surface right after go-live, but remain hidden. Examples of this are incidences during the monthly closing of books, when rolling over the budget (typically, yearly), or when the MRP (Material Resource Planning) is run. They will generally follow the same pattern, save for the delay. Particularly difficult are those that happen way-off from the go-live (such as during year end closing of books) as the project team may have been long gone, and the O&M team inexperienced still with the new setup.

As an example of a go-live that was stabilized, take when we implemented the single sign-on (SSO) system in a company, wherein the user would need to sign on to Active Directory and would automatically get the correct access and permissions for all systems (vs. having to have separate login and passwords for each system). To do this, several steps were undertaken

- A mapping was done for each application to the AD account. This means that every application's user account needs to be matched to its corresponding AD account. Sometimes the account name is distinctly different, so that matching these is not evident.
- Each application has to be "tied" to the AD controller, so that the credentials from the AD server are passed to each application
- Each end user in turn needs to have a security certificate in his endpoint, so that the single sign-on system can recognize the endpoint as valid.
- A single sign-on system is set up for some applications requiring this particular service. This now becomes the hub for authorizing these applications after checking with the authorization at the endpoint (certificate) and the AD server.
- The certificates need to be pushed to each endpoint.
- The new links to the SSO-enabled applications are now pushed to each endpoint.

WEEKLY TICKET TREND
YEAR 2014

CLASS	Tickets for the Week	Mar-15				Apr-15			
		3rd	4th	5th	Total	1st	2nd	3rd	Total
INCIDENT	Created	106	79	201	556	185	73	63	321
	Closed	6	8	4	26	4	4	5	13
	Cancelled	31	28	53	174	83	18	12	113
	Resolved	7	2	18	31	12	4	6	22
	Resolved (Waiting)	30	11	18	93	20	18	13	51
	Open	8	14	56	103	21	9	9	39
	Pending (Waiting)	24	16	52	129	45	20	18	83
	All Resolved Tickets	43	21	40	110	36	26	24	86
	Resolved %	57.33%	41.18%	27.03%	47.53%	35.29%	47.27%	47.06%	43.21%
	Resolved % (excluding pending)	84.31%	60.00%	41.67%		63.16%	74.29%	72.73%	
	All Carried Over Tickets From Last W	145	141	140	746	276	265	170	711
	Closed	5	2	2	19	10	8	3	21
	Cancelled	14	8	4	47	33	73	13	119
	Resolved	4	6	1	20	9	16	6	31
	Resolved (Waiting)	14	15	8	75	28	27	14	69
	Open	0	2	1	5	3	4	1	8
	Pending (Waiting)	108	108	124	580	193	137	133	463
	All Resolved Tickets	23	23	11	103	47	51	23	121
	Resolved %	17.56%	17.29%	8.09%	18.55%	19.34%	26.56%	14.65%	20.18%
	Resolved % (excluding pending)	100.00%	92.00%	91.67%		94.00%	92.73%	95.83%	

Fig. 6.4 Example of a go-live project and resulting incidence tickets

As you can see from above, it is both a technical deployment, and a data cleanup exercise, and several things can go wrong.

Upon going live on the 5th week of March, the resulting tickets were created as shown in Fig. 6.4.

As can be seen during the 5th week of March, the number of incidence tickets more than doubled, due to the extent of the change. Upon investigation, several incidences were found

- In some cases, the certificates did not push correctly, or the links did not. This was addressed by US in pushing those certificates again.
- Other cases were procedural; the users were accessing the old non-SSO-enabled link. SD reacted by advising each caller on this, releasing an advisory reminding people, as well as deleting wherever possible the old link.
- Some of the mappings were incomplete, so some users were not able to login to some of the applications because they were not initially enabled to do so. In this case, AM took each one case by case and validated that the user is indeed authorized to access such application.
- In some rare cases, there were technical issues with the AD and SSO, but these were minimal, so that in fact the networks group actually did not have to conduct much work.

As can be seen from above, tickets normalized after 2 weeks.

Further Reading

Cut-over forms part of IT Project Management, however, scant attention has been given to it, which is remarkable when one realizes that it is a very crucial part of the success of a project. The following publications touch on peripheral topics.

Kalaimani, J., 2016. Approach to Cut Over and Go Live Best Practices. In: *SAP Project Management Pitfalls*. Apress, pp. 93–105.

Morris, J., 2012. *Practical Data Migration*. 2nd ed. BCS.

Olson, T., 2015. *Digital Project Management: The Complete Step-by-Step Guide to a Successful Launch*. J. Ross Publishing, Inc.

Project Governance

Project governance is a component of IT governance as explained below, and sits side by side with IT operations governance. Many of the dimensions of project governance discussed in this chapter were also discussed in Chap. 5, but here we make more emphasis on what are the minimal required processes and documentation needed in order to comply with governance best practices.

7.1 Overall IT Governance

Governance refers to all policies, guidelines, and procedures which must be followed by the IT organization. In general, these are defined at different organizational levels and are cascaded down the organization by means of detailing them successively.

From Fig. 7.1, we can see on the left how company mission and vision is cascaded down the organization. Ideally, each division's mission and vision, as well as objectives should be aligned to its higher level, meaning that the attainment of each's division's objectives contribute to the overall company objectives, and in turn, to the company's mission and vision.

Company objectives, mission and vision are of course usually very high level in nature, so there is a need to operationalize them. On the right-hand side, we see a pyramid depicting the company policies cascaded all the way down to the work instructions. Company policies should be aligned with the overall company mission and vision. This policy in turn, must be defined in more detail in terms of HR, legal, regulatory, safety and health, and IT policies. IT policies are not only restricted by the former, so that they should not be in conflict, but even more, it should be in fact supporting them, as in today's business environment, IT is in fact used to operationalize company-wide, HR, legal, and regulatory policies, to ensure they are followed by means of business processes which reflect these, as well as monitor, control, and audit these. IT policies apply not only to the IT Division's personnel, but some also apply company-wide. Common IT O&M and project policies should cover:

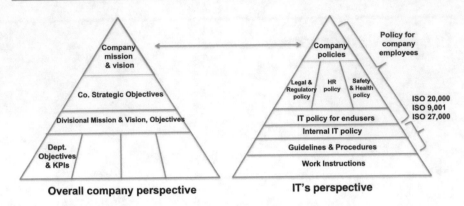

Fig. 7.1 Company governance and relation to IT governance, policy

- **Implementing new services**: how are new services requested, approved, created, and made part of the service portfolio
- **Service Delivery Management**: how are services delivered to the end users, SLAs by which they will conform to
- **Incidence and Problem Management**: what are considered incidences and problems, how do they have to be reported, how they are handled, resolved, and closed
- **Security**: policies on access, confidentiality, integrity of data, and systems
- **Service Continuity and Disaster Recovery**: manner in which service is provided and restored when a disaster occurs, when is the disaster recovery plan to be called, SLA that kicks in once the disaster has triggered
- **Customer Relationship Management**: policies relating to IT with regard to the company's customers and clients
- **Supplier Management**: policies relating to IT with regard to suppliers and contractors
- **Configuration Management and Change Management**: how configuration changes are requested, approved, created, and released
- **Release Management**: manner in which changes are released into production
- **Project Management**: policies related to projects which require IT resources, including IT projects themselves

From the point of view of the end users, the following are typical policies that apply to them:

- Email usage policy
- Internet usage policy
- Security policy
- Requests in accessing a service
- Requests for infrastructure
- Requests for new applications
- Requests for major enhancements

- Policy on requests for application modifications and enhancements
- Requests for PCs, laptop, printers, tablets, smartphones, scanners, and other endpoint and peripheral devices
- Service Desk policy

IT policies can in turn be taken one level down in the form of guidelines and procedures which are designed mainly for IT's internal personnel:

- Availability management. Including how to measure and manage it.
- Capacity management. Includes how to measure and manage it.
- Change and release management. The whole process for requesting, approving, planning, and releasing changes, including possible rollback procedures.
- System backup and recovery.
- Disaster Recovery Plan.
- Service Desk. Ticket categories, opening, escalating, and filling-up of ticket details until closing.
- Configuration Management. Including scope of the configuration management (servers, applications, switches, etc.) and definition of the Configuration Management DB (CMDB).

As represented on the right hand triangle of Fig. 7.1, the topmost policies apply to all the different employees of the company (end users from IT's point of view). Also, ISO certification including ISO20000, which focuses on IT O&M, ISO9001 which focuses on standards and procedures, as well as ISO27000 which focuses on IT security, will cover policies, operational procedures, but not go down to the work instruction level.

> To illustrate the difference in what each level means, take, for example, IT backup policy. At the policy level, it may be indicated that all major systems need to be regularly backed-up. Procedures will indicate the criteria for backing up, retention period, and how backup media is to be retained. Work instructions will indicate the exact HOW to undertake the backup, including what tools, specific media, how often, what type of backup, and how the media will be managed.

7.2   Project Governance and Operations Governance

Most ISO standards provide clear guidelines to O&M; however, they are quite weak on project governance.

Clearly, projects will eventually turned over to O&M, so that project policy and governance needs to be in sync with that of operations, however, the reality is that there are only few areas in operations which really have a direct effect on the project. To name these:

- Security policy
- Email and internet policy
- Endpoint policy
- Service Desk policy; and
- Request for infrastructure

Since projects are not in production, they may have their own particularities which make their requirements on the above, not exactly the same. The most important aspect thus is that upon *turnover to O&M*, the operational policies are followed, and all the necessary configurations to comply with these are implemented. Project policy may in fact differ, especially so because the project environment may be completely isolated from the rest of the infrastructure, users, and sometimes may even be in a different physical location.

It is thus important that the head of the project portfolio be the one to define project policy and governance for all projects, and the Project Manager apply these to his specific project. Variations from the general project policy may be acceptable, for as long as the PM seeks proper approval.

Project policy should cover the following:

- **Project Monitoring and Control**: How projects are to be monitored in terms of templates to be used, roles in terms of personnel that are involved in the reporting and control activities
- **Project team roles and responsibilities**: roles and responsibilities of different team members
- **Communication management**: explaining different stakeholders that require communication, frequency of communication, as well as media used for communicating
- **Scope management, including change requests**: how the changes in scope to be requested, costed, and approved.
- **Risk Management**: templates used in risk management, frequency of risk analysis, personnel involved in the risk analysis.
- **Asset Management**: policy regarding the usage of company issued assets for projects
- **Incidence and issue management**: how incidences and issues are identified, created, approved, and resolved
- **Release management**: how releases are to be managed within the project (typically from DEV to QA) and to production, as well as any other environments which may exist
- **Infrastructure capacity management**: manner in which capacity is to be measured and managed (in case additional capacity is needed)
- **Request management for projects**: how are new requests to be created, costed, approved
- **Code development guidelines**: do's and don'ts, code structure, documentation, security
- **Test guidelines**: how to test, who will test, formats for test scripts, including any tools utilized

Fig. 7.2 Standard project documentation versus project specific

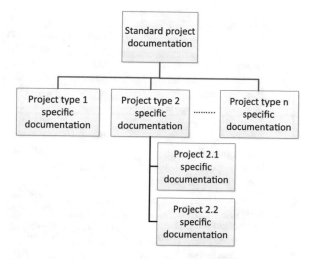

- **Training guidelines**: format and general content, method of training
- **Backup and recovery policy**: manner of backups, frequency, what to backup
- **Pre-go live guidelines**: minimum requirements before going live, verifications and actions to be conducted after going live. Who makes the final decision for go-live?
- **Service Desk usage policy**: manner in which projects will use the service desk system, access
- **Post-implementation support and warranty period policy**: minimum requirements for post-implementation support and warranty, definition of roles
- **Security guidelines** (these are normally the same as for O&M)

All of these policies and guidelines have in turn, a set of documentation, which should as much as possible, be standardized across all projects. However, as IT projects vary quite considerably in technology, process, application, etc. project documentation may be standardized according to TYPE of project as well, and, be further adapted to the needs of the particular project in question by customizing it to the project type, as shown in Fig. 7.2.

The exact project documentation should be discussed and agreed by both the vendor PM and the client PM, and then approved by the portfolio manager.

7.3   Project Monitoring and Control

It is imperative that both PMs (vendor and client), the Portfolio manager and the key stakeholders know exactly how the project is doing at any moment in time in terms of scope (quality), time, cost and resources. Communication to each party shall vary as discussed in the later section, but for the PMs and the portfolio manager, the same set of reports and tools can be used for reporting. Three essential tools can be defined here:

Task Name	Duration	Start	Finish	% Complete	SPI
⊟ BI Phase 2 Build	252 days	Wed 8/13/14	Fri 8/14/15	13%	0.13
⊟ Project Initiation	9 days	Wed 8/13/14	Thu 8/28/14	100%	0
⊞ Project Initiation	9 days	Wed 8/13/14	Thu 8/28/14	100%	0
⊟ Integrated System Design and Test Plan	10 days	Fri 8/29/14	Thu 9/11/14	100%	0
Document System Design and Test Plan	5 days	Fri 8/29/14	Thu 9/4/14	100%	0
Present System Design to customer	1 day	Fri 9/5/14	Fri 9/5/14	100%	0
Revise System Design	1 day	Mon 9/8/14	Mon 9/8/14	100%	0
Submit revised System Design	0 days	Mon 9/8/14	Mon 9/8/14	100%	0
Accept System Design	4 days	Mon 9/8/14	Thu 9/11/14	100%	0
Milestone: Signed off System Design	0 days	Thu 9/11/14	Thu 9/11/14	100%	0
Present Test Plan to Maynilad	1 day	Fri 9/5/14	Fri 9/5/14	100%	0
Revise Test Plan	1 day	Mon 9/8/14	Mon 9/8/14	100%	0
Submit revised Test Plan	0 days	Mon 9/8/14	Mon 9/8/14	100%	0
Accept Test Plan	4 days	Mon 9/8/14	Thu 9/11/14	100%	0
Milestone: Signed Off Test Plan	1 day	Thu 9/11/14	Thu 9/11/14	100%	0
⊟ Construction Waves	164 days	Fri 9/12/14	Fri 5/8/15	9%	0
⊟ Wave 1: Purchasing & Inventory	75 days	Fri 9/12/14	Mon 12/29/14	19%	0
⊟ System Development	52 days	Fri 9/12/14	Mon 11/24/14	28%	0
⊟ Out of the box implementation	31 days	Fri 9/12/14	Fri 10/24/14	51%	0
⊟ ETL (Development environmer	27 days	Fri 9/12/14	Mon 10/20/14	55%	0

Fig. 7.3 Sample project plan showing milestones, % completion and SPI

- **Project Management tool** (such as MS Project, Primavera, etc.): as defined in Sect. 5.1.4, this gives an updated view as to what tasks have been finished, what not, if there are delays, if it affects the overall timeline, CPI, and SPI calculations (S-curve), resource utilization, deliverables attained. In fact, in one brief view and snapshot, the PM can understand exactly the progress and status of the project. A sample is shown in Fig. 7.3.
- **Issue registry**: is a list of all issues encountered and/or reported for the project. These issues can be reported by any party (either PM, an end user, the O&M team, a stakeholder). It is registered into this sheet until it is resolved or canceled (because it ceases to be an issue, not relevant, or due to other reasons), the date identified, the person responsible for seeking resolution of the issue, status of the issue, and any remarks. An issue registry may be as simple as an excel sheet which enumerates all current issues and their status, as shown in Fig. 7.4.

The fields that are important include the status, who resolved the issue:

- **Request registry**: is similarly, a list of any and all requests for the project which affect/modify the original scope of work. This is again similar to the issue registry in which any party can raise the request, and carries the same set of fields as above. A request need or need not have monetary implication, may or may not be accepted, but is registered anyways, for as long as it was raised and

Bills Presentment Issue Register

No.	Issue	Updates	Status	Resolved by	Bills Presentment Team Notes
1	SMS Gateway - telecom co. unable to provide the transaction status for each of the SMS sent (Success/Fail); currently they are only providing numerical statistics of successfully and failed SMS sending	April 1 : customer has raised a request for telecom co. to provide the status per SMS sent April 17 : Meeting with telecom co. clarified items on the transactions status. customer will be able to extract SMS transaction status per SMS sent via web service	Closed	Joan	Impact: Reports on SMS sent status will not be available April 15 - A second meeting has been requested by telecom co. to answer previous meeting's questions and requirements as well as to clarify more the customer requirements from them. April 17 - telecom co. will ensure that the custom application and web services should be ready for Bills Presentment preliminary Integration Testing by May 15, 2016. Demo telecom co. accounts will be requested 2-weeks before the testing week.
2	SMS Gateway - telecom co. unable to filter incoming messages and has no automated facility to send to customer	April 1 : customer requested for telecom co. to find out if they can provide filtered incoming SMS and automated sending of this files to	Closed	Noel	Impact: Enrolment via SMS functionality will not be available should telecom co. not be able to provide incoming SMS file April 15 - A second meeting has been requested by telecom co. to answer previous meeting's questions and requirements as
3	Unified Payment Gateway - identification of the unfied gateway to link to	April 1 : customer arranged for a meeting with Treasury department	Closed	Tess	Impact: Availability of the link to payment gateway April 8 - There will be a dropdown box for the Pay Now option within the Bills Presentment System will contain the list of financial institutions customer has existing MOA. This list will be mantainable.
4	DSP/principal Technical Foreign Resource On-site work commitment to ensure functional and technical design are sound and ensure quality	April 22 : Advise was received from customer CIO, that architectural meetings with customer will be put on hold until the principal experts are present here in project site so that discussions will be more comprehensive and assuring that what is designed is feasible	Open	DSP	Impact: Scheduled architectural review (functional and design document) may be delayed due to the pending response from DSP/principal <April 22-29> same status <May 5> DSP has responded with a schedule of the resources working on-site and off-site. Sajid and Sathish went onsite to work with customer for the Blueprint/Design review sessions. <May 8> New project TO was given to company Continous monitoring of resource and resource work is going to be done.

Fig. 7.4 Sample issue register (partial register shown)

is within the project's influence area. Again, a simple excel sheet may be used to track requests as shown in Fig. 7.5.

With the above three, the PM can scan the project management status, check for delays, and how it affects the overall project timeline and cost, zero in on the task(s) causing the delays, and open the issue registry to identify the underlying cause for the delay.

An additional governance document proves to be very useful:

- **Deliverable checklist**—is a document with the list of all deliverables agreed for the project, the phase of the project in which it is to be generated (initiation, blueprint and design, development, …), who it will be prepared by, status, date submitted, who is to produce the document, description, whether it requires a sign-off, and who shall be the signatories and approvers.

Bills Presentment Request Tracker

No.	Portal Type	Request	Requestor	Updates	Status	Resolved by	Resolution Code (ticket#)
1	Service Desk Ticket# 9608	Infrastructure Set-up - Development	Tess	Infrastructure request approved 3/31 Completed 4/14	Completed	customer Infra Team	9608
2	Service Desk Ticket# 9608	Infrastructure Set-up - QAS	Tess	Infrastructure request approved 3/31 Completed 4/14	Completed	customer Infra Team	9608
3	Service Desk Ticket# 9608	Infrastructure Set-up - Production	Tess	Infrastructure request approved 3/31 Pending QAS performance	WIP		
4		Addition of Payment Status notification	John	4/10 - CR form being created by SI (estimates on effort and costs)	Cancelled CR		
5		Provision of additional drives for Software installation and DB	John	5/25 - Aligned with customer's requirements of no storing to Drive C; Request raised	Completed	customer infra team	
6	14445, 14728	Request for QAS environment provisioning update	Tess	June 16 - For Approval	Completed	customer infra team	
7		Telecom Test Accounts needed IP address	John	June 28 - Request raised	Completed		
8		Telecom Test Accounts needed IP address for Cloud	Anne	July 29 - Request raised. As per Max's response, it can only be provided once Cloud server set-up and definition has been completed	Completed		

Fig. 7.5 Sample request register (partial register shown)

One way to do this is through an excel sheet which already contains a predefined set of deliverables normally needed for IT projects as shown in Fig. 7.6.

This checklist would then be customized by the PMs in mutual agreement.

What this document allows is for the PM to quickly view the list of all submitted deliverables, and determine what is pending, so he/she can follow-up. Deliverables may be anything ranging from a kick-off meeting, a blueprint, technical design, actual code, UAT, training, manuals, meeting, etc. Again, since every project is different, the exact deliverables to be produced will be agreed upon at the start of the project by both PMs. Generally, technical projects carry less deliverables than applications that touch on process, and the more processes that span across different departments; the more documentation is usually needed.

Project Phase	Deliverable	optional?	Prepared By	Status	Date submitted or signed-off	Description	Undertaken by	Sign-off required?	List of Signatories
Blueprinting and Design	Process flows level 0,1,2,3 (up to level applicable)	No	Vendor	ON-GOING		Visio, explanation in word document. See standard document.	Vendor PM	Yes	Customer users, PM, IS Head, CIO. Optional as case may be: - Operations Head
	Functional Design	No	Vendor	DONE	22 July, 2015	Format varies per application and thus, should be agreed-upon at project start. This document however, shall contain details on the functional aspects of the solution in how it meets the BRD	Vendor PM	Yes	Customer users, Customer PM, IS Head, CIO. Optional as case may be: - Operations Head
	Technical Design	No	Vendor	ON-GOING		Format varies per application and thus, should be agreed-upon at project start. This document however, shall contain details on the technical aspects of the solution, and is a further elaboration on the IT infra discussion. PM must ensure that DEV, QA,Testing and PROD environments are all properly licensed (or if license is waved for some), so as not to have issues later on.	Vendor PM	Yes	TM Head, IT Head, Customer PM, CIO
	Backup procedure	No	Vendor			Should contain details of the backup procedure (instruction level) for the application should include procedure for changing admin passwords	Vendor PM	Yes	TM Head, CIO

Fig. 7.6 Sample deliverables checklist (partial list shown)

Aside from this, it is also important to choose proper deliverables so that the real progress of the project can be monitored. Deliverables are milestones which help to understand whether the project has progressed or not to that stage. Deliverables should preferably be:

- **Easily identified**
- **Objective**—either they are attained or not, there should be no room for ambiguity
- **Clear in terms of whether they have been achieved**. Is the objective attained upon submission? Approval? Sign-off by users?
- **Spaced along the life of the project**. In this way, it is easy to monitor progress. It is usually hard to place deliverables during the development phase, especially if development of different modules or functions occurs simultaneously.
- **Usable**. Preferably, the deliverable should be of actual use to the project, and not merely for the purpose of project tracking, so that the effort in producing this deliverable is not wasted.

Sample of badly defined milestones includes:

- % completion of development—because this is hard to measure and have to take the vendor's word for it, it is also normally too long a phase which would require milestones within it.

- % tested—if this is not measured by pass/fail, then it is a bad measure because it is not objective. Testing typically requires several iterations of testing.
- Blueprint defined—again, the blueprint may have been drafted, but there is no guarantee that the blueprint is correct nor accepted. If this immediately leads to development without proper acceptance, it is a "false" milestone.

From the PMs' point of view, projects will also be monitored and controlled by means of regular project update meetings, usually weekly. During these meetings, the documentation mentioned above is reviewed, analyzed, and major issues raised for clarification and decision-making. The risk analysis register, if utilized, will also be updated.

These project update meetings should be kept short (1 h), unless (exceptionally) there are a lot of topics that need to be covered. Mandatory in these meetings is the presence of the 2 PMs; the rest of the attendees will be invited depending on the communication plan decided. From time to time, key users, the portfolio manager, project sponsor, project team lead, key personnel from the Customer's Operations and support team will be invited, if and when their involvement, inputs or decision is required.

7.4   Project Team Roles and Responsibilities

Project team members, stakeholders should have clear roles and responsibilities. Generally speaking, the PM should be the single point of contact and singly responsible for the delivery of the whole project. He shall also be in charge of:

- Scope mgmt.
- Time mgmt.
- Cost management
- Quality
- Resources
- Risk Management
- Asset Management
- Governance and reporting
- Communication management
- Procurement and contract management

The roles and responsibilities of the other project team members (whether full-or part-time) shall depend to a large extent on the type of project, structure and model used by the client and vendor organizations. Some of the typical roles that exist are (those marked with * are more uncommon, V refers to a vendor role, C to a client role):

- **Business Analyst (V)**—is a functional expert that will be in charge of capturing and translating business requirements into functional specifications for the design and configuration of the application, as well as codes that need to be

developed. Many times, the analyst is also in charge of executing the configuration changes on the application.

- **Programmer** (V)—is the person that will code using the pertinent programming
  language as per the specifications developed by the Business Analyst.
- **Technical manager/System Architect** (V)—is in charge of determining the
  necessary infrastructure for the execution of the project. Will also be in charge
  of designing the overall architecture, as well as sizing servers, storage, and
  determining hardware and software components needed, including network
  requirements. Will coordinate extensively with the customer Technical Manager
  to ensure the architecture is compatible, and complies with the customer's
  technical infrastructure and policies. His role in the project is usually temporary,
  with a heavy involvement in the beginning when the overall architecture needs
  to be designed, the functional specifications translated to technical specifications, as well as shortly before the go-live.
- **Technical support personnel** (V)—may include a Database Administrator,
  Network Administrator, System Administrator(s) that will each be in charge of
  installing, creating, configuring, defining permissions and maintaining during
  the course of the project the Database, network, Application(s) used, respectively. Will communicate extensively with the client's counterparts.
- **Tester (V*)**—will be in charge of defining the test scripts and running the tests
  before UAT. These personnel may be a complement to the business analysts,
  and will work closely with them, or is a role taken on entirely by the Business
  Analysts.
- **Documentation writers (V*)**—will be in charge of the documentation of the
  project, including process flows, end user requirements, manuals, etc. Is a role
  also complementing that of the Business Analyst, and may be a role taken
  entirely by the Business Analysts.
- **Process experts (C)**—are the end users that are experts in the business or
  business processes that will be covered by the project. They will give information, data, interviews, and should be the main approvers for the deliverables
  of the Business Analysts, namely, the end user requirement documents, functional design and specifications, as well as the main te sters during UAT.
- **Technical support personnel (under the TM team) (C)**—the counterparts of
  the project technical support personnel, will be in charge of reviewing and
  approving their corresponding parts which will later on turned over to them,
  including sufficiency and clarity of documentation. They will also assist the
  project (on a part-time, as need basis) for any requests for infrastructure.

It is important that the project team's role be clearly defined from the beginning
of the project. A good moment to formalize these roles are during the kick-off, so
that especially the process experts are identified and they commit to the project (as
they are usually from the end users' side). Specific roles can be displayed on a
screen or board, and the corresponding name written down. Their exact role during
the project should be well explained, and by having their boss during the kick-off
meeting, their role formalized.

Aside from the project team itself, a steering committee may be needed for the smooth conduct of the project. The role of the steering committee is to act as a body that will guide, and if necessary decide and approve matters which cannot be decided at the project management level. Some of these may be:

- Disputes that cannot be resolved at the Project Management level
- Decisions which affect policy or in which policy changes need to be made
- Conflicts which exists between different departments and which need to be decided at a higher level (not a decision IT can or should make)

Aside from these, the steering committee meeting may also be called for:

- Progress updates
- Informing them of major changes that will happen due to the project
- Inform different departments that even though they are not directly part of the project, but will also be affected somehow.
- Seek clearance for additional budget, scope or resources, if necessary.

The exact role and times the steering committee is called for a meeting will depend on the type of project and the company culture. Some companies' senior management like to take a hands-on approach and be involved closely with IT projects, especially if the project is strategic for the business, while others may entrust the details to the IT Department, and just wish to be informed on major milestones and progress. In any case, this needs to be determined as explained in the Communications Management section.

7.5   Communication Management

Communication management policy indicates who should be informed and the means and regularity to which they are to be informed. This is generally very much project-dependent, but the policy should describe the bare minimum required. This would normally be in the form of:

- **Kick-off**: the first formal project meeting with end users, PMs, and other key stakeholders. This meeting is important in briefly describing the scope, timeline, table of organization, methodology to be used, disseminating the communication plan for the project, details of the project governance (if needed), identifying needed project resources and assets, as well as identifying and getting the commitment of stakeholders needed in the project. For example, getting the commitment in terms of time and dedication of the end users for the blueprinting sessions and testing. The requested commitment should be as explicit as possible.
- **Project update meetings**: normally weekly and preferably predefined in terms of the date and time these shall take place, but depending on the phase, risk, and

criticality of the project, may be called for more often (every day in the 2 weeks before going live, for example).

- **Steering committee meetings**—indicating the criteria to be used for calling the steering committee for a meeting, or if regularly scheduled. Also important is to validate the members of the steering committee meeting, which would generally depend on the type of project (e.g., CEO, COO, CFO, CIO may form part by default, Head of Logistics invited due to the project dealing with a logistics optimization).

7.6 Scope Management (Including Change Requests)

As stated before, scope management is usually the single, biggest source of failure in a project. Disputes commonly occur with regards to the inclusion and exclusion of certain functions, as well as the perceived quality of the solution. This means that scope should be as clear as possible upon the start of the project, and should be handled correctly during the whole lifecycle of the project.

All IT projects are successively elaborated with regard to scope, while usually maintaining quality standards and managing costs and resources to be as close as possible to the baseline. As such, the level of scope detail should progress as the project progresses in time. Take for example the standard documentation below, which is arranged in the order of project start to project finish:

- Terms of Reference (tender document)
- Proposal
- Proposal clarifications
- Contract
- End-user requirements
- Functional design
- Technical design
- Blueprint
- Coding design
- User manuals

With each successive step, the exact scope of the project is being further elaborated in details (scope, quality). As most projects would be turn-key (fixed price), the challenge of the PMs is to keep the scope within the reasonable bounds of what was tendered (and successively detailed), so that no additional price or resources are needed. Any specifications that do not conform to this are therefore called a change request, which means that these are additional specifications that were not part of the agreed-upon scope. Before we go into details of the change request, let us first review the list of documents above, and try to understand how scope discrepancies and misunderstanding between the two parties can be minimized.

Firstl, it must be understood that what is binding to both parties is the scope of work as detailed in the contract. This is a legally binding document which, in case of disputes, is the primary document to be consulted and defended in case of arbitration or any legal actions taken to resolve the dispute. As scope has been successively detailed from the moment the project was tendered, it is important that the contract correctly capture all these details appearing in documents elaborated and agreed upon by both parties between the moment of tender and the moment the contract is signed. One way to do this is to write into the scope of work (SOW) what was agreed, including all those agreements during clarification meetings and presentations, and include it as part of the contract. This may take time, first to draft, making sure all points discussed are reflected, then to review from both sides and agree. A simpler way to do this is to just mechanically attach all relevant documents as annexes being referred to by the main, standard contract (which should not be changed). Thus, the terms-of-reference released by the client, the proposal submitted by the vendor, and the minutes of the meetings between both parties with all agreements and clarifications should be attached, and their precedence (in case of conflicts between them), stipulated in the main contract. In this way, all agreements including clarifications are made contractually binding.

Another important advantage of this method is that the contract can be standardized (more in Sect. 5.1.3), and the vendors' commitments stated in the proposal made part of the tender contract. After all, who has not experienced of vendors indicating something in the proposal which is eventually "forgotten" as it was not explicitly indicated in the contract. Furthermore, having the vendor aware that all replies in the proposal are in fact contractually binding, they will in fact think twice before overcommitting or even bending facts just to win the contract.

Let us now go back to the topic of to change requests. Although change requests are a dirty word in many organizations, they need not be so. Properly managed change requests can in fact be very useful, as will be explained shortly.

The first and most important tool for identifying *possible* change requests is the request registry. As explained, any request that has been flagged by any stakeholder is to be registered into this document for further analysis. First, it needs to be analyzed whether the request is actually outside the SOW. If so the next question is whether this request is reasonable, in terms of:

- **Functionality and usability**. Is it really necessary or is it a nice to have? Is this only an individual's request or is a functionality which will be used by many?
- **Is it a key requirement?** Such that, not having it will be a major issue.
- **Cost**. How many man-days estimate? If not quantified yet, at last have an idea whether this is a major change or if it is just a small effort.
- **Timing**. Is this necessary now before going live or can it be taken as an enhancement in a subsequent phase? If included into the current project, will it affect the overall timeline? Will it form part of the critical path?
- **Resources**. Are they available for this within the project's current table of organization? Or should they be sourced externally? How long will it take to source?

Take note that cost is just one of the evaluation criteria, not the only one. Whether the requirement is key or not usually has much more weight as compared to other criteria. One needs to take into account the *overall* cost, not just the IT cost, which many times is forgotten. In other words, not having that additional scope may impair operations considerably, resulting in much more work, effort, lower customer experience or additional operational cost which must be weighed versus the IT cost. It is in fact the job of the CIO to weigh all these factors (especially if it is a big change request, otherwise it can be handled by the PM or Portfolio Manager.) and make a decision. It is also the job of the client PM to make a recommendation, and it is especially important for him to weigh the advantage of including that additional scope versus the additional cost, and very importantly, the additional time delay and risk that the change request will introduce. Sometimes, introducing the change immediately may not impact the overall timeframe too much, but it carries the risk that every whim and fancy from the end users to include additional scope (assuming here that they were the ones to raise the request) will be accepted. If that then becomes the culture, then all these additional requests will eventually delay or even derail the project. If just for this reason alone, it may be recommended to just keep the request in the request registry and have a subsequent enhancement project to address these additional requests.

A sample of well-managed project creep occurred in a Business Intelligence project which had its delivery outputs already signed-off by the users. When development started however, some users realized that additional details on the fixed assets reports were needed. Including these would have meant restarting the development, so that instead, it was negotiated with the users to maintain them as-is, test and approve, and have a subsequent phase for such modifications. This was possible as these additional requirements were nice to have and further refinements of the original scope, but were in no way essential in the sense that their non-inclusion would invalidate the outputs.

Once the request has passed the initial screening, it now goes on to a formal "change request status" and main responsibility for filling-up the details is now the vendor's PM. He now puts in motion his mechanism to formally propose the change request:

- Identify main person who can estimate the change request tasks and effort
- Identify the resources needed for the change request and check availability
- If not readily available, check the constraints or ability to source from other project pools or externally (subcontract)
- Identify the man-days for each resource needed to complete the change request.
- Cost the change request, including any margins applicable
- Get internal management approval

The change request proposal is then with the customer PM to evaluate, negotiate (if needed) and approve or disapprove. If the man-day rates were included as part of the contract then the money calculation of the change request is relatively easy and the customer PM need only to verify that the effort is reasonable versus the request.

In accordance with company and IT policy, the change request may need an additional contract, addendum to the main contract, or may be accepted as part of the main contract.

7.7   Risk Management

As explained in Sect. 5.1.7 risk management may be called for, depending on the complexity of the project. The basic tool for this is the risk management registry, which evaluates both (+) and (−) risks, their probability, impact, as well mitigation steps. This would normally be done during the weekly project update meetings. Special risk management sessions will also be called by the PM during times when high-risk activities are drawing near, such as cut-over, data migration, release of new enhancements, etc. The content of this report and techniques has already been explained in the aforementioned section.

Policy should also indicate when to conduct risk management.

An example of how risk management can be extremely useful is that it is able to identify actions for reducing the risk of commonly risky activities. From experience, risky activities include:

- Interfaces
- Customization of non-standard processes
- Data migration
- Cut-over from a legacy system to a new system
- Cut-over from a legacy process to a completely new process (even if within the same application)
- Revenue-generating processes (invoicing, billing, sales…): this is due to the huge impact it may have on the company
- Production-related processes (production planning, inventory, purchasing, logistics, delivery)
- Regulatory compliance processes and reports
- Significant custom code used in an off-the-shelf application
- Processes involving major user change management

By conducting a risk analysis way before the risky activity is undertaken, it is possible to come up with practical, mitigating factors to address them.

Take the example of migration from a legacy marketing system to a new marketing system. First, one of the risks identified was the quality and reliability of the customer data. As such, several actions were taken:

- Verify the accuracy of a sample of the data. From here it was determined that customer profile, address and contact numbers were dirty;

- Conduct a customer cleansing campaign where these details were verified via email and calls from agents trained appropriately
- Final cleansed data loaded, in order to minimize the risk of error, a sample slice of the data was also loaded into the new marketing system for testing and verification, not only of the loading process, but also of the subsequent marketing process triggered by this data

This actually minimized the number of errors in the data, which in turn minimized errors in the process due to wrong triggers, resulting in a much shorter post-go-live cleanup process and better customer image.

7.8 Asset Management

Assets assigned to a project are the responsibility of the PM until formal turnover to O&M. This means that servers, environments (which are not being used in production), switches, laptops and other devices are her responsibility. Not only is the PM accountable for the physical asset, but also for all intangibles such as installations, configuration items and the like, within these assets.

This has special relevance in the release management procedures because assets that are under a project (unless shared with O&M), are the full responsibility of the project team. In fact, as explained in the Chap. 6 under cut-over procedures, any environment will be the responsibility of the project team until going live, and will only go-live once accepted by O&M.

Why should O&M have a role on the go-live? This is to ensure that the project team has made enough effort to convey and document what has been done for the project in terms of the configurations, environments, etc. As one can imagine, the project team is in a hurry to finish and turnover the project, as any delays means additional cost or breach of the original planned timelines, however, as it is the O&M team that will eventually *support* the whole application and infrastructure, they must be able to understand what has been done, and this necessarily needs to be done before going live, even if there is a warranty period in which the vendor is still addressing project-related issues.

The other reason why O&M must have a say is to ensure that all work done by the project team conforms to IT standards and policies. While it is the job of the customer PM to ensure this is so, in reality, it is impossible for the PM to be knowledgeable of all technical details, because her knowledge is also limited. However, as the project will be turned-over to O&M, it is in fact a must that the O&M team understands the details of the application and infrastructure so that they can support it in the future. Either they would have the knowledge for the technology being used, or they should be required to acquire that knowledge before the turnover, in the form of trainings, handholding, and other transition activities.

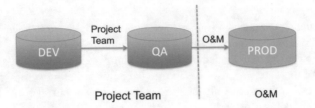

Fig. 7.7 Project team in charge of DEV, QA, while O&M in charge of PROD setup

The responsibility over an asset becomes more complicated when the asset and/or environment is shared. In this case, the policy "Operations rules" applies, which means that overall responsibility will fall under O&M because as the system is in production (or under O&M's responsibility), any changes, releases should not impair production, and thus, approval from O&M is needed for any release. How this is actually done depends on the situation. When it comes to applications and their environment, three possible scenarios exist:

Scenario 1: O&M not conducting any changes in DEV, QA environments

This may be because there are very few requests and releases being undertaken for the application, or it may be by imposition. The latter is when a moratorium on changes is asked for by IT in order to undertake this major project. This of course may not always be acceptable or possible, and must be consulted with the different user departments affected. It simplifies cut-over, but if used too often for major systems, it will irritate the users. This is however the most risk-free scenario. Figure 7.7 illustrates which team is responsible for what environment.

As the project team shall be managing directly the DEV and QA environments, it is wise for O&M to conduct a backup of both before the responsibility is handed over to the project team. In this way, full restoration of the previous configurations and data can easily be done in case something goes wrong.

Scenario 2: project team is given a separate DEV, QA environment

This solves the problem of changes being made by two separate teams which may have conflicts between them. Of course, there will be no conflicts initially, but once both changes are tested on the same QA server, that is the moment the conflicts will become apparent. This initial scenario wherein both are using separate environments is represented by the diagram shown in Fig. 7.8.

However, at some point the configurations and changes made by the project team must be tested all together along with those made by O&M as shown in Fig. 7.9.

The dotted line arrow from the Project DEV to the O&M Dev shows how the new project releases must be reproduced into the O&M DEV. These configuration changes must often times be done manually (would depend on the ability of the application to support releases), so there is a risk of course that changes not be reflected completely or correctly. The changes would be reproduced by the Project

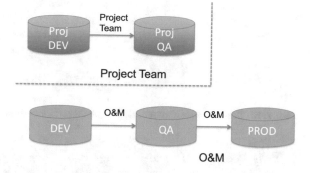

Fig. 7.8 Scenario with DEV, QA environments separate from O&M's

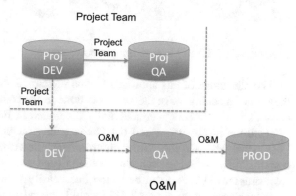

Fig. 7.9 Copying of releases from Project DEV into Operations' DEV

Team into the O&M DEV, and subsequent releases into QA and PROD will be done by the O&M team. Take note however that exhaustive regression testing needs to be done again both by the Project Team and O&M in the O&M QA, to ensure that no conflicts have occurred between the two teams' changes. Conflicts will need to be resolved by analyzing one by one their interdependencies, rolling them back, and retesting. Sometimes, this alone can be a major effort if changes were done on common functions or submodules.

An example of scenario 2 which we undertook is when we reconfigured the warehouse module of the existing ERP. Even while changes were being made in this module as part of operations (there were outstanding changes that could not be stopped) changes also were needed due to the warehouse module's major reconfiguration. To do this, a separate DEV and QA environment for the project were created and the project's development, testing and training proceeded independently to that of the releases and environment used by O&M. Once all the changes were accepted in the Project QA, these now had to be redeployed in the O&M DEV, by reproducing these changes manually (i.e., reconstructing each configuration change, one by one), then releasing them into the O&M QA and retesting all these changes again, as

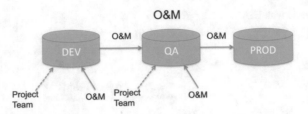

Fig. 7.10 Scenario with common DEV, QA shared by both project and O&M

well as doing a complete regression testing so as to guarantee that the changes
had no untoward impact to other CIs.

Scenario 3: DEV, QA environments are shared

The advantage of this approach versus scenario 2 is that conflicts are detected as
they arise, meaning, once the testing is done in the common QA and maybe even as
early as in DEV. This is conceptually illustrated in Fig. 7.10.

Both the project team and the O&M team conduct their changes directly into
DEV, and test on the same environment, however, all releases are O&M's
responsibility. Releases can thus be analyzed first for possible conflicts before
releasing into QA, and can be rolled back easily before the releases accumulate.

Which scenario to choose? This would depend to a large degree on the number
of releases being undertaken by O&M, the feasibility of calling for a freeze, as well
as an analysis of which scenario will ultimately be easier to manage.

For pure infrastructure projects, the approach may be different if the infra project
does not have the possibility of testing in DEV, QA environments. Attaching
infrastructure directly to the current infra usually has an effect, as it is not easy to
directly separate interdependencies. In such cases, what is usually recommended is
to test in some separate environments:

- Laboratory environment—a contained, isolated environment which is used
  primarily for testing
- Pilot implementation—a selected group of users to use the infrastructure

Lab environment and pilot implementation are not always possible, as there is
infrastructure which to really fully test, must be configured to run directly into
production. Sometimes as well, to setup a test environment is so much work that it
is not practical to do so.

Take as an example, a new firewall that is to be deployed. Even though the
defined policies may have been tested thoroughly in a contained environment,
deployment to production, when exposed to the live internet connection and

actual users, expose it to conditions which may not have been considered at all in the lab environment, and so policies and CIs would normally have to be tweaked once in production to fine-tune and attain the desired performance. Examples of this are policies which inadvertently created a loophole for traffic to pass through when it should have been blocked, (for example) due to authentication policy issues that were not apparent in the lab environment.

7.9 Issue Management

Project issues and related incidences are first and foremost managed using the issue registry as defined above. Issues may in fact be varied in nature, but all should be registered and handled by the respective PMs. Typical issue types include:

- **Infrastructure-related**: insufficient capacity, incorrect CI, performance issues
- **Configuration related**: incorrect configuration
- **Noncompliance to scope**: did not comply to blueprint or other detailed specifications
- **Test failures**
- **Availability of users**: no testers, no trainers, no sign-offs, delayed sign-offs, difficult users
- **Availability of training infrastructure**: no training rooms, PCs not properly configured
- **License-related**: license expired, no QA license

It is important to flag the issue and identify the person responsible for addressing it. This list will be reviewed as part of the regular project monitoring and control activities.

An important aspect to take into account for system application and infrastructure-related incidences (a subset of all issues), is that their resolution, root cause and any work-around applied need necessarily to be documented as part of the knowledge-base, this can follow the same document standard used for O&M's Knowledge Base (see Sect. 4.5). It is important to document these not only for the project team, but that these are turned-over to the O&M team as well.

7.10 Release Management

Release management for projects is much simpler than for operations as changes are not yet in production until the moment of go-live. As such, they should follow the release management procedures as defined in the earlier section (Asset Management). Once the project goes live or if the project is sharing some environment with O&M, then the procedures for release management used by O&M are then to be followed. Remember that the general rule is only 1 unit is responsible; there cannot be two responsible for releases. As such, O&M is always responsible for environments that are shared and has the last say in authorizing any releases.

Release requests are preferably handled through the Service Desk system and would follow the normal escalation procedures defined in it by O&M, and either direct access to the Service Desk is given to the vendor, or the client's PM raises the request on their behalf. Interdependencies between releases should also be taken into account when requesting for the release, such that any sequence that needs to be followed is to be indicated. All releases should also have a rollback procedure, as explained under O&M release management (see Sect. 4.4).

Releases that cause errors or incidences should be flagged and if needed, rolled-back, and they should trigger the issue management procedure including the documentation of solutions in the Knowledge Base, as explained earlier.

7.11   Infrastructure Capacity Management

Infrastructure needed by the project should also be defined during the proposal stage, so that the customer is made aware of the needed infrastructure, can provision for it, or start a purchase in case the hardware and other infrastructure is not available. Provisioning of infrastructure can be made using the regular request management process in O&M, which will undergo all the necessary approvals. It is of course important that even upon tendering, the vendor indicate how many environments are needed, as well as the particular requirements for each. Typically these would be DEV, QA, PROD, but additional TRAINING environments may be needed if development and testing is to continue in parallel with training. Other particular requirements should also be made clear.

Specifications for each environment given by the vendor is a starting point, however, as we all may very well know, sizing infrastructure is an art, not a science and is never exact. Most sizing tools ask for parameters which are hard to obtain, assumptions need to be made, some of which are wild guesses at best. As such, it is really upon going live that capacity aspects can be tweaked. In the past, since all servers were physical, this was difficult. Either you procured hardware with considerable buffers, or you would run the risk of falling short which would mean a delay in having to procure the additional hardware. Nowadays, with the prevalence of virtualization and cloud computing this endeavor has become much easier, as virtualization allows you to allocate resources on the fly, with little or no downtime. It thus becomes crucial to monitor hardware resources upon going live and tweak these accordingly till the desired performance is attained.

It is important that the technical specifications and architecture of the infrastructure be defined and agreed upon shortly after the project kick-off. This may seem difficult, but is necessary in order to avoid bigger problems later on. The architecture has to conform to several aspects of the client:

- Must conform to its standards in terms of hardware and software used
- Security compliance
- Sufficient capacity

It normally takes several sessions and discussions together before agreement of the final architecture is reached. This is a good exercise, because pros, cons are discussed, and the architecture dissected and analyzed for possible risks and noncompliance.

One particular painful experience which we lived was in a data mining project which had several software components running at the same time. In this case the vendor assumed that the ETL server could reside in the same machine as the data mining server and went live without previously verifying the architecture. The result was that the performance of the different applications was very slow, so that the whole architecture had to be redesigned, and all the different software components reinstalled, reconfigured, and the applications retested resulting in a 20 % delay in the project. All this could have been prevented by first verifying and getting a sign-off on the proposed architecture.

7.12 Request Management for Projects

Requests may be of many different types and forms. Generally speaking, there are two types of requests:

- Those affecting project resources only; and
- Those affecting O&M (production mainly)

Both are reflected into the request registry as explained earlier. The first type are handled and resolved by the two PMs, they are basically related to scope management as explained in the earlier section and thus follow the change request procedure as explained under the scope management section. The second involves O&M, and as such, it is best handled by initiating the request in the normal way any operations stakeholder does, usually through the service desk. Common types of such requests are:

- Request for release (to QA/PROD)
- Request for additional infrastructure
- Request for change (to be handled by O&M)
- Request for backup/restore
- Request for development. This is in case any development needs to be undertaken by O&M, a typical example of this would be for interfaces, in which development needs to be undertaken at the system being interfaced to, by the project
- Request for QA refresh. This is to refresh QA with updated data, which is usually a copy from production

The project team is seen by O&M as just another user, and its requests are thus handled in the same manner as all other requests, except that their requests need to be necessarily endorsed and approved by the customer PM, as well as approved by the authority defined to approve such project requests (either the Portfolio Manager or the CIO, depending on the type of request). Approval levels should be clearly delineated by the policy, as well as the priority levels as assigned jointly by the PM and the Head of Operations.

If the project requests are to be routed via the existing O&M Service Desk, then it should be clear that this is the method, and not just a verbal request.

7.13   Code Development Guidelines

Code development guidelines encompass the necessary aspects that need to be followed by the project code developers. These may include:

- Naming conventions for programs, objects, tables, variables, etc. Should also indicate common best practices, such as not hard-coding values into programs, using relative (vs. absolute paths), and others.
- Documentation format and details required. As it is very difficult for a person not involved directly in the development of the program, all code should come accompanied with a functional description of what the program does. Also, to make it easier, each program should contain a header with the mandatory information describing the program.
- Network Domain name conventions. Should also specify the avoidance of using IP addresses, as these change over time.
- Error and exception handling.
- Message types and convention.
- Tables and objects. Description of mandatory fields, as well as necessary descriptions for each.
- Indexing. When and how to create indexes.
- Performance standards. Includes treatment and usage of dead code, subroutines, nesting, conditions, CASE statements, SELECT statements, and all other code types which structure may have a significant impact on program performance.
- Use of standard interfaces. This should be used in interfacing the application.
- Code security. In order to avoid commonly known break-in mechanisms such as buffer overflow, SQL injection and the likes.

Nowadays, there are tools which check the validity of the code based on the defined standards, so that it scans through the code and detects noncompliance. It is highly recommended to use these tools as they save considerable effort in checking, and can be given to the project team for them to self-check.

7.14   Test Guidelines

Testing guidelines should specify the type of tests to be undertaken and by which party. Testing has been described already in Sect. 5.5 and Sect. 7.8 previously. As the types of testing are very much project-dependent, specific test guidelines need to be agreed during the project start. Types of testing required may include:

- **Unit testing**—mandatory, conducted by vendor.
- **Integration testing**—mandatory, conducted by vendor.
- **Regression testing**—needed only if change is undertaken on an application currently in production, or if a change is to be performed on an already accepted application (retest). Some amount of testing is to be undertaken by the vendor and O&M, more exhaustive testing by the end users. If the change is only a technical upgrade or patch, testing may be conducted solely by O&M.
- **User Acceptance Test**—mandatory, only after the above have been undertaken.
- **Stress testing**—optional, depending on the criticality of the application and feasibility for conducting stress testing.

Details on testing techniques can be found in Sect. 5.5.

7.15   Training Guidelines

Training is many times the make or break for the success of a project, as the project's success depends to a large extent on the acceptance by the users. Training however, is commonly neglected, rushed or is an afterthought of the PMs. It is commonly taken for granted.

As such, training guidelines should be as explicit and detailed as possible. Different trainings should be undertaken for different stakeholders:

- **End user training**. Main users of the system should be taught how to use the system. This means that manuals need to detail up to the transaction level, complete with screenshots and step-by-step guide on how to transact. User reference manuals also complement these, which is a manual of all commonly used functions and transactions in the application. It is however not enough to teach how to transact; the users must also understand why the process has been designed that way, so that an overview of the process needs to be explained to them. Different end users will use different transactions, so trainings must be specific for each particular user type.
- **System Administrators' training**. Knowledge transfer for the benefit of the O&M TM team. It should enable them to maintain, support, and in some cases reconfigure the applications and infrastructure in the future. It should cover architecture design, network specifications, databases, hardware, configuration, maintenance and upkeep procedures, and how to maintain the systems' roles

and permissions. These are the administrators of the system that will subsequently keep the systems running.

- **Operators' training**—focused toward the day-to-day operations that will need to be conducted by ITOM. They are normally the batch processes used in producing the necessary outputs.
- **Application Management training**—for the benefit of O&M's Application Management team, will cover the overall architecture of the solution, the processes implemented and the rationale for them, the current configuration setup, as well as how to maintain (change) the configurations when future changes are undertaken on the system.
- **Developers' training**—is a discussion on the code utilized for the project. If this is a technology new to the developers then, depending on the contract, should also include the necessary training on the technology. If not part of the contract scope, then the O&M developers shall have to undergo through a separate external training before the turnover trainings.
- **Overview trainings**—this may be sessions organized for the benefit of those O&M personnel and IT management not directly involved in the project nor in the turnover but which need to be informed on the general aspects of the project. It shall be a condensed version of the above mentioned trainings.
- **Train the trainers session**—this will not only consist of the training material for the final end users, it is also more elaborate in explaining the processes, and should also contain notes, guides and FAQs that will be used by the trainers in replicating the training. From experience, the more effective trainings are those that "tell a story" and not just give rote pointers on how to do things because people remember better when it follows a story line. This means normally following a process from beginning to end, even if they are not the user involved in all these steps. As an example, it is easier for a maintenance engineer to understand and follow what he has to do when the whole maintenance process is explained (From planning, scheduling, release of the maintenance orders, fulfillment, completion of the maintenance order details, closing, and analysis of reports), rather than just telling the maintenance engineer the different fields he has to fill, the click buttons he has to press, in a mechanical way.

All the trainings that are to be lined-up as part of the project need to be identified in a training plan. This training plan explains the training strategy and includes such details as:

- Type of training
- Recipients of the training
- Estimate on the number of trainees
- Person to conduct the training
- Approach taken for the training (Train the trainers, training of all personnel)
- List of associated material needed for the training

- Point in time the training will be imparted (before going live, during the support phase, etc.)

Reverse knowledge transfers (reverse KT) are also a very effective way to both train trainers, as well as verify whether they understood. This method consists of teaching the future trainer on what he has to do, and thereafter asking her to in return teach the trainer that taught her.

7.16   Backup and Recovery Guidelines

Should state when backups are to be conducted, by whom, and the type of backups (see Sect. 6.1) to be utilized. The actual execution of the backup may be performed by the O&M team; however, the project team must trigger the request. A typical point in time when a backup must be conducted includes:

- Upon finalization of the s/w installation
- Regularly for the DEV and QA servers (full and incremental backups as determined by the schedule)
- In case DEV and QA are also being used by O&M, right before any changes are started by the project team
- Upon finalization of the unit testing (DEV, QA)
- Before the release of the changes into production (PROD)
- Before applying any major patch
- Upon acceptance of the patch

Recovery can be initiated in case of major failures which can neither be fixed or take too long to revert without initiating a recovery procedure. If it is in an environment also handled by O&M, PM must necessarily seek O&M's approval.

7.17   Pre-go-Live Guidelines

These will encompass many of the points discussed in Chap. 6, which are needed as part of the cut-over plan. Pre-go-live guidelines will normally include the following:

- Approved cut-over plan
- Approved data migration plan
- Successful data migration sign-off—in case it must be executed before go-live.
- UAT completed and accepted
- List of manuals and other materials to be used by the users and O&M in support
- Preparation and briefing for the 1st and 2nd level support teams
- FAQ for the Service Desk personnel
- Full backup

- Pre- and post-go-live checklist. This is a checklist as prepared by Technical Management that indicates the condition of a resource, application or function before and after the release. It is used to verify that the release was successful, by comparing it to the prerelease condition, which should either match, or if not, have an acceptable reason for the discrepancy. It is the first check after completing the releases to make sure that these were successful
- Password change test—it is crucial that O&M's Technical Management group be handed over the new password. As such, they should test that it can be changed without problem, even before going live
- Operations Manual
- Acceptance by O&M of Knowledge Base from project team
- Advisories to users. Indicating any downtime, as well as informing them of the new releases
- Go/No-go signed decision by the CIO.

7.18 Post-implementation Support Policy

As explained as well in the cut-over Chap. 6, post-implementation support should be agreed-upon by both parties at the start of the project. Warranty for any hardware shall be processed by the project vendor (if procured through them) if any incidence occurs during the project.

Regardless of who actually conducts the first level post-implementation support, O&M or the vendor, any defects and incidences detected during the contracted period of post-implementation support is the responsibility of the vendor. That means that even though 1st level support was, for example, already transferred to O&M, if they are unable to resolve the issue, it now escalates to the vendor for resolution. The policy should be clear in that all tickets still OPEN at the end of the post-implementation support phase shall still be resolved by the vendor, even if after the contracted period.

As a practical example, if post-implementation support was 3 months in accordance with the contract, but on day 3 months—1 day, there were still 8 incidence tickets open with the vendor, then these shall have to be resolved by the vendor even after the 3 month period elapses. If this were not the case, then all the vendor needs to do is just sit it out and wait for his contractual period to lapse, without having invested any effort in their resolution.

Other aspects the policy should cover are:

- Required minimum handover sessions to the O&M team for the support. O&M team must sign-off its acceptance.
- Turn-over of all manuals and project documentation to O&M
- Turn-over of all Knowledge Base documentation to O&M
- FAQ session and materials to Service Desk operators so as to maximize first call resolution

- Uploading of all relevant documentation to the User support portal
- Formal handover and sign-off of first level support to O&M with the sign-off as well from the CIO.

7.19   Service Desk Usage Policy

Indicates the manner in which the project team shall be allowed access to the service desk, and how its requests will be escalated. Before the go-live, the project team shall be given access to the service desk for it to file any relevant project requests, just as any user would. After the go-live however, the service desk must be setup to process incidences and requests in accordance with the warranty support agreed upon, concretely, who will be in charge of first level and second level support as explained above.

7.20   Security Guidelines

Generally follows the security guidelines used by O&M and that for end users. Additionally, project security guidelines may explain the policy needed for granting remote access to systems. Generally speaking, no PROD access is to be given to project personnel and remote access to DEV and QA should have permissions limited to those modules or transactions strictly being developed. No Super user rights should be given to project personnel unless these environments are their sole responsibility, which should nevertheless be limited to DEV and QA only.

Further Reading

Harmer, G., 2014. *Governance of Enterprise IT based on COBIT 5: A management guide.* Ely (United Kingdom): IT Governance Publishing.

ISO, 2011. *IOS/IEC 20000-1 International Standard.* Switzerland: ISO/IEC.

ISO/IEC, 2015. *ISO/IEC 38500:2015,* Switzerland: ISO/IEC.

Kunas, M., 2012. *Implementing Service Quality based on ISO/IEC 20000.* 3rd ed. IT Governance Publishing.

Weill, P., Ross, J. 2013. *Executive's Guide to IT Governance: Improving Systems Processes with Service Management, COBIT, and ITIL.* Wiley.

Weill, P., Ross, J. R., 2004. *IT Governance: How Top Performers Manage IT Decision Rights for Superior Results.* 1st ed. Harvard Business Review Press.

Selig, G., 2008. *Implementing IT Governance: A Practical Guide to Global Best Practices in IT Management.* 1st ed. Van Haren Publishing

Agile-Scrum Project Management

8

8.1 Introduction and Basic Concepts

Agile-scrum methodologies have become very fashionable of late. Since most of us are familiar with the waterfall methodology, and most of this book's project management methodology is based on a waterfall approach, let me contrast the two project management methodologies for easy understanding, this is shown in Table 8.1.

One of the original attractions of SCRUM methodologies was in focusing on the output: delivering the application, rather than in intermediary tasks devoted to the analysis and documentation, it also gives a lot of importance to teamwork and informal organization in producing these outputs. More of this will be explained in the next sections.

8.2 Basic Components

Teams are formed based on concrete objectives that need to be attained, and each team is given a very general set of objectives. For example, an objective can be something as high-level as:

- Developing a fitness application
- Adding user feedback mechanisms to a social media application
- Improving interactivity in an adventure game.

The idea is not to start the project with a predefined idea and scope of what is to be done, but to iteratively develop this with the team. In order to do that, the end user devotes a lot of time in the project in validating and prioritizing outputs. As the eventual user of the system, his role is called "Product Owner." On the other hand, a "Scrum master" is basically the team member responsible for ensuring that the whole team is working well together and the agile-scrum methodology is being

© Springer International Publishing Switzerland 2016
F. Castillo, *Managing Information Technology*,
DOI 10.1007/978-3-319-38891-5_8

Table 8.1 Waterfall versus agile-scrum methodologies

Waterfall methodology	Agile-scrum
Has very distinct analysis and design, build, test phases	These phases exist, but not in sequential order as they are run iteratively within short, repetitive periods called sprints
Requires detailed documentation of design to be done	Requires minimal documentation, in extreme cases, the code is the documentation
End-users are consulted for their requirements during the analysis phase	End-user representatives are an integral part of the project and are involved during the whole duration of the project and regularly consulted
After the design is signed-off by the users, the build phase is conducted which will adhere to the signed-off specifications	Build is an inherent and iterative process, users are presented with the result, from which they critique and modifications or new features are added
Scope is clearly defined at the beginning of the project	Scope is iteratively decided upon as the project progresses
Project teams can be large, composed of many different skillsets of people	Project teams are composed of 6–12 people maximum
Heterogeneous team with distinct, specialized skills per team member	Homogeneous team, tasks can be accomplished by any team member

followed, and should preferably be certified so as to guarantee correct implementation of Scrum.

Figure 8.1 illustrates what a typical agile-scrum team would look like.

In this figure, the development team is usually composed of a small number between 4, but not more than 10 people who have cross-functional roles, meaning, they can all do the same functions and are not specialized. Some of the other characteristics of the development team are:

- **Developer**. Each team member is called a developer. This is basically due to the origins of the methodology, which was for custom development projects.
- **Self-organized**. Each team member can pick up a task for him to undertake, he need not wait for the task to be assigned to him. Furthermore, each task will require a complete iteration of design-development-testing-fixing, so that it is up

Fig. 8.1 Typical agile-scrum team

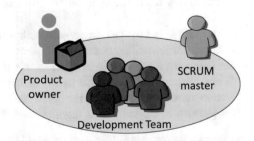

to her to organize these steps in order for her to complete the tasks she has in progress.

- **Own the sprint backlog**. As will be explained later, an iteration for developing tasks is called a sprint, and those tasks that have not been completed are essentially part of the backlog. Now aligned to the spirit of self-organization, this backlog is actually a common backlog for the whole team and each developer in facts "owns" it, so that each and every party has the responsibility for reducing the backlog to attain the desired, common objective.

On the other hand, the Product Owner has the following roles:

- **Owns the Product Backlog**. Similar to the developers, he also owns the product backlog and has a stake in the project, but he is in charge of prioritizing the backlog from most to least important.
- **Represents the users**. He is the main representative, and as such, is aware of what the users actually need, so that he prioritizes the backlog user stories (as will be explained later) and tasks that evolve in trying to meet the overall objective. He must have the vision of what the team is trying to build.
- **Communication**. He should be able to communicate and transmit to the team effectively the objectives of the project, and must be actively engaged with the project team. At the same time, he is also the key person for communicating to stakeholders outside the project team.

As not all products are deployed for internal consumption, in some cases, end users may actually be the general populace or consumers accessing the application. In such cases, the Product Owner may be someone from sales, marketing, or other department that has knowledge of what the users may be looking for or may want.

The Scrum master's role includes:

- Acting as facilitator to the team
- Promoting agile-scrum best practices and ensuring these are being followed
- Working with the team in removing impediments that may surface as part of the project
- Looking at ways to maximize the team's productivity.

Again, one of the basic precepts of agile-scrum methodology is emphasis on the interactions between individuals where each individual has quite a free hand in undertaking his specific tasks for as long the output is delivered. This is in contrast with the traditional Project Management approach in which a Project Manager supervises, and assigns tasks, and also has a very rigid, predefined hierarchy. In other words, there is more emphasis on the individuals' skill sets and their interactions in producing the work versus processes and tools to attain the work.

According to the Agile Manifesto (Highsmith 2001):

1. Our highest priority is to satisfy the customer through early and continuous delivery of valuable software.
2. Welcome changing requirements, even late in development. Agile processes harness change for the customer's competitive advantage.
3. Deliver working software frequently, from a couple of weeks to a couple of months, with a preference to the shorter timescale.
4. Business people and developers must work together daily throughout the project.
5. Build projects around motivated individuals. Give them the environment and support they need, and trust them to get the job done.
6. The most efficient and effective method of conveying information to and within a development team is face-to-face conversation.
7. Working software is the primary measure of progress.
8. Agile processes promote sustainable development. The sponsors, developers, and users should be able to maintain a constant pace indefinitely.
9. Continuous attention to technical excellence and good design enhances agility.
10. Simplicity–the art of maximizing the amount of work not done–is essential.
11. The best architectures, requirements, and designs emerge from self-organizing teams.
12. At regular intervals, the team reflects on how to become more effective, then tunes and adjusts its behavior accordingly.

As you can see, if one is used to the traditional way of managing projects, Agile is a radically different way of thinking and executing, and requires a different set of skills and principles which need to be applied.

The question now is if so much power is given to the developers, how do we now ensure that the project actually progresses, which brings us to the topic of:

- Product backlog
- Sprints
- Monitoring: Burn-down chart.

8.2.1 Product Backlog

First, when a product is to be developed a list of features or "user stories" are lined-up for development. These user stories are jointly developed by the SCRUM team, and are listed on a board. They are high-level statements of what the product should contain and can be contributed by any of the team members. These user stories are now in a pool and need to be prioritized for development by the project team.

It is the product owner that prioritizes the user stories based on his understanding of what users would like, and therefore applies a forced ranking from most to least

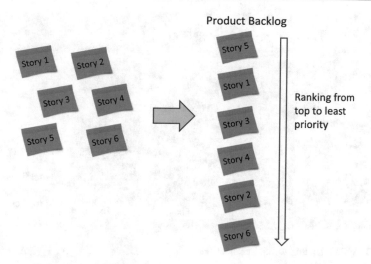

Fig. 8.2 Product backlog ranking

important stories on the product backlog, which conceptually, may be represented as shown in Fig. 8.2.

From the product backlog, the top stories will then be picked for development in the next sprint, as will be explained in the Sect. 8.2.2.

8.2.2 Sprints

Sprints are a basic component of Agile methodologies, and refers to a short period of time (usually 1–2 weeks, but sometimes can be as long as 1 month) in which a whole project timeline is sliced into. A sprint is a self-contained time capsule which is repeated cyclically until the project is completed. This is shown in Fig. 8.3.

It is also important to note that at the end of each Sprint there is a deliverable of the product which is basically in "Shippable" form. This means that although not all features have been incorporated into the product yet, it has enough for it to be released as a product, if the Product Owner would decide so. This is important, as not only is the product successively and iteratively designed, but at the end of each sprint or iteration, the product must be in working condition, even if limited in features (James 2016).

Take the example shown in Fig. 8.4 for a 2 week sprint.

It shows some of the major activities done within the sprint that are explained below:

- **Planning**. The first activity here is for the team to select the top backlog items (user stories) which are to be developed in the current sprint. These will now appear in the Sprint backlog, meaning, that these are the stories which need to be

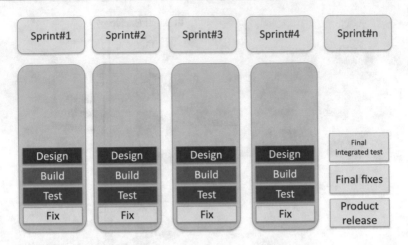

Fig. 8.3 Sprints leading to final product release

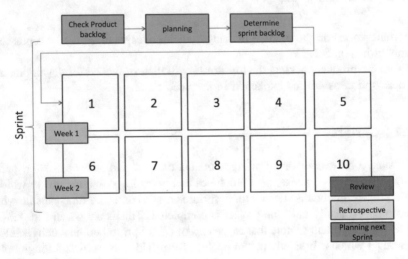

Fig. 8.4 Sample 2 week sprint

finished at the end of the current sprint cycle. These stories are then further subdivided into tasks. It is then ensured that the tasks committed for the Sprint are clear, and that they are attainable given the time duration. Each task's effort is also estimated by the team, either in man-days or in story points, which represent the relative complexity of the task.

- **Development**. This is when the Sprint has actually started formal execution work. During this period, each team member picks up specific tasks from the sprint backlog and moves them to the "on-going" or "Work-in-Progress" status. This can be done on a board which displays the status of each task (the so-called SCRUM board) as shown in Fig. 8.5.

Sprint backlog

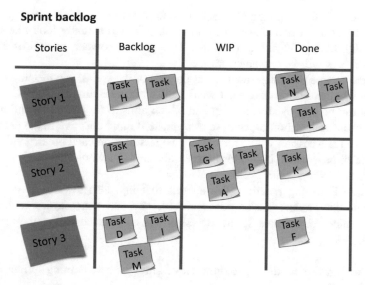

Fig. 8.5 Sprint backlog on a SCRUM board

Development in turn, can be further subdivided into the typical activities needed in order to develop (typically code):

- Design
- Programming
- Testing
- Fixing.

The developer would then move the task to "Done" once the whole development cycle for the task has been finished (final test).

Each task picked up by the developer passes through this design-program-test-fix process for the task until completed and the feature added to the product.

- **Daily Scrum**—at the start of the day and every day, a daily scrum session takes place in which each team member reports to the other team members what she has done the previous day in terms of work, and what she will do today. It is a short meeting (around 15 min), usually stand-up, which aims at informing everyone on the progress of the tasks.
- **Review meeting**. This is a meeting in which the team presents to the product owner and any other stakeholders interested in the product, usually toward the end of the sprint, the potentially shippable product. The product owner discusses which items are done, and which did not pass the acceptance criteria. It is also an opportunity by the stakeholders to give feedback to the team on features or changes they would actually want in the product. This is key, as stakeholders

tend to be better at giving feedback once they have a working prototype, rather than trying to conceive how the end-product would actually look like without actually having anything tangible. The product owner can also calculate velocity, as will be explained later.

- **Retrospective meeting**—happens at the end of the sprint, is a meeting between team members to discuss what went well with their current process, and also what can be improved. It is a session which aims to further refine and improve the whole agile-scrum process, so as to make it more effective in the next Sprint runs and is a session where members give feedback to each other. Typically, as the team progresses, it develops more cohesion and would tend to improve for each succeeding sprint cycle.
- **Release Planning meeting**. During this meeting, also toward the end of the Sprint, the product backlog is revisited, and the next stories reviewed in preparation for the next sprint. Based on the experience so far, the team may then:

  - Analyze the backlog to see how they fit into the next coming sprints, analyze dependencies.
  - Break some of the larger stories into smaller, more tractable ones.
  - Review the prioritization to see if it is still adequate, and update it.

8.3 Monitoring: Burn-Down Chart

The basic project monitoring tool used in agile-scrum is the burn-down chart, which in comparison with Waterfall approaches, is very easy to build, update and interpret.

First, it is built at the start of each sprint, and used for the current sprint till its very end; a sample is shown in Fig. 8.6.

The number of workdays is plotted on the x-axis, while the y-axis displays the measure of effort for all tasks that are to be developed within the sprint. It may be defined in terms of:

- Man-days
- Story Points—which are just an abstract amount time and effort needed to develop the task, and which gives a relative weight of the task versus others. This is usually preferred by experienced scrum masters due to the difficulty for people in assigning man-days realistically.

Ideally then, if the whole sprint backlog is to be finished at the end of the sprint with an equal distribution of effort for each day, it is then represented by a straight line (blue, continuous line in Fig. 8.6). During each daily scrum meeting, the sprint backlog is updated, and the burn-down chart is updated with all those "done" tasks.

Fig. 8.6 Sample burn-down chart

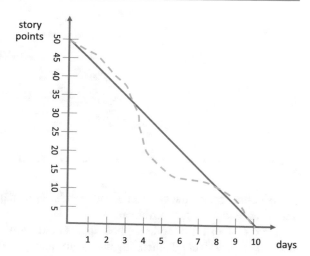

Say for example if on day 1, two tasks worth 1 and 2 story points are finished, then on day 1, the y-axis (story points) shall show 47 (burned down from 50 by 3 points).

This is done every day, and the plot updates and shows whether the tasks are on track, ahead, or delayed. In Fig. 8.6, we can see that the project was delayed from days 1–3, but caught-up and was ahead of schedule from days 4–8, after which it more or less followed the theoretical straight line.

Velocity can also be calculated at any given time, which gives you the burn-down per day that the project team is achieving. If evaluated at day 6, for example, the velocity would be 37 points/6 days = 6.17 points/day. The 37 points calculated by subtracting the 13 points at day 6 from 50. This velocity is actually faster than the initial estimate of 5 points/day.

8.4 Scope-Cost-Quality-Time Dimensions

First, let us examine the relationship between scope, quality, time, and cost in a waterfall approach. In such turn-key projects the scope is fixed and defined at the beginning of the project, and so is the quality by means of standards and other qualifying factors for the deliverables. Time and cost are defined by the contract, but it is the PM's role to manage these so that the project finishes on-time and within the contracted cost. He is to manage and minimize delays, project creep (increase in scope), and check if the deliverables are of expected quality, while keeping a control of the costs (usually due to the amount of resources committed to the project). This relationship may be represented by a triangle as shown in Fig. 8.7.

Resources assigned to the project are variable, if the project is of fixed cost, then cost overruns are to be absorbed by the contractor, if not, then these are picked-up by the client. The challenge in most waterfall-type projects is to be able to define the scope as detailed as possible in the beginning to avoid misinterpretation, as well

Fig. 8.7 Scope and the 3 dimensions for a turnkey waterfall project

as to define good quality criteria and standards (usually the task of the portfolio manager, under project governance).

On the other hand, agile methodologies start with no clear definition of scope, and it is successively defined, together with quality. What is fixed, however, is the number of resources assigned to the project (cost) and the time for the project to finish. This is represented as shown by Fig. 8.8.

Thus, depending on the ability and cohesion of the project team, the scope and quality may change accordingly as shown in Fig. 8.9.

This is not a problem because Agile project management is typically applied in projects in which it is fine to release a partial product at the end of the project, and can be compensated by a successive version of the product with more complete features, less bugs. This brings us to the question on the applicability of agile-scrum versus waterfall project management approaches.

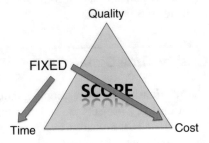

Fig. 8.8 Scope and the 3 dimensions for an agile-scrum project

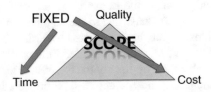

Fig. 8.9 Scope and quality varying in an agile-scrum project

Some of the basic criteria then for choosing agile would then be:

- **Project scope is allowed to be ill-defined**. This is of course applicable only for certain projects which can permit such an output. Typically, large and complex software development projects are very hard to define entirely at the start of the project, so these are good candidates. Other areas are those in which bugs and/or partial releases are acceptable to the end users. Examples of this are general consumer-market apps. Users have gotten used to the fact that the app will come with some bugs, and the fixes and additional features will be available in the next releases.
- **Project scope is difficult to define**. Here the alternative is to opt for a time and materials type of contract, or use agile methodology. Agile may be applicable when the users/product owners can devote sufficient time to successively define the product, as explained in the next point.
- **Users/product owners can devote time**. As agile-scrum requires regular feedback from them, they need to devote a significant amount of time into the project, necessitating their participation on a daily basis. The product owner needs to be empowered in making decisions as well, so this is a necessary prerequisite.
- **Time is a more important factor than scope-quality**. As there is a "hard stop" in terms of release date, agile-scrum guarantees the completion of the project at a particular date, what it does not guarantee is what the scope will be at that release date. Again, depending on the project, this may or may not be acceptable.
- **Development**. Most of the steps in the sprint are more applicable to programming or software development projects in which there is more reliance on the programmer's creativity and teamwork rather than on a structured hierarchy. On the other hand, Commercial Off-The-Shelf (COTS) software that requires configuration is generally harder to undertake using this methodology, also because it requires a heterogeneous team and because it normally touches on business process (which is both discussed further in the next points).
- **Visibility**. As product is presented to the stakeholders, these must easily understand what has been developed so far. This means that the product must have very tangible, usually visible outputs; otherwise the stakeholders will find it hard to comment and give feedback. It is for this reason that apps have also been popularly developed using agile methodologies.
- **Lack of complex business process**. On the other end of the spectrum from visibility lie deep business process functions and complex mathematical functions which are hard to appreciate simply from presenting the product to the end users. Business process cannot be simply "shown," it needs to be dissected and analyzed among many different end users of different departments affected, as business process moves across departments.
- **Homogeneous team**. The development team in agile-scrum is homogeneous in terms of skills, normally they are all programmers, albeit may be of different maturity, but they are conducting the same tasks: design-programming-testing.

This is fine for a pure software development project, but in cases of COTS where the programming is merely a small portion, and the larger portion of the work requires configuration and business process and domain knowledge, then team members are required to specialize, usually by module: finance, procurement, HR, and also by technology: Java, .net, etc. It is hard for team members to act collaboratively in picking-up tasks from the scrum board as by design, they have very different skills. Their skills in the project will also be called for during very specific points during the project.

In summary, agile-scrum is another project methodology which can be used under certain circumstances which require it, but is not a take-all methodology for CIOs and probably lesser-used one unless most of the applications are being custom-developed.

References

Highsmith, J., 2001. *Agile Manifesto*. [Online] Available at: http://www.agilemanifesto.org/ [last accessed February 2016].
James, M., n.d. *Scrum Methodology*. [Online] Available at: http://scrummethodology.com/ [last accessed February 2016].

Further Reading

As Agile and particularly, agile-scrum has become so fashionable as of late, there is a wealth of books and references on the matter, below ae just some of these.
Stellman, A., Greene, J., 2014. *Learning Agile: Understanding Scrum, XP, Lean, and Kanban*. 1st ed. O'Reilly Media.
Goodpasture, J. C., 2010. *Project Management the Agile Way: Making it Work in the Enterprise*. J. Ross Publishing.
Ashmore, S., Runyan, K., 2014. *Introduction to Agile Methods*. Addison-Wesley Professional.

IT Portfolio Management

9

An IT portfolio would normally be thought of as a collection of projects which need to be managed, however, this also normally includes IT Operations. A typical overall structure is shown in Fig. 9.1.

In this diagram the overall portfolio manager may be the CIO, while the sub portfolio managers either assigned clusters handling different sets of projects by volume and complexity, by type of project (such as finance related, sales related, etc.) or by technology (software vs. hardware/infrastructure). For all purposes, these sub portfolio managers shall have the same function and roles as the overall portfolio manager save for the fact that they do not handle operations. For the remainder of this chapter, I shall therefore not make any differentiation between portfolio and sub portfolio managers, with the understanding that their roles and responsibilities are similar. The IS and II heads are in fact the (sub)portfolio managers for applications projects and infrastructure projects, respectively.

In their entirety, all of these different sub portfolios and operations require and compete for different resources, such as

- Human Resources
- Tools and applications (may be limited due to licensing restrictions)
- Hardware (Servers, network bandwidth, storage)
- Funding

Therefore, some of the main questions that need to be answered by the portfolio manager are

- How do I assign resources across the different components in an optimized manner?
- How do I prioritize?
- How do I measure the different components' performance?

© Springer International Publishing Switzerland 2016
F. Castillo, *Managing Information Technology*,
DOI 10.1007/978-3-319-38891-5_9

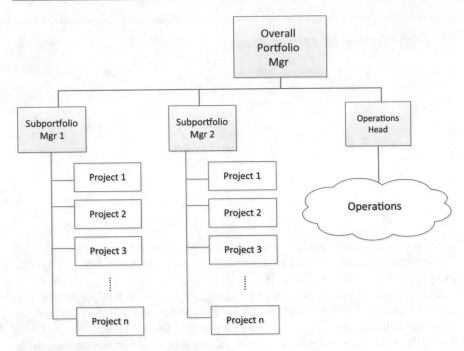

Fig. 9.1 Portfolio Manager's responsibilities

- How should performance be reported?
- How do I manage all these?

IT Portfolio management is different from IT Project Management in the sense that the latter has a distinct start and end, while a portfolio is a continuous process, even when some of its components end, as there are other components that start, and existing components evolve. Its management is therefore a continuous process, which may be represented as shown in Fig. 9.2.

The three bubbles in the middle show the continuous process of portfolio management

- **Planning and Design**: wherein the overall portfolio components are defined, and the design of each component defined in terms of scope, resources and assets assigned to them.
- **Measuring and Communicating**: wherein each portfolio component is measured against defined metrics that it has to meet, and this, together with the status is communicated to the different portfolio stakeholders.
- **Rebalancing**: wherein the priorities, resources, and assets are rebalanced across the portfolio based on the direction company strategy and tactical direction it is taking.

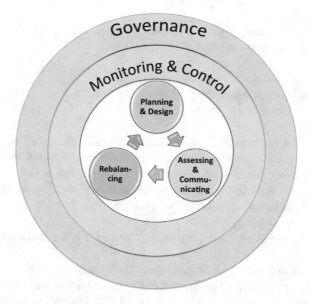

Fig. 9.2 Portfolio Management lifecycle

All of these are in turn managed in accordance with

- **Portfolio Governance**: following the policies and rules in which the portfolio must adhere to.
- **Monitoring and Control**: wherein the portfolio manager is monitoring the progress of the different components and applying control mechanisms to ensure governance and targets are adhered to.

9.1   Portfolio Planning and Design

Generally, the first step involves the creation of a portfolio(s) and identifying their components. These components would have their different Project Managers or Operations Managers identified. Among the different aspects that need to be identified for the Portfolio are

- Portfolio name and description
- Portfolio Manager
- Components: sub portfolios, projects, and Operations encompassed

- Component Name
- Component Manager (Sub portfolio manager, Project Manager, and Operations Manager attached to each component)
- Scope
- Resources allocated
- Tools and assets allocated
- Estimate Duration

Each portfolio component is then planned accordingly, mapping their dependencies (if any). This may be done using a Gantt chart, which will display the timing and interdependencies of portfolio components (Fig. 9.3)

The attributes for each portfolio component are usually embedded in the project/operations documents themselves, such as

- **Project charter**: Table of Organization, Scope of Work, estimated duration, and tools required.
- **Assets required**: which is drafted when the system architecture and their corresponding requirements are defined at the project level, will also be identified in the project or operations plan as to when they are needed in the project.
- **Assets assigned**
- **Project plan**: includes estimated start date, duration, and estimated finish. If project has started, the % completion, as well as the current SPI and CPI.
- **Issues**: as reflected in the issue registry. This gives an idea to the portfolio manager on the status of the component, and if there are delays or cost overruns, the cause for these overruns.

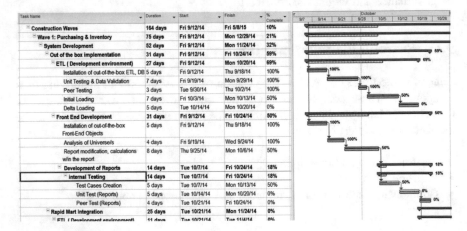

Fig. 9.3 Sample project plan with Gantt chart

- **Requests**: as reflected in the request registry. These may be valid or not, and their status will be classified by the corresponding project manager. For valid requests, these may be Change Requests (or not), and if so, may or may have a cost implication. Their escalation for approval will follow the policies as per the portfolio governance.
- **Checklist status**: the checklist as defined in Sect. 7.3, gives a list of all deliverables defined for the component. The checklist displays the status of the deliverable, whether it has been attained or not.

The portfolio design and its components will be continuously revisited as part of the monitoring and control and rebalancing operations, as will be explained later on.

9.2 Portfolio Assessment and Communicating

Portfolios need to be measured in accordance with some metric(s), to ascertain that they are doing well or not. Some metrics proposed by the Portfolio Management Professional Standard of PMI[TM] (Project Management Institute 2013) include measures like NPV, ROI, IRR, etc., which are very easily understood and measured by management as they have a clear financial impact. This may be well and good for major infrastructure projects, however, for IT projects; it is many times difficult to place a financial return for them. It is however encouraged that, if possible, such financial indicators be used as they will be better understood by higher management, in all other situations, alternative measures will have to be designed.

Traditional measures of component performance are time and cost, however, these measures alone fail to capture the significance of the portfolio component and its overall impact to the organization. Time and cost are measures that are important for the project manager, as they basically indicate how well or problematic his project is running, and many times (though not always) are an indicator of the PM's performance. At a higher level, however, these two measures just by themselves fail to convey much about the project.

Take for example a project that run on time and within the assigned budget, and yet, the project failed to deliver the intended purpose. To give a concrete example, a new payment gateway was put up to allow customers to pay conveniently online, project went well with respect to cost and time, however, because of the design of the interface to the customers, wherein the payment option (that management wanted to prioritize) was not evident to the customers, customers failed to make use of it. This may be considered a technical success, but from the point of the business, a large failure. The problem of course is that measuring this success varies from portfolio component to portfolio component in relation to its intended purpose, and many times the real benefit may be intangible or difficult to measure.

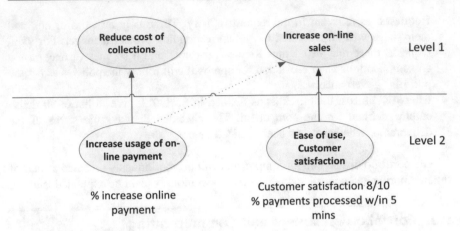

Fig. 9.4 Diagram showing interdependencies of objectives

Generally speaking, a portfolio component has to either

- Increase revenues in the long run; or
- Decrease costs

The above benefits may not be immediate, but should be the end goal, so that the indicator developed to measure the component success must be tied to the above. One way to derive that relation is to draw a relation diagram, in which the highest nodes are represented by either one of the above or both. For example, going back to our online payment example, a possible resulting diagram is that shown in Fig. 9.4.

At the topmost of the diagram (level 1), it shows two objectives to which higher management can easily relate to, that of reducing costs (of collections, in this case), and that of increasing revenue (through online sales). These can be easily measured, however, it is highly unlikely that both of these objectives, and most especially, the increase of online sales may be attributed only to the project which has gone live, as it is most likely part of a series of projects handled by other departments such as marketing, sales, logistics, etc., so that means that there is a need to measure some objective more directly influenced by the project.

Given the need to measure at a more tactical level, the next question to be asked is how is the cost of collections reduced and online sales increased as a direct effect of the intended project (these questions should be asked when the project is being drafted)? The answer may be that the online payment system as envisioned would reduce both the time and the cost involved in making payment transactions, leading in part for more customers to move to the online option, as a more convenient way to shop. This then results in the two objectives at level 2

- Increase usage of online payment; and
- Maintaining Customer Satisfaction via ease of use of the application.

Take note as well that the arrows above indicate an influence to, or in the case of the dotted arrow, a weak influence. The relationship is not mathematical at all.

These level 2 objectives can in turn be measured more easily as direct product of the project, the proposed measurements then are

- Increase usage of online payment

  – % increase in online payment usage

- Maintaining Customer Satisfaction via ease of use of the application

  – Customer satisfaction rating should be at least 8 over a maximum of 10
  – 90 % of online payments should be processed within 5 min

These indicators can then be measured easily and made part of the portfolio component's objective. See that to attain these indicators, not only technical work needs to be conducted, but most important, alignment to the business, and collaboration with other departments need to be undertaken during the execution of the project. Ideally, it should also be one of the KPIs to measure the PM's effectivity and form part of his personal scorecard.

During the normal course of the project, progress needs to be reported to the different stakeholders, and this should include

- % completion
- SPI indicating the % of delay or advancement the project has
- CPI indicating the % cost overrun or delay. If the project is fixed cost, then cost overruns will be basically due to Change Requests, so these will be reported as additional time delays, plus additional costs to the project (or portfolio, if charged at a higher level).
- Financial indicator chosen (if applicable): IRR, ROI, NPV
- Tactical indicator chosen: This tactical indicator may not make much sense until the project goes live, however, it is expected that the Portfolio Manager handle the component and ensures that these tactical indicators are met, well after the project goes live, as part of his turnover to operations.

In communicating results, it is important to identify all stakeholders and their particular influence on the project

- Stakeholder
- Influence/Involvement on the project
- Regularity in communicating results
- Mode of communication

This does not differ so much with what was discussed in Sect. 5.1.9; the main difference is that the concern of the stakeholders and the stakeholders themselves will change. Most likely, this being a portfolio, stakeholders are of a higher level, and communication can be made less personal (unless particular issues need to be resolved) by means of email with updates, a portal with the uploaded files and updates, and only when needed discussed at steering committee meetings or even management committee meetings.

9.3   Portfolio Rebalancing

Portfolios are not and should not be static because conditions surrounding it (the business) change constantly, so that a rebalancing of portfolios should actually be part of the normal procedure for managing them. Rebalancing may be due to

- Changing business strategy of the company
- Reorganization within the company
- Changing availability of Portfolio Assets

First and foremost, the portfolio should be aligned to the company's overall strategy. Failure to do so may result in projects which have no meaning to the company. Projects may be running efficiently (on time, within cost, giving the expected results), Operations handling the different applications efficiently, conducting changes on them efficiently as requested by the end users, and yet, the projects may be of little relevance to the overall business. The changes and improvements made by Operations may not align as well to the priorities of the company. These portfolio efforts will therefore not be recognized and ultimately fail in their end purpose—that of giving business value.

Generally speaking, company strategy may change over time, so that this has to be evaluated, and the different portfolio components prioritized in accordance with the strategy. Likewise, the company may reorganize, and certain components which may have been important now cease to be, and lastly, the assets made available, whether these are human resource assets, tools, licenses and others change, so that new projects may be possible, or conversely, not feasible due to lack of these assets.

One manner for prioritizing portfolio components may be to rank these in terms of priority based on the overall strategy and organization of the company versus the required assets. For IT portfolios, it is normally human resources and infrastructure which are the constraint in terms of which portfolio components can be undertaken. The latter is more an issue of budget and lead time to procure, but with the advent of the cloud, this is becoming less of a concern. The former however, qualified Human Resources, is more difficult to address and is commonly the constraint. Take the portfolio shown in Fig. 9.5 as an example.

As may be evidenced by the above, constraints on the resources make the originally planned portfolio timeline impossible to execute. Some alternatives exist

Resource Assignment per month

Portfolio name: Overall IT portfolio	Project Priority	Month 1				Month 2				Month 3				Month 4			
		DBA	Sysad	Java	.net	DBA	Sysad	Java	.net	DBA	Sysad	Java	.net	DBA	Sysad	Java	.net
Operations: support to LOB requests																	
Customer Automatic Debit Agreement	High	0.2	0.5	1		0.2	0.5	1		0.2	0.5	1					
Inventory usage reports	High	0.2	0.5	1		0.2	0.5	1		0.2	0.5	1					
Clearing of inventory reservation program	Medium						0.2	3			0.2	3					
Datawarehouse implementation for finance	Medium	1	1			1	1			1	1			1	1		4
HR training module	Medium	1	1			1	1		4	1	1		4	1	1		4
Automation of batch processes	Low									1	0.5			1	0.5		
CRM access to field personnel via tablet	High	1	1			1	1			1	1			1	1		
TOTAL		2.4	3	2	8	2.4	3.2	5	8	4.2	4.2	5	8	4	3.5	4	8

Resource Assignment per month

Portfolio name: Overall IT portfolio	Project Priority	Month 5				Month 6				Month 7				Month 8				Month 9			
		DBA	Sysad	Java	.net	DBA	Sysad	Java	.net	DBA	Sysad	Java	.net	DBA	Sysad	Java	.net	DBA	Sysad	Java	.net
Operations: support to LOB requests																					
Customer Automatic Debit Agreement	High																				
Inventory usage reports	High																				
Clearing of inventory reservation program	Medium																				
Datawarehouse implementation for finance	Medium	1	1			1	1			1	1			1	1			1	1		4
HR training module	Medium	1	1		4	1	1		4	1	1		4	1	1		4	1	1		4
Automation of batch processes	Low	1	0.5			1	0.5			1	0.5										
CRM access to field personnel via tablet	High	1	1	1		1	1	1		1	1	1		1	1	1		1	1	1	
TOTAL		4	3.5	1	8	3	3	1	8	4	2	2	1	4	2	2	1	4	2	2	1	4

Resource Assignment per month

Portfolio name: Overall IT portfolio	Project Priority	Month 5				Month 6				Month 7			
		DBA	Sysad	Java	.net	DBA	Sysad	Java	.net	DBA	Sysad	Java	.net
Operations: support to LOB requests													
Customer Automatic Debit Agreement	High												
Inventory usage reports	High												
Clearing of inventory reservation program	Medium												
Datawarehouse implementation for finance	Medium	1	1		4	1	1		4				
HR training module	Medium	1	1			1	1						
Automation of batch processes	Low	1	0.5										
CRM access to field personnel via tablet	High	1	1	1		1	1	1		1	1	1	
TOTAL		4	3.5	1	8	3	3	1	8	2	2	1	4

	DBA	Sysad	Java	.net
Max resource needed	4.2	4.2	5	8
Available resources	4	4	4	4

- month when project is running

Fig. 9.5 Sample portfolio showing timeline and resources needed

- Contract resources externally to beef up the portfolio components. This is possible; however, sufficient lead time for onboarding may yet be needed.
- Contract the project totally to an external party.
- Reschedule the portfolio components so that the maximum number of resources at any given time does not exceed those available. In this case, it is the lower priority projects which can be delayed, so that higher priority projects push through first. For the schedule above, for example, the Medium priority Operations component "Clearing of inventory reservation program" can in fact be pushed back by 2 months, while the automation of batch processes pushed back by 1 month, resulting in adequacy of resources for DBA, System Administrator (Sysad) and Java roles as shown in Fig. 9.6.
  However, the issue of .net programmers is still pending, and since both the datawarehouse and the HR training module projects take long to execute, then there is no alternative but to resort to any of the two aforementioned techniques, in getting external resources.

In all these discussions, there has been no mention of an additional constraint, that of funding. If resources are purely internal, then all costs are sunk costs and portfolio optimization is just a matter of trying to optimize the % utilization of internal resources. If however external resources are needed, then funding should be made available accordingly.

As portfolio balancing is an optimization of several variables: time, funding, go-live, resource availability, and resource competencies, it is generally complex and requires several iterations until optimality is obtained. Much simpler of course is if all projects are contracted turnkey externally, so that the only internal constraints now become funding and availability of Project Managers/Operation Managers.

As discussed earlier as well, company strategy changes with time, and it is the job of the portfolio manager to be aware of such changes and make the necessary reprioritization of components accordingly. Portfolio components may thus be added, reprioritized in either direction (made more important or less), or dropped altogether.

Take for example a company which prioritized having its own App available for customers to increase online sales. This project was allocated funding and resources however, 3 months after the 8 month project started, management found out that even with its current sales channels, severe logistical constraints were hampering the delivery of goods to its customers. Management then decided to initiate a third-party logistics handling program which necessitated an IT component so that it would seamlessly integrate the third party's information with the company's back-end logistics system. After careful evaluation, senior management, together with the portfolio manager decided to freeze the App project and reallocate funding and resources to the new logistics integration project.

Resource Assignment per month (Months 5–9)

Portfolio name: Overall IT portfolio	Project Priority	Month 5 DBA	Sysad	Java	.net	Month 6 DBA	Sysad	Java	.net	Month 7 DBA	Sysad	Java	.net	Month 8 DBA	Sysad	Java	.net	Month 9 DBA	Sysad	Java	.net
Operations: support to LOB requests	High																				
Customer Automatic Debit-Agreement	High																				
Inventory usage reports																					
Clearing of inventory reservation program	Medium		0.2	3																	
Datawarehouse implementation for finance	Medium	1	1		4	1	1		4	1	1		4	1	1		4	1	1		4
HR training module	Medium	1	1		4	1	1		4	1	1			1	1			1	1		
Automation of batch processes	Low	1	0.5			1	0.5			1	1			1	1			1	1		
CRM access to field personnel via tablet	High	1	1	1		1	1	1		1	1	1		1	1	1		1	1	1	
TOTAL		4	3.7	4	8	4	3.5	1	8	4	2	1	4	4	2	1	4	4	2	1	4

Resource Assignment per month (Months 1–4)

Portfolio name: Overall IT portfolio	Project Priority	Month 1 DBA	Sysad	Java	.net	Month 2 DBA	Sysad	Java	.net	Month 3 DBA	Sysad	Java	.net	Month 4 DBA	Sysad	Java	.net
Operations: support to LOB requests	High	0.2	0.5	1		0.2	0.5	1									
Customer Automatic Debit-Agreement	High	0.2	0.5	1		0.2	0.5	1		0.2	0.5	1					
Inventory usage reports																	
Clearing of inventory reservation program	Medium														0.2	3	
Datawarehouse implementation for finance	Medium	1	1		4	1	1		4	1	1		4	1	1		4
HR training module	Medium	1	1		4	1	1		4	1	1		4	1	1		4
Automation of batch processes	Low									1	0.5			1	0.5		
CRM access to field personnel via tablet	High									1	1	1		1	1	1	
TOTAL		2.4	3	2	8	2.4	3	2	8	3.2	3.5	2	8	4	3.7	4	8

Resource Assignment per month (Months 5–7)

Portfolio name: Overall IT portfolio	Project Priority	Month 5 DBA	Sysad	Java	.net	Month 6 DBA	Sysad	Java	.net	Month 7 DBA	Sysad	Java	.net
Operations: support to LOB requests	High												
Customer Automatic Debit-Agreement	High												
Inventory usage reports													
Clearing of inventory reservation program	Medium		0.2	3									
Datawarehouse implementation for finance	Medium	1	1		4	1	1		4	1	1		
HR training module	Medium	1	1		4	1	1			1	1		4
Automation of batch processes	Low	1	0.5			1	0.5			1	1		
CRM access to field personnel via tablet	High	1	1	1		1	1	1		1	1	1	
TOTAL		4	3.7	4	8	4	3.5	1	8	4	3.5	1	4
Max resource needed		4	3.7	4	8								
Available resources		4	4	4	4								

▨ - month when project is running

Fig. 9.6 Realigned portfolio

As can be seen, rebalancing is needed in regular intervals so as to ensure

- Portfolio components stay relevant to the company' business strategy and objectives.
- Revised timelines as required by management.
- Company Organization.
- Resource availability.
- Funding reallocation.

9.4   Portfolio Governance

Portfolio governance refers to all policies and procedures which should govern the portfolio and its components. It sits at a higher level than projects and operations, and therefore, both project and operations are necessarily guided by the portfolio governance rules.

As such, both operations and project policies and guidelines must align with the overarching portfolio guidelines. Guidelines would normally cut across all portfolios and be standardized, and would also normally align with general IT policies and procedures as discussed in Chap. 7. Aside from these general guidelines, some guidelines would be specific for the portfolio

- **Guidelines for officially incorporating a component into the portfolio**.
- **Manner and regularity in which components report their performance**. In this case, and as discussed under portfolio assessment and communication, each component will have its own set of indicators that have been agreed upon with the PM and higher management as those that will be regularly monitored.
- **Portfolio Component documentation**. This will specify the minimum documentation that is required for each project/operation component and is also discussed in Chap. 7. Projects shall have a different set of documentation from operations, so that typical documentation is discussed separately here for each.

  - Project documentation

        Issue registry
        Request registry
        Updated project timeline in standard format
        Deliverable checklist
        Risk registry (optional)
        PM task activity report

– Operations documentation

    Operations report
    Team activity report
    Ticket summary report

- **Asset request/release guidelines**. This describes the manner in which a particular asset (normally human resources) shall be requested by the PM to be assigned (released) from his project, and includes the approval process.
- **Change request guidelines**. Will describe the procedure for requesting and approving change requests, this shall include all necessary details for the change request including

  – Reason for the change request
  – Requestor (PM, user, vendor)
  – Scope of work.
  – Estimated man-days and breakdown of resources needed for the CR
  – Cost (if any)
  – Duration
  – Functional and technical details, including any customizations if needed

- **Guidelines for requesting a change in scope**. Additional scope will be covered by Change Requests, however, from time to time, a change in the scope of the project may be needed due to

  – Obsolescence
  – Change in the direction of the users/company management
  – Technical limitations
  – Difficulty in meeting requirements, not initially foreseen
  – Reprioritization of scope

- The reasons above should be carefully examined and validated, at it is not good practice to change scope in the middle of the project, however, such possibilities do exist. The change request should include

  – Reason for the change
  – Requestor (PM, user, vendor)
  – Scope of work changed.
  – Estimated man-days and breakdown of resources needed
  – Impact on project cost (if any)
  – Impact on project duration
  – Functional and technical details, including any customizations if needed

- **Request for additional funding**. This should be raised by the PM and justified accordingly.

  - Reason for the request
  - Amount
  - Reason and Details on the cause for the delay

- **Risk registry**

  - When risk registry should be drafted
  - Procedure and frequency of update

One practical way to monitor all portfolio documentation in a timely manner is through the use of a Document Management System (DMS) in which different folders are kept for the different portfolio components, which are updated in regular fashion (usually weekly). Nowadays many DMS have a web interface so that the documentation is available as a Portfolio portal, which maintains different authorizations depending on the user, as well as approval workflows.

9.5 Portfolio Monitoring and Control

The Portfolio Manager is in charge of monitoring and controlling the portfolio. His role is somewhat similar to that of a PM in terms of this function in a project; the portfolio manager must ensure that the portfolio is

- Aligned with overall strategy, structure, and objectives of the company
- Has sufficient resources and other assets assigned to each component so that work can be accomplished on time and with the necessary quality
- Being undertaken on time
- Being undertaken within budget
- Delivering or will eventually be able to deliver its intended benefits

  As well as

- Ensuring that requests from the PM or Operations manager are being evaluated and approved/rejected on time. This includes

  - Request for assets
  - Request for additional funding
  - Change Requests
  - Changes in scope

- Ensuring that there is no issue which cannot be handled by the assigned PM and his current HR assets. In case the issue is deemed to be beyond the PM's capability, then the portfolio manager needs to step in and facilitate resolution. Typical issues which may need to be resolved by the Portfolio Manager includes

- Lack of knowledge by the PM on the issue at hand. This may be technical, functional, or a business challenge
- Lack of pertinent resource(s)
- Conflicts between the PM and the users
- Conflict between the PM and the vendor
- Mismatch of skills or underperformance by some of the resources assigned
- Nonconformance with IT, Portfolio, or Project Management guidelines and policies
- Underperformance by the PM/Operations Manager
- Delay or non-provisioning of infrastructure
- Conflict or non-prioritization of task requested by the PM to another team (typically, a request to O&M)
- Delay in the formal approval of deliverables

The idea of monitoring and control is to ensure that the different portfolio components are running smoothly, and if not, be able to first, detect the issue, and thereafter address the root cause of the issue.

Part of this monitoring and control process includes internal communication between the Portfolio Manager and his Project Managers and Operations Head. Typically these will come in the form of

- **Operations Meeting**. This meeting should be conducted by the Portfolio Manager, the Operations Head, together with the different O&M Team Leads. During this meeting the operations report is reviewed, tickets and their statistics are analyzed, and each team leader is given the chance to present his regular operations update. During this meeting, any of these sources of information will be the basis for determining issues and will then be discussed and resolved jointly by the team.
- **Portfolio projects update meeting**. Takes place between the Portfolio manager, sub portfolio managers, the different Project Managers, and if needed, the Operations Head. The latest standard documentation discussed in Chap. 7 is presented, statuses discussed and any issues brought up for resolution.
- **Stakeholders' meeting**. This may actually be the management committee, normally the highest management level meeting, in which all operational, tactical, and strategic initiatives are discussed and updates from each department head given. Alternatively, it may be a different meeting altogether, called or regularly held, in which the different portfolio stakeholders are updated on the status. These meetings are normally quick, and focus on

- Status of the portfolio components in terms of % completion.
- Project estimated completion dates.

- If delayed, a discussion on the reason for the delays. If issues can be resolved at the stakeholder level, then these are brought up and guidance, resolution, or assistance sought.
- Performance review for operations, may include SPI, CPI, summary of cost overruns.
- Discussion on possible strategy change by the company, impact and rebalancing at the portfolio level.

Governance is a common discussion at portfolio meetings between the portfolio manager and his operations head, PMs. This is to review if governance policies are being followed correctly and in a timely manner (such as the filing of Project information), as well as the regular review and improvement of these policies. Review of governance policies will again follow a PDCA cycle shown in Fig. 9.7.

In these review meetings, policies and guidelines are reviewed, tweaked and released again. Any of the PMs and Operations Manager is actually free to come up with suggestions on how to improve, and these are deliberated and if approved, made part of the guidelines. These should be improvements, not radical deviations of the previous rules, otherwise this will cause consternation.

Another optional component, depending on the complexity and exposure of the portfolio to risks, is to conduct a risk analysis. This is similar to that discussed for projects, in which a qualitative risk analysis can be performed and each risk identified versus possible impact and probability. The difference here is that this should be conducted at the portfolio level versus project level. Examples of project level risks are delays in approval from the users of deliverables, failure of a module during testing, or project creep. At the portfolio level these would be risks that can affect one or many components. Examples of this are unavailability of certain resources, obsolescence of some of the portfolio components due to a new direction taken by the company, irrelevance of some projects due to repeated delays in going live.

Fig. 9.7 PDCA cycle

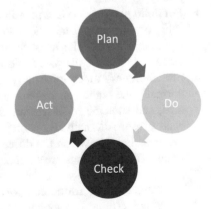

Reference

Project Management Institute, 2013. *The Standard for Portfolio Management*. 3rd ed. Atlanta: Project Management Institute, Inc.

Further Reading

Unfortunately, there is a dearth of good portfolio management books for IT, below are just some references, though good material is hard to come by.

Sanwal, A., 2007. *Optimizing Corporate Portfolio Management: Aligning Investment Proposals with Organizational Strategy*. 1st ed. Wiley.

Maizlish, B., Handler, R., 2005. *IT Portfolio Management: Unlocking the Business Value of Technology*. 1st ed. Wiley.

Hughes, D.L., Dwivedi, Y.K., Simintiras, A.C., Rana, N.P., 2016. *Success and Failure of IS/IT Projects*. Springer.

Appendix A: Sample Terms of Reference (TOR)

VM (Virtual Machine) Backup Solution

10

1 Company Profile

XXX

2 Background

XX

All applications were virtualized using XXX which started in 2012 and completed by 2013. Backup and restore procedures were implemented using XXX Backup but mainly for file and database backup and recovery only and this does not include the entire system backup of each and every virtual machines which is also considered essential to business continuity process.

The proposed VM Backup Solution should focus on the following criteria:

1. Backup speed;
2. VM image consistency check after backups;
3. Multiple restore capabilities;
4. Point-in-time recovery;
5. Replication to complement colocation strategy for disaster recovery;
6. Data deduplication to reduce backup storage requirements;
7. The ability to target any storage device.

Below is the identified number of VM Host with their respective number of CPU Sockets that requires implementation of VM Backup Solution.

Site	# of servers	# of CPU sockets per server
Data Center	2	4
	8	2
Head Office	9	2
Remote Sites	15	2

© Springer International Publishing Switzerland 2016
F. Castillo, *Managing Information Technology*,
DOI 10.1007/978-3-319-38891-5_10

3   Objectives

This Request for Proposal aims to achieve the following:

- Ensure that the proposal meets the requirements stated in the Scope of Work.
- Ensure compatibility with our current systems.

To fulfill the above objectives, the Bidder is expected to bring experience and expertise in the area of implementing backup solutions for virtualized environment.

4   Scope of Work

The scope of the project includes the following:

4.1   Implementation and configuration of all needed software solution proposed should be all-inclusive and not require any additional hardware, software, or services aside from those in the vendor's proposal, for the solution to function. Off-the-shelf software and hardware may be purchased separately by the company, so that their corresponding costings should be itemized separately.

4.2   All hardware will be provided by the company, the bidder should include all hardware specs for Development, QA/Testing, and Production environments, whichever are relevant to the project.

4.3   Creation of detailed implementation plan to include the duration of the project and number of resources.

4.4   Provide user and administration training that covers Installation, configuration, and management course for three (3) participants.

4.5   Complete documentation of the project including user manuals, training manuals, presentations, and source code (wherever applicable).

4.6   Post-implementation support and maintenance.

5   Submission of Proposals

The company reserves the right to

- Reject any or all offers and discontinue this RFP process without obligation or liability to any potential vendor,
- Award a contract on the basis of initial offers received, without discussions or requests for best and final offers, and

- Consider all responses to this TOR as binding, and have them form part of the contract
- Disqualify and/or blacklist any vendor due to misrepresentations or misinformation provided in the proposal.

Vendor's proposal shall be submitted in the format as set forth below. Responding service providers will confine its submission to the matters sufficient to define its proposal and to provide an adequate basis for the company evaluation of the Vendor's proposal.

The proposal should contain three parts

5.1   Company Profile
5.2   Client references—references with similar products/services provided including description of what was provided.
5.3   Cost and Technical Proposal
    5.3.1   Technical Proposal—the technical proposal should be limited to ten (10) pages + appendices with the following information:
        5.3.1.1   General Description of the proposed solution.
        5.3.1.2   General description of the base software of the proposed solution (e.g., web services, portal software, etc.), if any. This may be complemented with an exhaustive description of the solution architecture with detail work flows in an Appendix (soft copy only is acceptable)
        5.3.1.3   Project Timeline—Detailed schedule of activities and identified deliverables per activity. Please use MS Project 2010.
        5.3.1.4   Methodology—should describe the general methodology to be used in the project implementation with description of concrete activities to be undertaken, including expected involvement from the company's personnel (if any).
    5.3.2   Relevant credentials (e.g., Gold Partner, etc.)
    5.3.3   Project Team composition with detailed CV's of assigned key personnel including information on project implementation experiences, at least 3 years relevant experiences, similar to this project and roles. Supporting Training Certifications should be provided.
    5.3.4   Cost Proposal—the cost proposal should be detailed per component.
        5.3.4.1   If discrepancies occur between the total cost and itemized costs, the company shall make use of whichever price is lower.
        5.3.4.2   Price quoted should be inclusive of ALL TAXES except VAT. Price quotations that indicate otherwise will be assumed to include all taxes or risk being disqualified.

Example:

Component	Unit cost	Metric	Amount (VAT Ex)
Software licenses			
Backup Software		Per VMHost	
		Per Core	
		Per VM	
Services			
Installation/Configuration			
Others (If any)			
Total Cost			

Prepared By: XXX
Endorsed By: XXXX

List of Functional Requirements

Item	Requirements	Comply (yes/no)	Remarks/Work Around Substitution
1	Backup and replication solution in a single product		
2	Leverage vSphere API (Application Programming Interface) for Data Protection		
3	Integrate and leverage on Changed Block Tracking		
4	Agentless deployment without the need to install individual agents inside each Guest VMs		
5	Full support for VMWare ESX and ESXi editions		
6	Ability to backup via vCenter or directly from individual ESX or ESXi servers		
7	Support for LAN-free data backup		
8	Support for thin and thick provisioned VMs		
9	Provide a centralized web-based enterprise console to monitor and manage all the backup servers with dashboard statistics view		

(continued)

(continued)

Item	Requirements	Comply (yes/no)	Remarks/Work Around Substitution
10	Ability to add datastore object as a dynamic container for backup which will include new VM when it is added into the datastore during backup job run		
11	Ability to exclude specific virtual disk for backup as per VM selected in a backup job		
12	User profiling to allow role segregation to perform full administration, backup operations, backup viewing only, or restore operations		
13	Customizable block size for optimal deduplication across different networks (SAN, LAN, WAN)		
14	Deduplication and compression bundled in software without additional option to purchase		
15	Ability to utilize forward and reverse incremental backup methodology		
16	Ability to utilize full backup methodology		
17	Ability to provide application-consistent backups (utilizing Microsoft Visual Source Safe or VMware Tools)		
18	Support for continuous job schedule to immediately start the backup job once upon completion to provide near-Continuous Date Protection (CDP)		
19	Backup VM can be manually or automatically removed from the backup image file to reduce backup storage space		
20	Single, consistent method of image-level backup but provides granular full or item-level recovery		
21	Ability to perform full VM restoration and Guest OS file-level recovery		
22	Ability to perform application-item level recovery (for MS SQL, MS Exchange, MS Active Directory, and other applications)		
23	Ability to perform transaction log pruning after successful backup of VM running MS SQL		
24	Automated verification of backup images by starting up required VMs, checks performed on VM, OS and Application to ensure integrity without the need of human intervention. Verification report to be emailed automatically to administrator can be configured		
25	Provide near-CDP-level replication bundled in software without additional option to purchase		

(continued)

(continued)

Item	Requirements	Comply (yes/no)	Remarks/Work Around Substitution
26	Ability to create isolated environment for on-demand Sandbox with required VMs running for testing/troubleshooting. In addition, this isolated environment will be able to interact with the production environment		
27	Offsite storage of backups with built-in WAN acceleration		

Curriculum Vitae

Dr. Francisco Castillo is currently Senior Vice President and Chief Information Officer of Maynilad Water Services, Inc., the water concessionaire for the West area of Manila's greater metropolitan area.

Francisco previously worked in a major multinational IT consulting firm as Managing Consultant for Asia-Pacific, where he worked for over 12 years in various capacities. In 2013, he was named "Outstanding ASEAN CIO" by the IDG group, and also appeared in the 2014 and 2015 CIO 100 Listings published by CIO Asia Magazine. This 2016 he is one of three finalists in the ASEAN Strategy Forum IT as "Influencer of the Year" for his contribution in the convergence of IT and OT. He is also a founding member of the Philippine Internet of Everything Consortium and a member of its Board of Trustees.

Francisco has over 25 years experience in Information Technology, and has undertaken projects in over a dozen countries in Europe and Asia. He holds a Ph.D. in Electronics and Telecommunications Engineering from the Universidad Politécnica de Catalunya (Barcelona, Spain), where he was also Associate Director for the Technical Engineering College (Vilanova), and Associate Professor. He is currently an active speaker and panelist in many Asian IT events, and in his previous role as researcher published over 50 papers in international journals and conferences, and presented in over 20 international seminars.

Index

Printed in the United States
By Bookmasters